796.332 K95 9 40

KUECHLE OLIVER
ON WISCONSIN
WITHDRAWN

P9-CAA-734

0964500 0024 FD 1977

MAR 2 1 1989

D A T E   D U E

FEB 06. 90	SEP 19 2012	
MAR 22. 90	SEP 28 2017	
FEB 06. 91		
AUG 29. 91		
NOV 05. 92		
NOV 28. 92		
JUN 16 94		
APR 0 1 1999		
FEB 2 - 2005		PUBLIC LIBRARY
MAR 17 2009		HOLSON AVE.
		S, WI 53207
		-READ (40)

FL-28-2

ON WISCONSIN
Badger Football

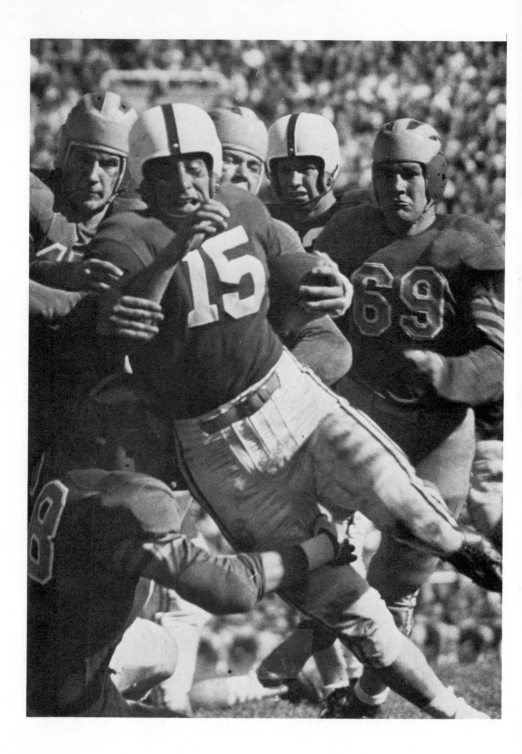

ON WISCONSIN
BADGER FOOTBALL

by Oliver E. Kuechle
with Jim Mott

796.332
K95

THE STRODE PUBLISHERS, INC.
HUNTSVILLE, ALABAMA 35802

011881

Photographs Courtesy Of The University Of Wisconsin
Athletic Department

Copyright 1977 By
Oliver E. Kuechle And Jim Mott
All Rights In This Book
Reserved Including The Right
To Reproduce This Book Or Parts
Thereof In Any Form—Printed In U.S.A.
Library of Congress Catalog Number 76-19973
Standard Book Number 87397-093-4

Acknowledgments

To acknowledge widespread help in preparing this book about University of Wisconsin football is at once both the easiest and hardest part of the pleasant chore. It is easiest because no one can describe 94 years of football at the university without help. There are old university yearbooks and newspaper files. And there are faded individual clippings of an era long gone. All provided invaluable help. In this last I give particular thanks to Mrs. Edward Gerhardy, daughter of Ikey Karel, the Red Grange of his day at the university. The collection of clippings which her father had turned over to her was an education in what football was like in the nineties. I likewise acknowledge such help from Jack Ryan, son of Wisconsin's coach in the twenties, and Howard Stark, a star tackle on some of Wisconsin's greatest teams about the time of World War I and immediately after.

The hardest part of acknowledgments is not to forget any of those hundreds whom, in my 50 years as football writer and later sports editor of the *Milwaukee Journal*, I got to know and listened to as they spoke of things they knew or had heard about. In many instances what they said was only a clue to further investigation, but nonetheless invaluable aids. To all of them my blanket thanks and particularly to a colleague of mine in my reporting days, Lloyd Larson, sports editor of the *Milwaukee Sentinel,* and to the Wisconsin coaches and athletic directors with whom I have had personal contacts—George Downer, Graduate Manager of Athletics shortly after the turn of the century; Athletic Directors Tom Jones, George Little, Dr. Walter Meanwell, Irvin Uteritz, Harry Stuhldreher, Guy Sundt, and Ivan Williamson, and Coaches John Richards, Jack Ryan, George Little, Glen Thistlethwaite, Dr. Clarence Spears, Harry Stuhldreher, and Ivan Williamson. All of them have passed on. And thanks also to those still living—Athletic Director Elroy Hirsch and football coaches Milt Bruhn, John Coatta, and John Jardine, and certainly to Bill Aspinwall, business manager of the Athletic Department and also secretary of the Athletic Board for almost 50 years, and Professor Mark Ingraham, who supplemented what appears in his book, *The Golden Vector*, about some of the most tumultuous days in the university's history.

I likewise acknowledge with deep appreciation the invaluable assistance and cooperation of Jim Mott, a Wisconsin graduate and the university's sports information director since 1966, before which he was assistant director for 12 years.

Oliver Kuechle

Dedication

To Bucky Badger, the belligerent little mascot whose antics on the sidelines have delighted thousands of Wisconsin fans, is dedicated this book by one of those thousands of Wisconsin fans. Bucky Badger was conceived by the Athletic Department's publicity director, Arthur Lentz, after the original Badger mascot on a chain had become too vicious to control and was retired to the Madison Zoo. A student in the University's Art Department, Connie Conrad, was commissioned to mold a papier-mache head of a badger, and cheerleader and gymnast Bill Sagal was directed by homecoming chairman Bill Sachse to wear the outfit at the homecoming game of 1948. A campus contest among sororities was held to give the new mascot a name, and Delta Gamma and Delta Zeta suggested Buckingham U. Badger. The committee in charge felt that this was a bit too formal and changed it to Bucky Badger. It was also decided to dress the new "badger" in a blazing cardinal sweater with a big white "W" and to put boxing gloves on his paws as a suggestion of a real badger's belligerency. The new type of mascot became a hit at once and has remained so for 29 years. He particularly delights in running across the field between halves, capturing one of the rival girl cheerleaders, and carrying her to his "lair" on his side of the field.

BADGER BALLAD

If you want to be a Badger,
Just come along with me,
By the bright shining light,
By the light of the moon.
If you want to be a Badger,
Just come along with me,
By the bright shining light of the moon.

Chorus

By the light of the moon,
By the light of the moon,
By the bright shining light,
By the light of the moon,
If you want to be a Badger,
Just come along with me,
By the bright shining light of the moon.

A score of student generations have sung this Badger Ballad, composed in 1919 by Julius Emil Olson, a Wisconsin graduate of 1884 and later professor of Scandinavian languages and literature. Dr. Charles H. Mills, director of the music school in 1919, arranged the music.

Contents

Foreword
1. "In The Beginning" 13
2. Coaches As Officials And A Forfeit 34
3. Early Giants In Cardinal 56
4. Financial Troubles And Jeopardy 68
5. The Slow Descent Begins 84
6. A Rally Under Little 102
7. The Two Doctors Feud In Public 122
8. Regents Clean House 138
9. Ivy's Ivy-Covered Record 161
10. Williamson Goes To The Rose Bowl 176
11. VanderKelen To Richter 194
12. The Bittersweet Coatta Years 215
13. In Retrospect 231
    Appendix 247

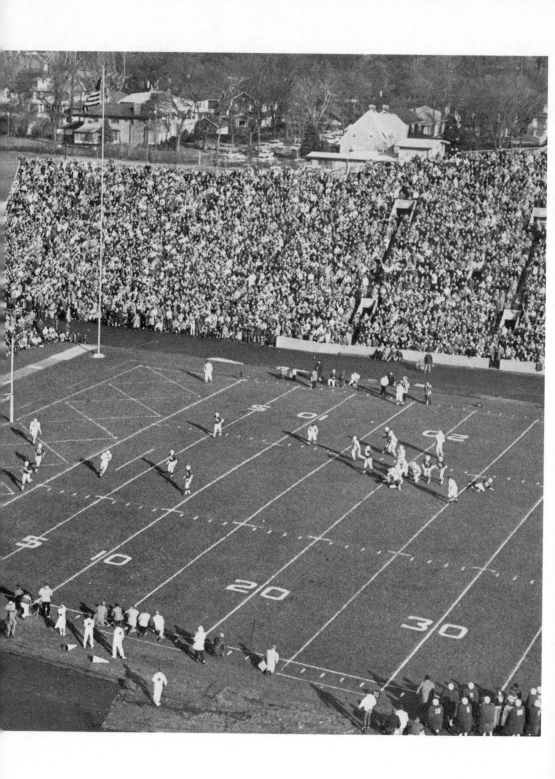

Foreword

I can think of no man better qualified to write a history of the University of Wisconsin's football fortunes than Oliver Kuechle. "Ollie," as we all know him, has covered Wisconsin football for more than fifty years. I first started to read his news stories while I was still at Wausau High School, and, of course, have read them ever since.

"Ollie" has been more than a reporter; he has had a deep-rooted interest in the university itself and has understood well the university's philosophy. Wisconsin by every design is first an educational institution. Intercollegiate sports and especially football have always had a place in its curricula but only a place. The larger places have always been for the university's primary purposes.

It has been a delight to read this presentation of Wisconsin's triumphs and heartbreaks, some of which I shared in as a player.

I shall never forget the victories over Ohio State and Minnesota in 1942 or the defeat at Iowa's hands which kept Wisconsin from an undefeated season and probable national collegiate championship.

I congratulate Ollie for this presentation and the research on the very early days before either of us was even born.

Elroy L. Hirsch
Director of Athletics
University of Wisconsin-Madison

"In The Beginning"

Out of the old Northwest Territory which had been under successive French and British rules until ceded to the United States by the Treaty of Paris (1783), out of this vast wilderness of pine-scented forests and sparkling glacial lakes, the state of Wisconsin was created in 1848. A year later a land grant college, the University of Wisconsin, was chartered by the first state legislature and began operations. With campus buildings still to be constructed, the first classes were held in the old Madison Female Academy of territorial days. The first class had two students, Levi M. Booth and Charles T. Wakeley.

The charter creating the university gave it unsurpassed grounds for a campus, including more than 240 acres for a mile along the picturesque shore of Lake Mendota. The lower part of the campus on Langdon Street, across from what is now affectionately known as the "Little Red Gym," afforded a wide open field for play and recreation. Buildings of the State Historical Society and Memorial Library now stand on these grounds with a class gift fountain between them.

Wisconsin's very early intercollegiate football games, through the 1894 games, were played on this field with cardinal-beribboned coeds and their pennant-waving escorts standing along the sidelines. The field, of course, had no stands. Even in later years, long after football games had been transferred to Camp Randall, the lower campus was used for rallies.

Campus life in those early years was not without organized

Ikey Karel, an outstanding halfback in the early nineties, was later dubbed the Red Grange of his day.

sports, although the only intercollegiate competition at first was in baseball. In the early 1880s Wisconsin competed in baseball with Beloit College, then known as the "Yale of the West"; Lake Forest College; Northwestern; and Racine College in the Northwest College Baseball Association. The first recorded baseball game was played against Beloit in 1883. A program of intramural sports grew around baseball and, to a lesser extent, around tennis, track, crew, and football. According to *Trochus*, a campus publication in 1883, there were class teams in all sports, each with its own student governing association, and an all-around university field day which was an annual event of the joint associations. The latter included a three-legged race, a football kick, a tug of war, a baseball throw, a potato race, a bicycle race, and the usual running and jumping events.

The joint individual associations made up the all-embracing athletic association, which through the years underwent various changes of face although always student-dominated. In 1901, for instance, the constitution of the athletic association spelled out membership as: "All students, former students, and members of the faculty shall be members of the association. The officers shall be president, vice president, secretary, and treasurer, and a board of 18 directors. Three members of the board shall be chosen from the faculty, one from the alumni, one from the Board of Regents, and 10 from among the undergraduates." In addition the athletic association always included a faculty-dominated athletic council of restricted authority. It ruled only in matters of eligibility.

Carl T. Veltner in his book *A History of the Western Intercollegiate Conference* tells of this student administration which all schools at this time relied on.

"The faculties," he wrote, "wedded to classical rather than to social or educational philosophy, commonly regarded athletics as a nuisance, a means of irritation rather than of education, and, at best, a waste of time and interest. Faculty indifference gave the athletic management to interested students. As time passed the carry-over of this system and the interest of the general graduate body produced strong alumni influence. Gambling which involved students and alumni added to the concern which outsiders had. A former football manager states that seven members of the team which was under his charge at Michigan in 1893 were not enrolled on the books of the university during the football season. (Wisconsin beat this Michigan team, 34-18.) Recruiting of high school players became more troublesome as many secondary schools took up the game. (And played college teams.) Trailing the coach like a poor relation was the ever present school and public pressure for a winning team. There was practically no curb on migrant athletes."

The *Trochus* in 1883 listed 11 students as members of Wisconsin's first Football Association: W. A. Aitchison, C. L. Allen, J.A. Aylward, A.C. Briggs, S.A. Connell, T. English, J.B. M. Connel, G.S. Parker, A. Schroeder, J.R. Thompson, and R.G.

15

Werner. In the beginning these men, with the student manager whom they appointed, administered the sport with little faculty interest or control. They hired and fired coaches, scheduled games, and took care of all the finances, which more than once meant going into their own pockets or asking Madison businessmen for contributions. In time, shortly after the turn of the century, the student manager gave way briefly to a graduate manager, whose unhappy experiences led to Wisconsin's first athletic director in 1906. He was Dr. C. P. Hutchins, appointed by President C.R. Van Hise. But that came much later.

It was not until 1889 that the university had a football team which played a recorded intercollegiate game. George F. Downer—a student manager of Wisconsin football teams in the late 1890s, a track athlete, the last graduate manager of the athletic association shortly after the turn of the century, sports editor of the *Milwaukee Sentinel*, and later still publicity director for the university's athletic department—wrote in his memoirs which appeared in football programs of 1931: "A group of students decided to form a team in 1889 (obviously within the framework of the Football Association organized in 1883). Andrew A. Bruce, later a member of the law faculty, is generally credited with being the father of the project but L. D. Sumner of Madison who played fullback for three years gives that credit to Charles Mayer of Madison. Mayer was captain at any rate. Bruce, who had learned rugby at English schools in India, was, however, the only one who knew much about the game and taught these first Badgers the rudiments."

A group of young men in Milwaukee, 85 miles away, hurled the challenge for this first intercollegiate game. They had attended college in the East, where football as an intercollegiate sport was already well established. The Football Association accepted their challenge to a contest in Milwaukee. On Saturday morning, November 23, 1889, the morning *Milwaukee Sentinel* told its readers about the game: "The Milwaukee graduates and Madison University football team will play a match at National Park this afternoon. There promises to be plenty of excitement as the University team will be accompanied by a delegation of students, each of whom will bring two sound lungs with him."

National Park, a privately owned recreation area of 50

acres (at the southwest corner of what is now Layton Boulevard and National Avenue), included a half-mile track for harness racing, a shooting range, a small artificial lake for boating, a deer park, a roller coaster, a small three-story frame hotel and, most important, a cricket field. The football game was played on a gridiron (110 yards by 160 feet) laid out on the cricket field. P. C. Brand was proprietor of the park.

It is not hard to imagine the young Milwaukee blades of 1889 in their surreys or tallyhoes and the students from Madison with their cardinal pennants and ribbons lining the field at the three o'clock kickoff of this new-fangled game.

The "Milwaukee Graduates" who faced Wisconsin were all members of the Calumet Club in Milwaukee who had attended colleges in the East and who in most instances had played football there. Foremost among them was Alvin Kletsch, who organized the Calumets and who this same year both coached and played with Wisconsin against Beloit three weeks later.

Kletsch, who had attended Stevens Institute of Technology in Hoboken, New Jersey, and had played the game there, both coached and played with the Calumets. The club was not an athletic club as we know such today but a social club devoted largely to beer drinking, if its own written history may be believed. A game like football or any other athletic activity was incidental.

A club report prepared in later years and reported in the *Milwaukee Journal* said: "There existed at that time (when the club was organized in 1884) no club for young men in moderate circumstances where they could meet socially among themselves. There was only one public institution then that invited the young men within its portals—the saloon. The young and old were welcome in the club and spent the fleeting hours in conversation or card playing but with the expectation of quaffing the foaming beverage whether to a greater or less degree."

It is not inconceivable that a bunch of the Calumet boys including Kletsch, of course, sat around dutifully quaffing their beer one night and decided to hurl the football challenge at the Madison university. Wisconsin accepted, so the game was arranged.

It was hardly an impressive beginning. The Calumets won,

17

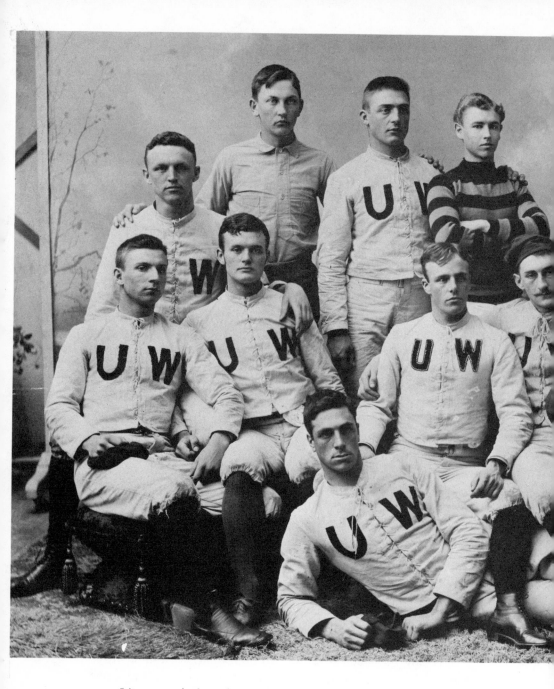

Wisconsin's first football team, 1889. Members were A. A. Bruce, fullback; F. W. Prael and W. C. Brumder, halfbacks; C. M. Mayer, captain and quarterback (with football above); W. H. Blackburn, snapback; B. N. Clark, right guard; J. B. Kerr, right

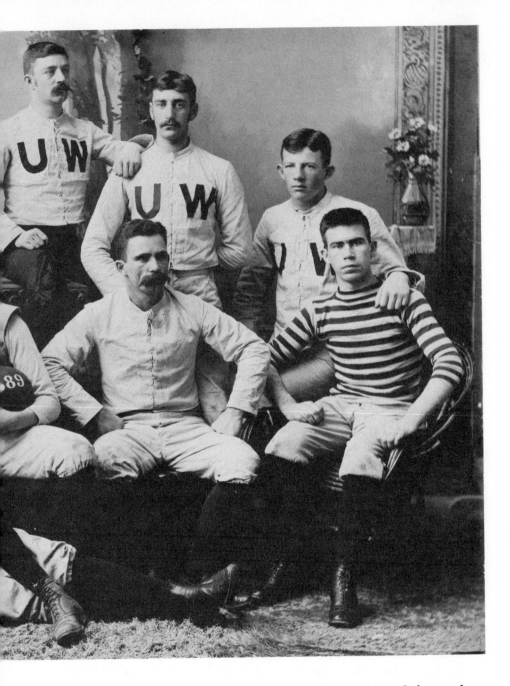

tackle; T. E. Loope, right end-rush; W. D. Sheldon, left guard; R. Logemann, left tackle; W. L. Brooks, left end-rush; L. D. Sumner, J. E. McNaught, and G. W. Ackward, substitutes.

27-0, although the scoring of that rough and tumble day in 1889 should be explained. A safety counted two points, a touchdown four points, a goal after touchdown two points, and a goal from the field five points. Clearly the foot was in football. These values remained until 1897 when they were changed to make a touchdown five points and a goal after touchdown one point. A goal from the field remained five points and a safety two points. The field was 110 yards long, with two 50 yard lines, and 160 feet wide. There were no end lines and hence no end zones, only goal lines. The team had three downs in which to make five yards. The time was divided into two halves of 45 minutes each and was changed to two halves of 35 minutes each in 1894. The restriction of 11 men on a side instead of the mob scene of 20 or 25 men of paleolithic days in the East had been introduced by Walter Camp in 1880.

A yearbook picture of the 1889 team shows the men who faced the Calumets: snapback or center, W. H. Blackburn; right guard, B. N. Clark; left guard, W. D. Sheldon; right tackle, J. B. Kerr; left tackle, R. Logemann; right end rush or just end, T. E. Loope; left end rush, W. L. Brooks; quarterback and captain, Charles Mayer; halfbacks, W.C. Brumder and F.W. Prael; fullback, A. A. Bruce; and substitutes, L. D. Sumner, G. W. Ackward, and J. E. McNaught.

To the best of confusing records, the Calumets took the field with A. F. and H. G. Kletsch, Schultz, Forsyth, Weinbank, Krueger, and Miranaham as rushers or linemen; Anderson, quarterback; Lacke and W.L. Mauch, halfbacks; and Blackstrand, fullback. Less confusing in the records was the name of the referee, E. Brown. He handled the game alone.

While there was certainly nothing encouraging about the 27-0 licking by the Calumets, there was no feeling by Wisconsin to forget the whole thing. These first Badgers immediately challenged nearby Beloit, which accepted. Moreover, having been highly impressed by Alvin Kletsch's strong play in the Calumet victory, the Badgers invited him to Madison to coach the team for a few days. He would go to Madison from Milwaukee by the morning train, drill the team in the afternoon, and return by the evening train—all at his own expense, which in his enthusiasm for football he had gladly agreed to. Three weeks after the Calumet game, the Badgers played Beloit at Beloit—and lost again,

20

but this time by a respectable 4-0.

What football was like in those days was described in the *Milwaukee Sentinel* under a New York dateline, November 24, 1889, as follows:

Football furnishes the all absorbing topic in American colleges at the present time. Every year increases the interest taken in the sport by the colleges and since the suspension of slugging by the resolute action of the faculty of Harvard in 1883 there has been a marked improvement in the game. In the early days of football, Yale and Princeton led all other colleges at the game. Their elevens were little else than sluggers and when they got the ball they rushed it through the lines of their opponents without mercy. Harvard played more gentle and with some show of science. The result was it was left far behind in the race by other universities and not until Harvard encountered repeated defeats did it decide to adopt the tactics of its rivals. Six years ago (1883) Cambridge trained a team of giants to meet Yale and Princeton and determined to beat them at their own game. The team was instructed to defeat their rivals even if they had to play every man of the rival team, "hors de combat." In other words it was to be a "free fight." News of this arrangement reached the ears of the Harvard faculty and they immediately took steps to prevent the members of their team from being subjected to the brutal handling that was clearly in store for them. The faculty demanded that the rule then in force that a player be warned three times before being disqualified for slugging be rescinded and that instead he be thrown out after the first offense. This demand and all protests were unavailing and the game was played under the old rules (Princeton won, 26-7). But this was the last game played that way. In 1884, the suggestion of the Harvard faculty was adopted generally. (No three warnings any more, a man was ejected after the first infraction.)

Kletsch is generally credited with bringing to Wisconsin the first egg-shaped pigskin football that replaced the round rubber ball used in the earlier age of Association ball in the East. As a

21

former star center, guard, or fullback at Stevens Institute, Kletsch naturally taught his Calumets and later the Wisconsin team what was called the Eastern style of play. It emphasized running wide, smashing through the line with mass power, actually heaving the ballcarrier over the line at times, or lateral passing to get around the ends quickly. On defense his teams used a nine-man line with one roving linebacker and a safety. (The forward pass was not legalized until 1906.)

Uniforms were simple, although they had evolved, indeed, from what Princeton and Rutgers used in their first intercollegiate game in 1869. In fact those Princeton and Rutgers players used no uniforms at all. They simply removed their jackets and played in street clothes. After all, football in that day and until the turn of the century was a "free fight" or slugging match, and a young man could fight or slug as well in street clothes as in a uniform. Kletsch later told how in his college career at Stevens he had suffered broken ribs, a broken nose, and a broken collarbone.

Pictures of Wisconsin's first team in 1889 show what the men wore against the Calumets—heavy quilted pants, black stockings, and white canvas vests laced tight and sometimes smeared with grease or vaseline. Emblazoned on the vests in cardinal were the letters "U" and "W." Since players had to buy their own uniforms there was a slight difference in the cut of the vests at times, although each bore the bright "U" and "W." The shoes were ordinary heavy street brogans laced or buttoned with do-it-yourself strips of leather tacked to the soles for traction.

Long hair was a desirable adjunct to the pads, and the Badger yearbook of 1899 referred to it in a poem:

How long should the halfback wear his hair?
Asks the coed young and gay,
As she views his locks so long and fair.
Why, till after Thanksgiving Day.

Thanksgiving Day, of course, was the traditional last day of the season.

The football player of this day was a heroic figure indeed. The *Sentinel* described him like this:

The football player is a broad shouldered, smooth faced, bright eyed, long haired young man and is a good fellow to know, if he has not grown egotistical through his victories. He is really our modern knight errant who fights for the honor of his alma mater instead of his family name and for the praise from his lady in laces as he stands before her in his ripped, mud bespattered and sometimes blood bespattered suit, bruised but triumphant. And now he wears armor as the old knight. He has a rubber mask for his nose and mouth, pads for his ears, leather caps for his shoulders, pads for his stomach, shin protectors and bandages for his legs and arms to prevent him from being mauled or bruised. Yet with all of these to protect him he sometimes loses his life. But more American college men die of causes traceable to lack of exercise than to football. The world is bound to have its knights and our footballist is of a better sort than the blustering, threatening swashbuckler or the insipid creature sometimes met at an afternoon tea.

After the loosely organized and certainly modest beginning in 1889, Wisconsin in the 1890s embarked on an era of great significance in its football history:

1. Intense rivalries were established with Minnesota, Chicago, Michigan, Purdue, and Northwestern.

2. The 1890 team rolled up the first football victory, and the highest score in Wisconsin history, with a 106-0 defeat of Whitewater Normal at Madison.

3. In 1895 Wisconsin took a charter role in the organization of the Western Conference, subsequently known at different times as the Big Seven, Big Eight, Big Nine, or Big Ten, depending on the number of members.

4. In 1896 the wandering feet of Pat O'Dea were directed to Wisconsin. O'Dea was the great Australian kicker who was regarded by most, certainly by Wisconsin men, as the greatest kicker of all time. The appraisal is one in which Walter Camp himself joined when he wrote in one of the early Football Guides, "O'Dea put the foot in football as no man ever has or as no man probably ever will again."

All of the rivalries were bitterly fought from the beginning and have continued to be so to this day, except the Chicago series. Chicago abandoned football after the 1939 season and 22 games with Wisconsin. The Wisconsin-Minnesota contests, dropped for one year in 1906 by faculty order, constitute the oldest football rivalry in the Middle West. The faculty order was in response to the public revulsion nationally over football's brutality, with its flying wedges and mass power plays, and to widespread corruption. (A survey by the *Chicago Tribune* showed 18 deaths from football in 1905 and scores of serious injuries.)

In the era up to and just beyond the turn of the century, Wisconsin had a succession of coaches, all understandably from the East, where football had been born in 1869. Most of them were seasonally employed by the Football Association. After Alvin Kletsch came Ted Mestre of Yale in 1890; Herb Alward, Harvard, 1891; Frank Crawford, Yale, 1892; Parke H. Davis, Princeton, 1893; Hiram Stickney, Harvard, 1894-95; and Phil King, Princeton, during 1896-1902 and again for one year in 1905.

Davis, a magnetic personality, was the first full-time coach. Because he felt his Badgers needed a little help at tackle, a position he had played at Princeton, he enrolled as a graduate student in English and played with the team. His enrollment satisfied the only eligibility requirement of the time.

Minnesota was a constant nemesis to Wisconsin in those years, starting with the first game in 1890. Minnesota won, 63-0, destroying any illusions the Badgers might have had following their 106-0 victory over Whitewater two weeks earlier. Minnesota also won, 26-12, in 1891; 32-4 in 1892; and 40-0 in 1893.

The 1893 game had an incident that Christy Walsh used in his *Intercollegiate Football 1869-1933* to reveal what the game was really like in that day. He wrote:

In the early nineties college teams received absolutely no support from school funds. (At Wisconsin the student Football Association, as mentioned, handled everything from schedules to finances.) Hence it was necessary to select well-to-do managers who could finance the team when receipts were at low ebb. In 1893, the Wisconsin

24

Charles Kendall Adams was university president in the nineties when Wisconsin helped lay the groundwork of the Intercollegiate Conference of Faculty Representatives now known as the Big Ten.

team, managed by C. B. Culbertson, journeyed to Minneapolis for its annual tilt with the Gophers. The team finances at the Badger institution were in bad shape, Mr. Culbertson holding the bag to the tune of several hundred dollars. Minneapolis buzzed with excitement and at the 2 p.m. kickoff the Minnesota field was filled to capacity. Minnesota won, 40-0. After the game the Wisconsin manager entered the Badger dressing room loaded down with two bags of money representing Wisconsin's share of the gate. "Well, boys," he shouted, passing out a ten dollar bill to each player and taking a few nips from his bottle of good cheer, "we are slaughtered, but solvent and satisfied."

If Culbertson and the Football Association were "solvent and satisfied," however, Badger followers were getting restive. Wisconsin in those first four meetings had scored only 16 points to Minnesota's 161. But the day of reckoning was at hand, however slow it might have been in coming. In 1894 under Coach Stickney, in the last game to be played on the lower campus before the games were moved to Camp Randall, Wisconsin beat Minnesota, 6-0.

Actually the game was brought about only after much bickering between the rival student managers who handled all arrangements, L. W. Myers of Wisconsin and J. E. O'Brien of Minnesota. Minnesota, having mauled Wisconsin in the four previous meetings and holding the Western Championship (as it was called since there was no conference as yet), at first flatly refused to play in Madison. The correspondence between the two managers tells the story.

After earlier discussion, this was the letter Myers sent to O'Brien, dated October 30, 1894:

I have delayed replying to your last hoping that I would be able to accept your invitation and come up to Minneapolis to talk with you about a game. I might be able to do so yet but I'm afraid it would be fruitless. If you adhere to your determination not to come down here a game will be impossible because we cannot go up there. As you place the matter on financial grounds I will make a

26

financial arrangement with you. I understand you have no game scheduled for Thanksgiving Day; now if you will play us here (Madison) on that day, I will make you this offer which is more than double what I give any other team. I will give you a guarantee of $500 for the game and will give you the option of one half of the gross receipts. I think this offer is certain proof of our bona fide desire to meet you and I hope I may hear from you at your earliest convenience. Signed: L. W. Myers.

Several days later, Myers received this answer:

Yours received. I asked you to come here and we would talk business. Instead you resort to the same old methods of chewing the rag on paper. I am through—was through long ago for that matter. We have no game on Thanksgiving Day but we play in Denver on the 24th and will probably play another game near Denver on Thanksgiving Day. At any rate we will not be back in Minneapolis much before that date. Mr. Myers, there is one thing you can be assured of and that is Minnesota will not play in Madison this year or any other year until we have something to gain by going there.

I assured you long ago that we stood pat and if you wish to play us you must meet us here (Minneapolis) and I care little whether you play us or not. I know of no date on which we can play except November 10th and for that date I can meet your offer but I do not care to carry on so much needless correspondence. If you are as sincere as I am, believe me there is no hope for a game. Minnesota will not play in Madison until there is something to be gained by doing so. And you will gradually appreciate the truth of this statement. Signed: J. E. O'Brien.

Minnesota, it turns out, had no game in or near Denver as O'Brien claimed. At least the record shows none. In fact, Minnesota, which had an undefeated and untied team in five games in 1892 and in six games in 1893, had only three games on its schedule at the time Wisconsin tried so desperately to arrange a game for 1894. Minnesota had games with Grinnell,

Purdue, and Beloit, all of which it won by respective scores of 10-2, 24-0, and 40-0.

The apparently adamant O'Brien eventually relented, however, and took the $500 guarantee to play in Madison, November 17. The guarantee, which had to be paid in advance, was drawn from the meager Football Association treasury and supplemented by contributions from students and Madison merchants.

The game finally decided upon, the college and the city spared no efforts to make it a success. Windows were decorated in the cardinal and white and maroon and gold as never before. Madison newspapers, of course, gave the game major attention. One barbershop even had its barbers decked out in cardinal jackets. Temporary stands were built on the lower campus field, and fraternities and sororities fought over seats in these choice locations.

The newspapers paid attention to every small detail, as this account in one of the Madison papers the day before the game reveals:

> The Minnesota players left their Gopher home early Friday morning and after a pleasant day's ride reached the capitol city of their enemy, the Badgers. Their ride down was for the most part passed in quiet, the responsibility of doing credit to their state weighing down their otherwise lightened spirits. They were heartily received at East Madison by a half thousand partisans of the cardinal who after greeting the visitors with the "Ski-U-Rah" gave their own stirring "U-Rah-Rah-Wisconsin." The team was escorted to the Park Hotel. Here they were soon registered under the flaring title, "Minnesota Football Team."
>
> After supper and a little lounging the team was disposed of in bed. Here the spirit of fun showed itself and a general pillow fight was engaged in.

On the day of the game attention to every detail was just as complete as this further excerpt from a Madison paper reveals: "Early this morning, the rest of the Minnesota contingent arrived, 200 strong, headed by the Minnesota cadet band. The procession formed in the middle of the street, four abreast and two blocks long, and started their Indian zigzag up the street to the Park Hotel."

Continuing the recitation, the newspaper said the field was as hard as pavement at an early hour but turned to sticky clay as the sun's rays struck it.

Long before 2 o'clock the temporary stands, holding about 500, were filled, and people were refused admission. Even the nearby trees and rooftops were occupied by spectators. Notables in the crowd included former Governor Fairchild, Governor Peck, and Senator Vilas.

No special provisions having been made for Minnesota rooters or the college band, those visitors were compelled to find what standing room they could. Flimsy ropes kept all others off the playing area.

At 3 o'clock the teams lined up. Wisconsin started with Walter Sheldon, left end; Walter Alexander, left tackle; George Bunge, left guard; Fred Kull, center; John Patsy Ryan, right guard; J. F. A. Pyre, right tackle; H. F. Dickinson, right end; T. U. Lyman, quarterback; Oscar Nelson, left halfback; Ikey Karel, right halfback; John Richards, fullback; and G. H. Trautman, H.F. Cochems, W.H. Bunge, J. Major, and F.W. Bosendahl, substitutes. Pyre later joined the faculty as an instructor in English.

H. O. Jacobs, Wisconsin's regular right guard, could not play because of typhoid fever. His loss also had a side effect, because it was his additional duty to kick the 225-pound Kull occasionally to stir him up, the center being a gentle sort of soul.

Wisconsin used only 12 men in the game. When Sheldon dislocated his shoulder early in the second half, Major replaced him.

Minnesota's lineup included John Harrison at left end; John Dalrymple, left tackle; A. T. Larson, left guard; G. E. Finlayson, center; E. F. Harding, right guard; Will Walker, right tackle; Will Dalrymple, right end; Van Campen, quarterback; Charles Adams, left half; Walter Southwrath, right half; and Reuben Cutler, fullback. The substitutes were Parker, Pettibone, Kehoe, Conchet, Mathews, Slussen, and Winkjer.

The newspaper went on to praise the two coaches, T. Cochran of Minnesota (Yale '94) and Stickney of Wisconsin, and the two trainers, John Warren of Minnesota and John

Hickey of Wisconsin.

The game naturally produced heavy betting. And betting was different from what it is today. No points. Would a team win or not at odds? Would a team score or not? The *Chicago Record Herald* had this comment about wagering on the game: "Minnesota's form has been so good that their friends are willing to wager almost any amount that their team will win. Wagers of 2 to 5 are also offered that they prevent the Badgers from scoring."

On the same matter, a Madison paper said the day after the game, "It is impossible to estimate how much money changed hands on the game but it is safe to say that it was probably in excess of $5,000. Mr. Thomas Morgan held stakes in the neighborhood of $700 and a similar sum was put up at the Park Hotel but these were probably insignificant sums as compared with the money that found private stake holders. Minnesota businessmen were represented largely in pools. Some heavy bluff bets of large dimensions were offered before these pools were tapped on the side by small and sundry incisions."

The money in the Park Hotel was made known by a notice posted in the lobby: "We the undersigned have money to put on the Minnesota team. We take this means so that Madison people cannot say they had no chance to bet. Signed: A. C. Johnson, E. L. Clifford, E. S. Stevens."

The Mr. Morgan referred to as a holder of stakes, or "Dad" Morgan as he was better known to generations of Wisconsin students, owned a student gathering place and billiard parlor on State Street which before prohibition served sandwiches and imported beer. During and after prohibition it dispensed sandwiches and malted milks. "Dad" was a ready friend to any student who might need bail money or any other kind of help. A board in his place of business stated the betting odds.

As for the game itself George Downer, who was a spectator, never tired of talking about it. He wrote in his program memoirs:

The story of that 6-0 victory over a great Minnesota team has often been told. T. U. Lyman, Wisconsin captain and quarterback, dazed by a blow on the head early, played the entire game in a mental blank—which should

Thomas (Dad) Morgan's eating and drinking place on State Street was a hangout for generations of students.

prove something to students of the subconcious mind. Big John Richards, fullback, gave the signals for the first time in his life, then whispered to Lyman his part in the play, shoved him back into position, and called for the ball before the bewildered captain had time to forget his part. The Badger line fought heroically and held the heavier Gophers at all stages (once holding Minnesota on the five yard line) forcing the game into a kicking contest. Richards, who had never been able to catch punts, did not trust Lyman to do so and went back and handled a score of kicks himself. Finally in the second half, Ikey Karel, the Red Grange of his day, went around end behind beautiful interference (when was interference anything but beauti-

31

ful?) and ran 50 yards for a touchdown from which Richards kicked goal. The game was played on the lower campus muddy from heavy rain before 8,000 persons, the largest crowd which had witnessed a game in Madison up to that time.

The *Madison Democrat* went into rhapsodies to describe the game under the headline, "Great is Wisconsin." It said, "The game was the prettiest, the most manly fought and at the same time the most desperate of contests ever seen in the West and was as close and exciting as the hardest fought battle of its kind ever fought in America. Never but once was Wisconsin sure of victory and that was when time was called at the end of the last half."

The *Milwaukee Journal* had this comment on Karel's winning touchdown: "When little Karel had done it, he sat down and wept. The excitement was too much for him." The same story pointed out that Karel had been tackled by Van Campen, Minnesota's safety, on the five yard line and that the momentum of the two clashing bodies had carried Karel over the goal line. It added that Karel said it would take a month to recover from his bruises.

The Wisconsin campus was bedlam all through the night. A huge bonfire was kept burning on the lower campus with any kind of wood the students could find. This included Dean Birge's wooden sidewalk a block or two away, for which they later had to pay. President Charles Kendall Adams was serenaded at his home until early morning. And the student newspaper, the *Daily Cardinal*, printed an extra edition on cardinal paper.

Not only the campus but also the entire city revelled in the victory, and one of the Madison papers implied what the victory had meant economically to the community: "Up to 2:30 p.m. 64 had registered at the Park Hotel, 55 at the Van Etta, 12 at the Capitol and 8 at the Schulkamp. The Minnesota team will leave Madison by the 9:45 train over the St. Paul road." The Van Etta offered fricasseed gopher on the menu that night and had the Wisconsin team as its guest.

The western title was immediately claimed by Wisconsin— there was no Big Ten as yet—but Michigan, defeated only by

Cornell of the East and tied by Orchard Lake, disputed this. Attempts to bring the teams together for a showdown in December were futile. Wisconsin challenged, suggesting an indoor game in Chicago, but Michigan ignored every approach.

Coaches As Officials
And A Forfeit

A game which Wisconsin forfeited to Purdue, 1-0, early in the season clearly did not help Wisconsin's title claim. It was one of the two games the Badgers lost that year, the second being against the Chicago Athletic Association. The Minnesota victory and others over Chicago, Iowa, Beloit, and the Chicago Athletic Association in a second meeting more than offset the defeats.

The forfeit was an unfortunate incident. The coaches had agreed in arrangements for the game that they would officiate as referee and umpire, changing roles between halves. Stickney of Wisconsin was to be referee the first half and D. W. Balliett of Purdue, umpire.

Wisconsin led, 6-0, late in the first half on Norsky Larson's touchdown early in the game when Balliett ejected Wisconsin captain Lyman for alleged roughness. The ejection caused an uproar on the field, and the Badgers simply refused to continue without their captain. As umpire, under the rules of that day, Balliett alone had the authority to kick a man out.

The uproar, of course, continued in the press. Wisconsin's student paper, the *Cardinal*, had this to say about the game: "Balliett ruled Lyman off for what he called unnecessary roughness. A ranker, more unjust decision than this was never made on any field. In less than two minutes the half would have been over and Balliett's power of ruling anyone off would have been at an end. He knew this and his decision, utterly without foundation, was the result. The game was not forfeited to Purdue

but left unfinished. No time was called. Mr. Balliett made no request of Referee Stickney to ask the teams to continue and under the rules only the referee can award a game."

Under the heading, "UW Boys Home from Purdue Disgusted," the *Madison State Journal* had this story: "The 'UW' football team returned from Purdue this noon. Every member of the team says the game was unfairly umpired. Balliett, the Purdue umpire, gave the game to that college. Said a UW man, 'The score of the game still stands at 6-0 in favor of UW and no decision of Balliett can change it. Stickney, the UW umpire, in the second half, decided it although the game was declared off.'"

One Madison paper saw an end to the relationship with Purdue:

It is not probable that Wisconsin university and Purdue will meet again on the football field unless the latter team agrees to play this fall with an unprejudiced referee and umpire. The Madison boys returned home last evening and were bitter in their denunciation of the Purdue men. They claimed that Umpire Balliett exceeded his power on all occasions and deliberately robbed Wisconsin of the game by ruling Lyman out when there was no cause for such action. Bachman, the player who was supposed to have been slugged by the Madison captain, stated that he had no complaint to make at all; that Lyman had played a fair and gentlemanly game. The Madison boys offered to remain over in Lafayette and play Purdue again with the understanding that they would not receive any of the gate receipts unless they won the game, the referee and umpire to be selected from outside the colleges. There has been considerable hard feeling between Purdue and Wisconsin, the trouble dating back two years when the Madison team also went to Purdue. The Badger boys were handled without kid gloves and received a severe shaking up. (Purdue won 32-4.) When Purdue visited Madison last year the old feeling broke out again but this time Wisconsin players had the long end of the score. (Wisconsin won, 36-30.) It seems that Purdue tried to work the same racket on the Madison boys as two years ago.

The paper did not mention what this "racket" was or that in the Purdue game at Madison the year before Wisconsin had a Wisconsin law student, Joe Turner, as referee. He was one of two Turners in the game. He worked the game in top hat, tan topcoat, pearl gray spats, and cane. Purdue's Turner, a 300-pound center, played in new tight pants which he had had tailored back home and which split when he bent over the ball. The tailor had made them too tight. The game was halted while repairs were hastily made on the field with shoe strings and a pen knife.

After numerous ups and downs which characterized most of the early years, Wisconsin embarked in 1895 on the "winningest decade" of victories in its history. From 1895 through 1905, under Phil King in seven of these years, Wisconsin won 81 games, lost only 19, and tied three. It ran up a winning streak of 17 straight at one point, longest in the school's history; made off with three championships, one of them shared with Michigan; and contributed a dozen names to the pantheon of Wisconsin's football immortals. It was also in 1895, on January 11, that Purdue President James H. Smart called together the presidents of seven other middle western schools to discuss common athletic problems, which eventually led to the formation of the Western Conference.

King became coach in 1896, succeeding Hiram Stickney under rather unusual circumstances. Stickney coached in 1894 and 1895 and in keeping with the common practice of that day played with the team whenever he felt his presence was needed. Just before the Chicago game in 1895 and for an unrevealed reason, Captain Lyman announced to the press that Coach Stickney would not play with the team in Chicago the next day but act as umpire.

The stigma of professionalism had attached itself to Stickney's name in his undergraduate days at Harvard, and it kept popping up at Wisconsin. Princeton had protested him as a pro, and Harvard undertook a study of the charge but cleared him. A couple of years later Walter Camp of Yale, familiar with the situation, wrote to a friend in Madison who had inquired about Stickney's days at Harvard: "'Not proven' I believe was the verdict in the case of Stickney," Camp wrote. "To tell the truth the charges of professionalism can hardly ever be proven

Phil King, a Princeton graduate, gave Wisconsin a record of 65 victories, 11 defeats, and 1 tie in a coaching career from 1896 through 1902 and then again in 1905.

in the case of college men and before any tribunal which must always be partisan. It must be the spirit within the university that keeps things clean. A captain can elect his own team and if the public feeling and his are for a clean team, he will get one; if not, he is liable to place immediate victory over principle."

Lyman's announcement hit the campus like a bombshell and a Madison newspaper commented like this:

Captain Lyman of the University stated today that Coach Stickney would not play with the eleven tomorrow in the game with the Chicagoans but would umpire. Mr. Lyman's intention to play college football and not a professional game is altogether commendable. Much has been said of Stickney's playing with the eleven although every one understands that the brilliant young player (and coach) is ineligible. The fact that mere love of the game brought him to Madison will not silence the carpings and protests of other colleges but will justly and otherwise attach to the state university an odium as an encourager of professionalism that friends of the university do not desire. The fact that the University of Minnesota has a shady record in the matter of inserting professionals in her athletic teams and Ann Arbor (Michigan) even a shadier one is not justification for vying with those institutions. Nor is the fact that Wisconsin is supposed to have a poorer team than usual pertinent. It increases the temptation to run Stickney in but does not warrant the impropriety. This is the attitude of the best friends of the University. College football at its best is football by students—young men whose first devotion is to their books, who are in their respective colleges with a single hearted, earnest endeavor to get an education and fit themselves for life in one of the world's recognized occupations.

Football in such hands is an unobjectionable diversion and may become a heroic contest engaging the best physical and mental powers of any man. This is the football the University of Wisconsin should adapt and maintain; it can afford to leave all other kinds to inferior institutions where lower ideals obtain. The determination of Captain Lyman to go down to defeat if necessary to maintain honor will, if persevered in, be applauded by the faculty and alumni and the more conservative of the student body. It would doubtless be possible to smuggle Stickney in the lineup but Captain Lyman has taken high ground in the matter. The incident should cause the men of the University of Wisconsin to be proud of their captain, their team and their college and to get sharply after their rivals to see that the teams to be met are equally honest in competition.

Chicago won the game, 22-12, and although Stickney had done nothing other coaches of his day had not done, he left

Madison several weeks later. In the last game of the season following the Chicago game, Wisconsin, again without Stickney in the lineup, lost to Minnesota, 14-10. So King became coach in 1896.

The 1901 team was the only undefeated eleven of this "winningest decade" with a 9-0 record. The 1900 team won eight of nine games, losing only to Minnesota on a kick after touchdown, 6-5. The 1899 team won nine of 11 games, yielding only to Yale at New Haven, 6-0, and Chicago, 17-0. The 1898 team was victorious in nine of 10 games, losing only to Chicago, 6-0. The 1897 team won nine of 10 games, defeated only by the alumni, 6-0, in a regularly scheduled contest which was supposed to become an annual event. And the 1896 team, King's first, captured seven of nine games, downed only by the Carlisle Indians in an indoor game in the old Chicago Coliseum, 18-8, and tying Northwestern, 6-6, in rain when Chet Brewer fell on the Northwestern center's high pass into the end zone for Wisconsin's touchdown. Those were glorious years, indeed, in which tradition was built and fine, lasting rivalries were established.

Within what was then the Western Conference, Wisconsin rightfully claimed the championships in 1896 and 1897 and tied with Michigan in 1901, when both teams won every game both in and outside the conference. This was the first of Michigan's awesome "point-a-minute" teams which not only ran wild in scoring (550 points) but did not allow a point in 11 games. Wisconsin in nine games, meanwhile, scored 317 points but allowed little Knox College a touchdown in a 23-5 romp.

The championship team of 1896 had a few returning stars from the great 1894 team that had beaten Minnesota. Four- or five-year playing careers were not uncommon because of the graduate work players often took after their senior year. This '96 team took the field with Walter Sheldon and Chet Brewer at ends, William Atkinson and J. F. A. Pyre at tackles, Jerry Riordan and John Patsy Ryan at guards, Nathan Comstock at center, John Gregg or Charles McPherson at quarterback, Oscar Nelson or Hereward Peele at left half, Ikey Karel at right half, John Richards at fullback, and Walter Cory, substitute lineman. Lewis Alsted was manager and Richards, captain.

Most of the 1897 title team's players also overlapped from

39

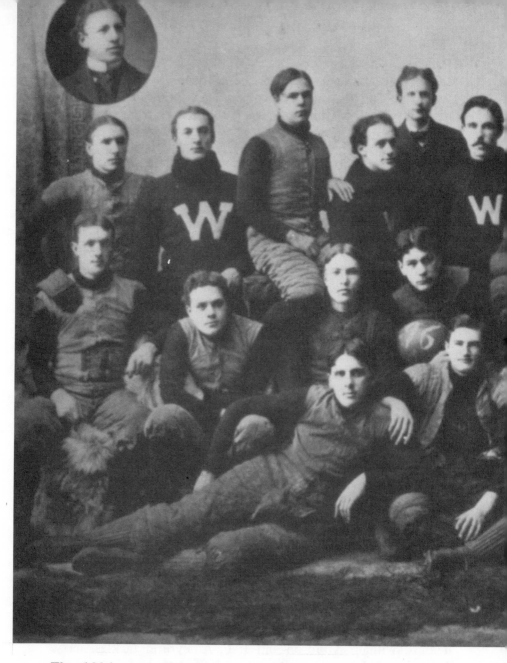

This 1896 team, with a 7-1-1 record, gave Wisconsin its first Big Ten championship. Phil King was the coach. John Richards, in middle holding ball, was captain. Inset: Coach Phil King. Top row, standing, left to right: Harry G. Forrest; Paul Tratt; Lewis L. Alsted, manager; Nathan Comstock; Pat O'Dea; and assistant manager William Mann. Middle row: Charles W. McPherson;

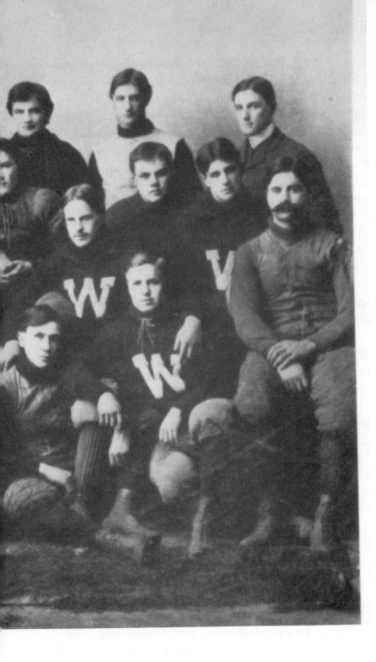

*Frank Bean; Walter Sheldon; J.F.A. Pyre; Walter Alexander;
Chester L. Brewer; Walter B. Cory; and Earl S. Anderson.
Seated: Hereward J. Peele; Jerry P. Riordan; Captain John R.
Richards; Oscar M. Nelson; John P. Gregg; and William A.
Atkinson. In Front: John C. "Ikey" Karel and John E. Ryan.*

41

earlier teams. It had W. C. Hazzard at center, Nathan Comstock and Jerry Riordan at guards, H.G. Forrest and Harvey Holmes at tackles, E. S. Anderson and Joe Dean at ends, Henry Cochems at right half, Hereward Peele at left half, John Gregg at quarterback, Pat O'Dea at fullback, C.T. Fugitt, as substitute end, and W. M. Jolliffe, substitute halfback. H. Kendall Clark was the team manager, Carl Geilfuss, assistant manager, and Jerry Riordan, captain.

The undefeated, untied team of 1901 which shared the Big Ten title with Michigan is always classed with Wisconsin's greatest. It not only allowed Knox the only points scored against it but won every game by at least three touchdowns. It was a team of "power, speed, stamina, and smartness" as one observer put it. It lined up in its big games with Emil Skow at center, Arne Lerum and Ward Westcott at guards, Art Curtis and Emil Hammerson at tackles, Bill Juneau and Red Abbott at ends, Norsky Larsen and Eddie Cochems at halfbacks, Joe Fogg at quarterback, and Earl Driver at fullback. Fred Vogel was manager, Henry Cole, assistant manager, and Curtis, captain. In early games Earl Schrieber had been one of the starting guards, but a week before the Minnesota game, second to last of the season, the Gophers protested that he had taken $12 for coaching a high school team for three days in 1900. Schrieber admitted this and was disqualified. Wisconsin still won, 18-0, Curtis blocking a punt for a safety in the first two minutes and then leading on to an easy victory.

Except for Michigan and Chicago, Wisconsin held its own or more with other conference teams in this "winningest decade." The Badgers split 10 games with Minnesota, won five and tied two in seven games with Northwestern, and won two and tied one in three games with Illinois.

In games outside the conference, the team beat Notre Dame twice, 54-0 and 58-0; Iowa State twice, 28-6 and 45-0; Nebraska, 18-0; Kansas twice, 50-0 and 38-0; Marquette, 33-0; and fattened up on an assortment of smaller colleges and high schools. High schools in this era were often good teams, strengthened as they were by Spanish-American War veterans just back from service seeking to continue their interrupted secondary school educations. Wisconsin beat Madison High School three times, once 8-0 in a game called at the half because of rain. It defeated Hyde Park (Illinois) High School twice in games in which it first encountered Walter Eckersall, a 115-pound quarterback who later enrolled with Alonzo Stagg at Chicago.

The Carlisle game in Chicago's Coliseum in 1896 was something special. It was Wisconsin's only appearance in an indoor game and only meeting with the fabled Indians. The Chicago Press Club arranged and sponsored it. At intervals far too frequent, a punt would go booming up and lodge in the rafters or bounce out of play into the stands. The game would then come to a halt until the ball was retrieved. Between halves an Indian band played. M. Wheelock, a regular Carlisle guard, left the playing field to lead the band with baton while still in football uniform. At one point a foul tackle below the knees was claimed, and play was stopped while the players argued with the referee. (A tackle below the knees was illegal then.)

Carlisle was a 2-to-1 favorite in odds posted at the Chicago Stock Exchange and substantiated the odds, winning 18-8. The *Milwaukee Journal*, in covering the game which was played on a mixture of tan bark and clay, reported: "The Indians seemed to glide along like swallows; they hardly touched the ground but fairly flew. They swept the interference of Wisconsin with a single sweep of their arm and went plunging down the field which they left strewn with Wisconsin men in the dirt."

The game was a society affair of lorgnette magnitude and drew a crowd of 15,000—women in boas and men in derbies and ascot ties. Preliminary announcements said that President-Elect William McKinley would attend and there see his first football game. Later reports did not tell whether the great man actually arrived. He probably did not.

The postgame rehash strikes a distinctly modern note. The losers complained about the referee, Frank Gould of Amherst.

"We are not going to play the baby act," said Wisconsin right guard Ryan. "The Indians were too much for us but the score would have been different with any other referee. We feel we received very unjust treatment."

Sentiment was different in the other dressing room. "The best feature of the game was the fine officiating," says a book on Carlisle football. "The officials received a great hand for their work."

Coach Phil King followed up his first championship in 1896 with another in 1897 with this team. It had a 9-1 record. Jerry Riordan, in middle holding ball, was captain. Top row, left to right: H.R. Chamberlain; C.T. Fugitt; Harry G. Forrest; W.C. Hazzard; E.S. Anderson; Coach Phil King; and Carl F. Geilfuss, assistant manager. On end, at left: James Temple, team trainer.

Seated, in middle, left to right: Harvey Holmes; Captain Jerry P. Riordan; H.F. Cochems; and Andrew O'Dea, trainer. Second Row: W.M. Jolliffe; Joseph Dean; Pat O'Dea; John P. Gregg; Paul Tratt; Harry E. Bradley; and Alonzo A. Chamberlain. Front Row: Manager H. Kendall Clark; Hereward J. Peele; Albert C. Shong; and Nathan Comstock.

The Yale game in 1899 which Wisconsin lost, 6-0, on the first invasion of the East was so well received by Easterners that the suggestion was made that the game become an annual event. But for one reason or another it never did. (Wisconsin waited until 1947 to square this particular score, winning at New Haven, 9-0.)

Wisconsin's 17-game winning streak began with the first victory over Notre Dame in 1900, 54-0, and ended in 1902 with a 6-0 licking at the hands of Michigan's second great "point-a-minute" team. Wisconsin never did beat any of those fabulous Wolverine teams, losing in successive years starting in 1902 by 6-0, 16-0, 28-0, and 12-0. But they still generally fared better than most of Michigan's other challengers.

In Michigan's incredible five-year era which ended when Chicago won 2-0 in 1905, the Wolverines scored 2,771 points, this before the forward pass was introduced. They allowed only 42 points, including the two on a safety that Chicago used to break the string. The 1901 team did not permit more than a 12-yard gain and never allowed any opponent closer to Michigan's goal than the 35 yard line.

Although this was the "winningest decade" in Wisconsin's history, Michigan was not the only nemesis. There was also Chicago, which won six of 10 meetings in this period, much to the chagrin of Wisconsin's campus, which expressed itself with this poem in the Badger yearbook:

> You've the cleanest team on earth
> I don't think Mr. Stagg;
> They've been amateurs from birth
> Aber ni't Mr. Stagg.
> We were doubtless very mean
> When we didn't have you screen
> Their past history that's so clean
> So we think, Mr. Stagg.
>
> Oh, you played a nice, clean game,
> I don't think Mr. Stagg;
> And the slugging was quite tame
> Aber ni't Mr. Stagg.
> But we'd only like to say

of the man who kicked O'Dea
He'll go without delay
So we think, Mr. Stagg.
And he'll ride home in a dray, Mr. Stagg.

Of course, you won with ease,
I don't think, Mr. Stagg.
And for you it was a cheese
Aber ni't Mr. Stagg.
But although we feel quite sore
We are thirsting for your gore
In another year or more
So we think, Mr. Stagg
We will turn about the score, Mr. Stagg.

Stagg had made the mistake of saying publicly after Wisconsin had scored a 23-8 victory over Chicago's Maroons in 1897 that the better team had not won, emphasizing that Chicago was "purely amateur." Wisconsin's campus had not forgotten the slur. Incidentally, Stagg himself, as all other coaches of the day, had played with his team in 1894 when the Maroons also lost to Wisconsin, 30-0.

One of Chicago's own immortals, Walter Eckersall, a mighty mite who never weighed more than 145 pounds, was largely responsible for Wisconsin's difficulties with the Maroons in this "winningest decade." In 1903 "Eckie" almost singlehandedly beat the Badgers, 15-6, with three dropkicks (35, 30, and 8 yards), which at this time still counted five points each. A year later he helped beat Wisconsin again, 18-11, with a 106-yard punt return for a touchdown.

His winning goals in 1903 prompted a Chicago newspaper to headline the story of the game, "Eckersall 15, Wisconsin 6." As a Big Ten referee in a game between Wisconsin and Michigan at Madison in 1923, Eckie supported his field judge, Colonel Mumma, on a controversial punt return and allowed Michigan a freak touchdown which beat Wisconsin, 6-3. Students then paraded around after the game with signs proclaiming, "Eckersall 6, Wisconsin 3, Michigan 0."

In the pantheon of Wisconsin football heroes of this early era, none occupies a higher niche than Pat O'Dea. "The Paul

Pat O'Dea, legendary kicker, came to Wisconsin in 1896 from Australia.

Bunyan of football" somebody once aptly called him. Only one word can describe his kicking feats: prodigious. The mere recitation of what he did almost boggles the mind:

O'Dea kicked a 110-yard punt against Minnesota in 1897. (Bear in mind that the field in his day was 110 yards long.)

He kicked a 57-yard goal against Chicago in 1897.

He kicked a 62-yard drop kick against Northwestern in 1898.

He kicked a 100-yard punt against Yale at New Haven in 1899.

He kicked a 57-yard place kick against Illinois in Milwaukee in 1899, with a curve applied to compensate for a strong wind.

He kicked a 60-yard drop while on a dead run against Minnesota in 1899.

It is understandably hard for today's generation to accept without a smile all that O'Dea did. The testimony of reliable witnesses is too strong to dispute in his case, however. Pat kicked with a snubnosed ball, which they say, is easier to kick than the pointed ball of today. But others in the nineties also kicked a snubnosed ball, and none, at least in the Middle West, ever approached him.

Gil Dobie, the famous Navy and Cornell coach who was an end at Minnesota from 1899 through 1901, always maintained that the greatest individual play he ever saw was O'Dea's 60-yard kick while on the run in the 1899 Wisconsin-Minnesota game at Minneapolis. Describing it, Dobie said that O'Dea, after eluding him in handling a punt, ran toward the sidelines and with other Minnesota players bearing down kicked a drop that sailed over the crossbar. The kick was at a difficult angle made harder because O'Dea, a right-footed kicker, was running to his left. The *Minneapolis Journal* had this comment on the play: "Great was the surprise of the Minnesota men to see O'Dea dodge an attack from Dobie and then deliberately kick a drop from the center of the field. A nicer kick could not have been made, and Wisconsin had a score, 5-0." (Wisconsin went on to win, 19-0.)

Bob Zuppke, Illinois' famous coach who spent his youth in Milwaukee and attended Wisconsin, always delighted in telling of O'Dea's 57-yard place kick against Illinois in 1899. "Zup" saw it while a little shaver from a rooftop across from the field in Milwaukee. "I couldn't believe my eyes," he once said. "The ball took off and just sailed higher and higher. It cleared the crossbar and carried clear out of the park."

The late Juste Lindgren, who played for Illinois in that game and later coached the Illini, always maintained that the kick went more than 60 yards. Wisconsin won, 23-0.

New York writers naturally raved about O'Dea's 100-yard punt against Yale the same year. In fact, one writer called it a 117-yard punt. O'Dea almost missed that game. He smashed his index finger on a door the morning of the game and bled so freely that Coach King at first was not going to let him play.

O'Dea is a story by himself aside from what he did kicking a football. He arrived unannounced on the campus at Madison from Melbourne, Australia, in the fall of 1896. He often explained how he happened to land in Madison.

"I was taking a trip around the world as a youth, keeping my eyes open for my brother, Andy, who had left home three years earlier," he said. "In Vancouver I heard that an O'Dea was coaching the 'yara-yara' stroke as crew coach at Wisconsin. Now there might have been a thousand O'Dea's in the world but only one who could be coaching crew and the distinctive 'yara-yara' stroke at that, so I took a train to Madison."

Pat further described the first meeting between these two. "I just said, 'Hello Andy,' when I saw him bending over a shell at the boathouse, and he just said, 'Hi kid, when did you get in?'" That was between two brothers who hadn't seen each other for three years and who had been separated by thousands of miles.

Andy naturally took Pat around the campus. Pat liked what he saw and decided to attend Wisconsin and study law.

How Pat came to Coach King's attention was still another bit of chance. Watching the team work out on the lower campus one afternoon in what he at first called "this crazy American game," Pat picked up a punt which happened to bounce his way and kicked it back. It must have been a tremendous kick because King could not get over to him fast enough.

"I thought I had done something wrong," Pat used to say. He soon found out. King had him in uniform the next day, and he began the career which lasted through the 1899 season. He appeared long enough in the opening game against Lake Forest to get off an 85-yard punt. In practice the next week he broke his arm and did not get into the lineup again until the Carlisle game, which closed the season. He captained the team in both 1898 and 1899.

King, of course, knew at once what he had in this kicking kangaroo and used him sparingly to carry the ball. However, as a fullback he ran 100 yards for a touchdown in the 36-0 victory over Beloit in 1899.

Upon graduation from law school in the spring of 1900, Pat went into coaching, going first to Notre Dame for two years, then to the University of Missouri for one. At Missouri old-timers still talk of the kicking feats he performed just to entertain students and faculty. In 1903 he gave up coaching and went West, settling in San Francisco. At this point his career became as bizarre as anything in football. Shortly before World War I he disappeared.

Pat himself later explained his disappearance as something he was driven to by the insistence of people to have him recount or demonstrate his kicking feats. "I just couldn't take it," he told friends later. "I couldn't stand it."

Be that as it may, for years no one knew what had happened. For a long time it was thought he had enlisted with an Australian outfit on its way to France and had been killed in action. The university alumni association made a world-wide search. Nothing turned up except that the Australian War Office did have a casualty by the name of "Pat O'Day." The spelling was different from that of Pat of Wisconsin, but that was presumed to be a mistake. It was reasonably concluded that Pat had been killed in the war.

Through all the years, however, Pat was very much alive. He had taken the name of Charles Mitchell, had moved to the small town of Westwood in northern California, and had started to work for a lumber company.

Why Charles Mitchell?

"I had a favorite cousin whose name was Charles," he explained. "My mother's maiden name was Mitchell."

The years of anonymity were not always happy. Pat retained his avid interest in football, but he had to be careful. The burden of having a concealed identity became as great as the burden of fame, and in 1933 he sought out the man who employed him, Willie Walker, and asked for advice in his plight. Walker, a Minnesota football player of the era just before O'Dea, was sympathetic. He advised O'Dea to reveal himself and offered to help through a sportswriting friend in San Francisco, Bill Leiser of the *Chronicle*.

So Leiser broke the story with authentication which included Pat's diploma from Wisconsin, a certificate Pat had received from an Australian society before he had left his homeland, and a scrapbook which recounted his kicking deeds.

The skeptics, so certain Pat had been killed in the war, at first refused to believe; even Pat's brother, Andy, was doubtful. Ikey Karel and Walter Alexander, both of whom had played with Pat, also doubted and regarded him as an impostor. But Pat persisted in efforts to make himself known.

"Who called signals when you played?" he was asked. "Where did you room in Madison?" "On what field were the games played in the nineties?"

The answers came easily: "I called signals at first but not my last year." "I roomed at George Borchsenius' house." "The games were played at old Camp Randall although we often practiced on the lower campus."

Slowly, unmistakable identity was established. Even brother Andy, when shown pictures, came around.

"That's my brother," Andy finally agreed. "I can tell by the indentation on the side of his face. He got that when a thug broke his jaw in Chicago, and I couldn't get a doctor to fix it up as it should have been."

As a special aside to Karel who used to hold the football on some of his occasional placements, Pat in turn asked, "Do you remember the bitters I had in 1898?"

The question referred to a case of bitters which he and some of the other boys nipped at before some of the games. "Remember what demons we would be when we took the field?"

To the *Journal*, questioning his identity because brother Andy had at first denied it, he sent this wire: "If Andrew O'Dea who expresses doubt will send me his address I will send him a letter that will remove any doubt. My identity has been established beyond any doubt. Also ask Judge Karel whether I didn't

One of the approaches to the Camp Randall Stadium is through this Civil War arch. The stadium site was the training ground of Wisconsin's famous Iron Brigade and later a prisoner of war camp.

make a reservation for him at the Dale Hotel in San Francisco in 1914 or 1915."

In 1934 the university brought Pat back to Madison as honored guest at the homecoming game with Illinois. In Chicago, Milwaukee, and Madison, he was feted as few football heroes have ever been. Here was a man back from the dead. (Underdog Wisconsin beat Illinois in the homecoming game, 7-3.)

Pat returned to Westwood after this new hour of glory and remained there for a few years before moving back to San Francisco. To the end he retained his interest in football and particularly in Wisconsin football. Wisconsin, in turn, maintained a constant interest in him.

Pat was an all-around athlete. In addition to football and track he also pulled a good oar and boxed. Despite his light weight—he weighed around 180 pounds on a six-foot frame—he was a bruising tackler in football and a safety in running back punts.

During his four-year college career (1896-99), Pat averaged better than 50 yards on punts and got off punts of 100 yards several times. He drop-kicked 31 field goals including 13 in one season (1899), drop-kicked four goals in one game (Beloit, 1899), a 62-yard goal against Northwestern (1898), a 60-yard goal against Minnesota (1899), and a 57-yard goal against Chicago (1897), and place-kicked a 57-yard goal against Illinois (1899).

The Badger yearbook went into rhapsodies with a poem about him in his junior year:

> The grandstand is a howling mass,
> The lines are crowded thick,
> Now center makes a clever pass,
> When Pat goes back to kick.
>
> Ten giant frames protect in front,
> Like twenty tons of brick,
> The captain signals for a punt,
> And Pat goes back to kick.
>
> Unerringly the pigskin flies,

Above the goal cross stick,
The rooter's "Rah Rah" rends the skies,
When Pat goes back to kick.

Say, you, who never yet have seen
The skillful kicker's trick,
Come out upon the white washed green,
Watch Pat go back to kick.

The author did not win the poetry award for the year, but he did reveal Pat's impact on the campus.

Early Giants In Cardinal

While Pat O'Dea was the most spectacular of the Badgers in this winningest decade of Wisconsin's early football history, there were others who have become an everlasting part of the university's lore and legend. They include Ikey Karel, John Richards, Art Curtis, Jerry Riordan, and Eddie Cochems, by all means; and T. U. Lyman; Keg Driver; Oscar Nelson; Alfred Larsen; Hereward Peele, a rugged Canadian; Paul Tratt; Joe Fogg; Walter Sheldon; Chet Brewer; Red Abbott; Sonny Pyre; Bill Juneau; Fred Kull; H. G. Jacobs, an ordained minister; Emil Skow; T. P. Crenshaw; A. C. Lerum; Walter Alexander; and R. Logemann. The list could go on.

"Give Ikey the ball," was a common chant of spectators while Karel played. He was, as George Downer described him, the Red Grange of his day. There was hardly a game, a victory or defeat, in which he did not star as a ballcarrier. He played as a freshman in 1892 and then four more years through 1896, the last of these after he had switched courses and entered law school. Karel never weighed more than 160 pounds and stood just under six feet. What he lacked in speed he compensated for with great spirit and an elusive stride. On defense he often played safety, in which position he handled punts. A familiar trick of his was to lay back, feigning indifference to the kick, then rush up at the last instant and catch the ball on the dead run. In later years, as a highly regarded county judge in Milwaukee, he was a "must" at all alumni functions, where his enthusiasm for football always pervaded the room.

Jerry Riordan was a contemporary guard who helped clear the way for Ikey. He played in 1894-97. In 1898 and 1899 he helped Phil King coach, then returned to school for a master's degree and played again in 1900. Linemen were eligible carriers in those days, and aside from being a good blocker, he was a better-than-average ballcarrier. In later years he coached football at Milwaukee South Side High School, turning out a succession of good teams for six years. He then gave up coaching and managed a large stock farm near Milwaukee.

John Richards won 11 major letters—more than any other man in Wisconsin history. In addition to football in 1892-96, and as captain the last two years, he was a hurdler on the track team from 1893 through 1897 and rowed on the crew in 1894. He began his football career as an end in 1892, then was switched to fullback the last four years. As a ballcarrier at 185 pounds, he was always marked on the field by his high knee action and generally reckless play. In 1911 he returned to coach the team but resigned after one season after a run-in with the commandant of the ROTC, who refused to excuse players from their military drill for spring football. He returned as coach in 1917. In 1918 he joined the war effort in Washington but came back as coach in 1919 and remained through 1922. In coaching he was best known for his emphasis on defense and his development of the screen pass, which the rulemakers outlawed after the 1922 season. As a player, he is generally credited with being the first man to use a helmet with earflaps. He had a Madison horseshoer make one for him.

Any list of Wisconsin's greatest tackles through the years must begin with Arthur Curtis, a legitimate star the first day he reported for practice as a freshman in 1898. He played as a regular on every team through 1901 and captained that undefeated team in his senior year. Though he never weighed more than 175 pounds, he was a terror, with quickness, spirit, and football savvy. He also played first base on the baseball team for three years. An honor student in the classroom, he became a distinguished doctor in Chicago and head of a department in Northwestern's Medical School after a brief but unhappy fling as a head coach at his alma mater in 1903 and 1904. His first team lost to Chicago, Minnesota, and Michigan, and he took the defeats so hard he resigned, but was persuaded to reconsider when the squad signed a petition asking him to stay. His 1904 team fared no better, and he did then resign. In 1905 Phil was recalled from his business in Washington, D.C., to succeed Curtis.

Eddie Cochems was more than a great halfback or end on the strong Wisconsin teams at the turn of the century, including the undefeated team of 1901. He was also the coach at St. Louis University a few years later which first developed and used the forward pass in a regular game. His historical impact on the game has never been fully recognized although well authenticated by Knute Rockne of Notre Dame. After his playing career which included a 100-yard kickoff return in the 35-0 victory over Chicago in 1901 and four touchdowns against Notre Dame in 1900, Cochems went into coaching immediately. In order, he was head coach for the North Dakota Aggies in 1902 and 1903, briefly an assistant with former teammate Art Curtis at Wisconsin in 1904, successor to John Heisman as head coach at Clemson in 1904 and 1905, and finally head coach and athletic director at St. Louis University in 1906.

The forward pass had just been legalized in 1906. Cochems, an Irishman with imagination, did something with it at once in his first year at St. Louis while others more firmly established in coaching stuck with the bruising old running or kicking game. For several weeks before the season opened Cochems drilled his strongest armed players on how to hold the ball and throw it, not end over end but like a projectile—a spiral. In fact, he preferred to call this new weapon in football's arsenal a "projectile pass."

As part of the practice, at a preseason training camp at Lake Beulah, Wisconsin, Cochems arranged a series of practice games with several nearby Wisconsin schools—Carroll College, Lawrence College, St. John's Military Academy, and Marquette University in that order. In the first game Carroll offered stiffer competition than anticipated in the scoreless first half, and in the second half Cochems had his team come up with its devastating "projectile." It did the trick, the Billikens completing seven of nine passes and winning easily 22-0. With his new weapon used sparingly to save it for the regular season, St. Louis then defeated Lawrence 6-0, St. John's, 27-0, and Marquette, 30-0. Through the regular season, using the pass

58

Eddie Cochems was a star halfback at the turn of the century, and later, as coach at St. Louis University, was the first college coach to make extensive use of the forward pass. He called it a "projectile pass."

extensively, St. Louis went undefeated, rolling up 407 points and allowing only 11.

Rockne wrote in his autobiography: "The forward pass came in quietly, almost obscurely. Eddie Cochems, coach at St. Louis University, enrolled a few boys with hands like steam shovels who could toss a football almost as far as they could throw a baseball. St. Louis played and defeated several big teams using the forward pass. One would have thought that so effective a play would have been instantly copied and become the vogue. The East, however, had not learned much about Midwest and Western football." (The East did learn when Notre Dame beat Army 35-13 in 1913.)

But while these men, Karel, Richards, Curtis, Riordan, Cochems, and the others were writing such winning pages in Wisconsin football history, there was also a growing feeling among the Wisconsin faculty that the way the pages were being written was an embarrassment to the educational purposes of the university. Faculty indifferences in the beginning had permitted student control, which, with its "anything to win" approach, invited evils and irregularities of all kinds.

Midwestern universities had long deplored what was happening. In 1895, in fact, President James H. Smart of Purdue had invited the presidents of Wisconsin, Chicago, Minnesota, Northwestern, Illinois, and Lake Forest to meet with him in Chicago to discuss their common problems. All had accepted. Charles Kendall Adams represented Wisconsin. An organization for regulation and control was set up consisting of one appointed faculty representative from each institution, and a rough set of rules was drawn up. Professor C. D. Barnes of the botany department became Wisconsin's faculty representative. On February 8, 1896, the appointed faculty representatives met in Chicago for the first time. Michigan replaced Lake Forest. What we today know as the "Western Conference" was born, although the idea of a league had not been the purpose of the presidents when they first met. All they had wanted were common rules by which to clean up intercollegiate athletics and to establish faculty control, ridding themselves of student practices inconsistent with higher education.

But a league it turned out to be and something much better than the loosely organized, little-known, and unacceptable Intercollegiate Athletic Association of the Northwest formed in 1892 by Wisconsin, Michigan, Minnesota, and Northwestern. To emphasize the faculty control they were determined to have, they called themselves "The Intercollegiate Conference of Faculty Representatives," which is still the official name. "Western Conference" is merely a convenient abbreviation, and "Big Seven," "Big Eight," "Big Nine," or "Big Ten" are even more convenient abbreviations, depending upon the number of members.

Casper Whitney, writing in *Harper's Weekly* in 1896, reflected the public's approval of what schools in the Middle West had done. "The most notable clearing in the atmosphere is to be seen in the West," he wrote. "Football—indeed all middle western college sports—was very near total extinction last year because of a rampant professional spirit that had ranged through nearly all universities, leaving corruption in its wake.

The meeting in Chicago last winter marked the beginning of a new and clarified era in Western college sports."

But Whitney, for the moment at least, did not look deep enough. After the meeting of 1896 the conference schools had common rules, but individually and collectively they did not live up to them because of the loopholes available. It was a simple matter, they all found out, to subscribe to the rules in good faith in a Chicago hotel room but quite another to apply them, especially to themselves. So the evils grew.

At Wisconsin, as guilty of irregularities as any, the faculty had had a light hand in athletics from the beginning but never faculty control, as the conference in these later years insisted upon. As early as 1889, the year Wisconsin played its first football game, the faculty had established a faculty committee on athletics as part of the student-dominated athletic association, which in the beginning was composed of the various individual sports associations. The faculty committee consisted of Edward T. Owen, professor of French, as chairman; Lt. James Cole of the military science department, and Charles Slichter, professor of mathematics.

In 1894 this faculty committee's title had been changed to Athletic Council, with slightly greater powers within the Athletic Association but not nearly enough for true faculty control. The council members in this year were Dr. James Elsom, professor of physical culture; Lieutenant Cheynowith of military science; Professor Barnes; Professor Charles Van Hise of the geology department; and Slichter.

The council had authority in matters of eligibility and could also exempt athletes from gymnasium and military drill. All other matters—schedules, finances, hiring and firing of coaches—remained in the hands of the Athletic Association composed in 1901 of "all students and members of the faculty with a board of directors made up of one regent, three faculty members and ten students." Slichter at various times was referred to as supervisor of athletics, probably an ex-officio title borne by the chairman of the Athletic Council.

In addition to the lack of faculty control, there was always a hard core of faculty men led by Professor Howard L. Smith of the law department who believed football a nuisance and saw no viable place for it in a university's curriculum. Still another

61

group showed indifference, hoping that whatever was wrong would become so bad that it would eventually destroy the whole. (It almost did.) Compounding the difficulties was the ever-present determination to recognize the student's role in the administration of sports, and a difficult role it had become indeed.

University president Charles Adams described the situation in a letter to the regents on April 7, 1900.

"I see no reason for changing anything I have said in regard to athletic matters," he wrote. "The reign of politics among students is unabated, and the athletic board recently chosen appears to be in hearty accord with the business manager whose accounts were found by Professor Slichter in so chaotic a condition that he declared they could not be audited. They also baffled the skill of Mr. Burd of the Treasurer's office, and Professor Van Hise after working over them for some weeks was obliged to leave them unsettled. No public statement of the results has yet been made. It is evident that very large numbers of those who heretofore have subscribed liberally for the boat crew and for other athletic matters will absolutely do nothing more until a change of one kind or another in the directorship takes place."

Things did not get much better rapidly, not only in finances but also in other athletic matters. Slowly, however, the faculty began to rouse itself, although it took several years to achieve anything. In 1903 Van Hise, who had just been named president, proposed to William Rainey Harper of the University of Chicago that something be done to clean up the game. Nothing happened—at least of record. Later the same year at a conference meeting, Slichter proposed a one-year residence rule for athletes for adoption a year later. That entailed waiting. In 1904 Van Hise called separate meetings of students, alumni, and faculty to discuss reorganization of the Athletic Association. In the school year of 1905-06, Slichter resigned from the Athletic Council, and Professor Thomas Sewell Adams was named to succeed him.

In November 1905, *Collier's* magazine came out with a blistering exposure of athletic conditions at Wisconsin, Michigan, Chicago, Illinois, Minnesota, and Northwestern. *Collier's* article about the demoralizing conditions, authored by Edward

President Charles R. Van Hise straightened out extensive irregularities in university football shortly after the turn of the century. He was also a prime mover in setting the Big Ten's feet on a new straight course.

S. Jordan, undoubtedly hastened reforms. All of the schools were equally condemned.

The *Collier's* article painted Slichter as a man who believed in absolute athletic decency but "lacked the nerve to use his absolute powers." In this *Collier's* may have erred, for Slichter did not have "absolute powers." Above him still was the student-dominated Athletic Association with its politics and corrupt ways. *Collier's* observations on Slichter were unfortunate, as he himself favored reforms.

Collier's early in 1905 decided to prepare the series of articles on athletics in the Middle West which Slichter himself had earlier proposed. He had written to Lloyd Jones, an associate editor of the magazine:

> As chairman of the Athletic Council at the University of Wisconsin I know something of the difficulties connected with getting the facts. As soon as a member of the faculty is appointed on the athletic committee, it seems to become everybody's business to keep him in as great ignorance as possible concerning the real situation, both at his own university and at others. After the athletic season is closed, a good many things come to light that prove to such a person the great extent to which he has been kept in ignorance. I have a strong conviction that publicity should be given to the situation in intercollegiate athletics in the West as well as in the East, and I would be glad to see *Collier's Weekly* take the lead in such a movement.

The extent of athletic corruption and chicanery at Wisconsin was, as *Collier's* exposed it, an athletic Watergate. Fullback-captain Ed Vanderboom of the 1905 team, for instance, gave early notification to George Downer that the manager was expected to recruit players by any means.

When Downer failed to get Wallie Steffan, a Chicago high school phenomenon, Vanderboom notified him of the team's displeasure and threatened him with his job. (Steffan had enrolled at the University of Chicago where, indeed, he was a phenomenon. He helped beat Wisconsin in 1908 with a 100-yard kickoff return.)

Collier's also cited several examples of graft accepted by

64

players on the 1903-05 teams.

Only Downer, who was graduate manager, was exonerated by *Collier's*. Writing of him, Jordan said: "This man has something of the old fashioned idea of college honor, works with a business head, and has disbelief in college spirit that depends on feats of gladiators who are not college men. He proposes an athletic structure that is clean, permanent and business-like. Enduring fame will be the fortune of Wisconsin if George Downer realizes his aims; pity will be her ultimate portion if brainless brawn frightens her president to non-support of this man."

Collier's actually challenged President Van Hise to do something at Wisconsin, saying, "If colleges will follow the course which President Charles R. Van Hise can scarcely evade, there will be a return to athletic decency, a return to legitimate athletic aims and a reversion to the old definition of college honor."

Van Hise, a great friend of football who would ride his horse to watch practice, accepted the challenge. There was little else he could do.

In December 1905 President Van Hise proposed to the faculty that a committee be named to study the condition of athletics at the university and make recommendations. On the committee were Deans Birge and Turneaure and Professors Turner, Slichter, Munro, Trowbridge, and Jackson.

The committee pulled no punches and wasted no time. *Collier's* exposure had had a tremendous impact on the public and the faculty.

Van Hise's committee recognized the need for drastic action and proposed that football be suspended for two years, with the suggestion that any such reforms be extended to other universities. To achieve this it suggested that President Van Hise approach President James B. Angell of the University of Michigan, enlist his help, and obtain conference action. Angell joined in, according to Voltmer's book on the Big Ten, and wrote a letter to the conference which expressed not only his feelings but also those of Van Hise.

"The general complaint in the public press is of the roughness and dangerous character of the game. Now, while it is desirable and I hope practicable to remove some of the objections to

the present style of playing, I think that we who administer universities will agree that there are other objections to the present mode of carrying on the game quite as serious as the roughness of the play. Let us notice some of them...."

In enumerating his objections, President Angell stated that he believed the football season was too long, encroaching on the students' academic interests; that football held up "false ideals of college life"; that the sport emphasized athletic over intellectual training at the universities; and that the expenditure for football was "out of all proportion...."

With this letter President Angell also called for a meeting in January 1906 in Chicago of regular faculty representatives and any other especially appointed faculty to discuss the difficulties. Professor Turner represented Wisconsin with specific instructions from the faculty that he propose a public condemnation of the evils of football and a two-year suspension of intercollegiate contests "to the end that rational, moral and normal relations between athletics and intellectual activities may develop in each institution."

In their two-volume history of the University of Wisconsin, Curti and Carstensen describe the results: "At Chicago the conference had little difficulty in agreeing to abolish football 'as now played' and quickly came to agreement on a number of proposals intended to reduce the number of contests and the expense of coaches and equipment and strengthened the eligibility rules. The Wisconsin proposal to suspend all games for a period of two years was not pushed vigorously or widely supported."

The recommendations agreed upon were referred to the respective faculties. Another meeting was held on March 10, and these regulations for participation in and control of intercollegiate athletics were officially adopted:

1. One year of residence was necessary for eligibility. This rule also required the meeting of all entrance requirements and completion of a full year's work.

2. Only three years of competition were allowed, and no graduate student was to be eligible.

3. The season was limited to five games (former schedules had included twice this number or more).

4. No training table or training quarters were permitted.

5. Student and faculty tickets were not to cost over fifty cents.

6. Freshmen and second teams were not to play outside games.

7. Coaches were to be appointed only by university bodies in the regular way and at moderate salaries. (There had been a strong sentiment for doing away with paid coaches entirely.)

8. Steps were to be taken to reduce receipts and expenses of athletic contests.

The faculty at Wisconsin passed a resolution approving and accepting these changes, then declared (as Curti and Carstensen reveal in their book): "The faculty of the University of Wisconsin express their preference for the suspension of intercollegiate football for a period of two years by agreement of the conference."

By this time the anti-football segment of the faculty had really provoked the football-rabid students, and 1,500 of them signed a petition to retain the game, promising to cooperate in eliminating graft and corruption. This promise the faculty accepted, and there were no further attempts to suspend or abolish football at Wisconsin.

President Van Hise appointed Dr. C. P. Hutchins of Syracuse as athletic director and coach, let it be sternly known that Wisconsin henceforth would live by the new Big Ten rules which the faculty had just approved, and decreed that all coaches and directors would, for the first time, be full members of the faculty.

His unequivocal position, coupled with the fact that athletic department finances which depended solely on football receipts (and still do) were going to be a new problem, naturally had immediate repercussions. The football, baseball, track, and crew coaches all resigned, as did graduate manager George Downer. And so, a little tragically and shamefully, the end had come to the "winningest decade" in Wisconsin's football history.

Financial Troubles
And Jeopardy

After his appointment as football coach and athletic director, Dr. C.P. Hutchins wasted no time in setting Wisconsin's feet on a victory path. His first team in 1906 won every game it played, beating Lawrence, North Dakota, Iowa, Illinois, and Purdue. The team scored 78 points, allowing only 15, and tied with Minnesota for the Big Ten championship.

There were problems, however. Without the "big" games of earlier years—Minnesota, Chicago, and Michigan had all been dropped as part of the great reform of 1905—interest and receipts fell off alarmingly. Phil King's last team in 1905 had season receipts of about $34,000 and Hutchins' championship team of 1906 only $3,400.

Department finances geared solely to football income became a grave problem, and for several years the entire self-supporting intercollegiate program, football itself, was in jeopardy. In 1907 the faculty permitted Minnesota back on the schedule and in 1908, Chicago. This for the moment solved the financial difficulty; Wisconsin needed those "big" games.

The 1906 team was not unaware of the critical situation in this first year of reform. In a report in the *Badger* yearbook at the end of the season, Captain W.A. Gelbach expressed the feeling of the squad: "We do not request our names be written along with those of O'Dea, Driver, Karel, Curtis, Larsen, Cochems, Bethke, Findlay, Vanderboom, Remp and the rest of their line; we only ask that it may be said we have engraved a little deeper upon the escutcheon of our alma mater those fine old words, 'There are no quitters at Wisconsin.'"

Gelbach wrote for a squad of lettermen that included Ewald (Jumbo) Stiehm and Elmer Whittaker, centers; Gelbach, Charles Bleyer and Lee Huntley, guards; John Messmer, Albert Johnson, and Fred Dittman, tackles; Harlan Rogers, Joe Curtin, Harry Hosler, and Arthur Frank, ends; George Zeisler, Floyd Clark, and Rudolph Soukup, halfbacks; Charles Miller and John Howard, fullbacks; and Carl ("Coots") Cunningham and Ernest Springer, quarterbacks.

Hutchins coached again in 1907 with Messmer, a fine tackle, as captain. Wisconsin beat Iowa, Indiana, and Purdue, tying Minnesota and losing only to Illinois. Illinois, with Pomeroy Sinnock, the Big Ten's first passing sharpshooter, won easily, 15-4.

The Illinois defeat was significant because Hutchins learned firsthand what a devastating weapon the newly legalized forward pass could be and emphasized its use himself the rest of the season.

The Minnesota tie, 17-17, was achieved only with a whirlwind comeback after Harry Capron of the Gophers had run the opening kickoff back 75 yards for a touchdown and subsequently kicked three field goals, accounting for all of Minnesota's points. Capron was one of three Caprons who played for Minnesota in this era. It was on this 1907 Minnesota team that the first Negro played in the Big Ten. He was Bobby Marshall, an end. The distinction has commonly been given to Duke Slater of Iowa.

In the 12-6 victory over Purdue, quarterback Coots Cunningham intercepted a pass and ran it back 105 yards for what proved to be the winning touchdown. The run still stands as the longest with an interception in Wisconsin's history.

The dual job of athletic director and coach became too much for Hutchins, and after the 1907 season he turned the coaching job over to J.A. (Tom) Barry of Brown University. Barry remained for three years with moderate success. His first team finished with a 5-1 record, his second with 3-1-1, and his third with 1-2-2. His second team, that of 1909, became known as the "On Wisconsin" team, because it was preceding the Minnesota game that year in Madison that the school's famous marching song, "On Wisconsin," was introduced to the student

Dr. C.P. Hutchins became Wisconsin's first full-time athletic director in 1906. He was also the football coach and gave Wisconsin an undefeated team, tying Minnesota for the Big Ten championship.

body at the campus homecoming rally. It became an instant hit. (Wisconsin lost, however, 34-6.)

The music was composed by William T. Purdy, and the original words were written by Carl Beck. Purdy actually wrote the music for a song to be entered in a University of Minnesota song contest but was prevailed upon by his friend Beck to submit it to the University of Wisconsin. Purdy and Beck lived in the same boardinghouse in Chicago at the time. Purdy taught piano and voice at the Drexel Conservatory of Music, and Beck was a Wisconsin student staying out a year to earn money to continue his education.

The music has been adopted by hundreds of high schools and colleges, each writing words to fit its own needs. The state of Wisconsin adopted "On Wisconsin" as its official state song in 1959.

The original words as written by Beck went like this:

On Wis-con-sin, On Wis-con-sin,
Plunge right through that line,
Run the ball clear 'round Chicago,
A touchdown sure this time.
On Wis-con-sin, On Wis-con-sin,
Fight on for her fame—
Fight, fellows, fight, fight, fight.

In 1909 Chicago was Wisconsin's foremost rival, and no season could really be called a success unless the Maroons were beaten. Maybe the song helped, for a week after the Minnesota shellacking Wisconsin tied a strong Chicago team, 6-6.

While Barry's years were not especially happy ones for Wisconsin, better ones were immediately ahead. John Richards, a fullback star of the nineties, became coach in 1911 and immediately turned out a team with a 5-1-1 record. Richards had only a few proven veterans back, but he drilled his young material exceedingly well, and his team scored 111 points and allowed only 14. Quarterback Keckie Moll, a star of the first magnitude, scored Wisconsin's touchdown on a 60-yard punt return in the 6-6 tie with Minnesota. Then in the closing seconds he almost won the game with another great run on an interception. The *Wisconsin State Journal* described the finish like this:

Just five seconds before the call of time in the final

71

quarter, J. Keckie leaping high in the air grabbed a Minnesota forward pass in midfield and started for the goal line at full speed. He was over the line at the corner of the field, and the stands believing the game won, forgot everything. Hats and pennants were thrown into the air. Pandemonium reigned for fully two minutes. The ball was called back to the one yard line, however, Field Judge Benbrook claiming Moll had stepped outside the bounds on the one yard line. The Badgers held a short consultation and then Tandberg was given the ball for one more play. When the players got up, the ball was found to be just six inches from the goal line and the whistle ending the game blew.

The game was almost cancelled at the last minute because of what was known as the "Pickering Affair." Earle G. Pickering, captain and star fullback of the Gophers, was formally protested by Wisconsin as a professional for having played baseball for pay in North Dakota two summers. The protest first appeared in the newspapers four days before the game. It was formally made to Minnesota by Athletic Director George Ehlers of Wisconsin, Hutchins' successor, on a hurried visit to Minneapolis two days later.

All hell broke loose at this, and the newspapers were filled with the charges and countercharges each school hurled at the other. Minnesota said that it certainly was not very sporting of Wisconsin to wait until four days before the game to make its charges. Wisconsin retorted that the charges had first been made the year before and that nothing had been done about them. It also said that Minnesota had waited until a week before the 1901 game to file a similar protest against Earle Schreiber; the star Wisconsin guard had been dropped the night before the game. The climax to the whole affair was reached when Minnesota announced that Pickering would not play and then formally protested Moll, William Mackmiller, Al Tandberg, and Merrill J. Hoeffel of Wisconsin as pros.

The official report of Minnesota's eligibility committee after studying documented charges against Pickering follows:

The charges against Mr. Earle C. Pickering were not prepared until four days before the game, whereas the spirit of the conference requires sufficient notice so that an adequate investigation can be made. In view of the shortness of the time it has been impossible to investigate the charges before the game of Saturday, but at the same time we do not wish to take a chance of playing a man who may be ineligible. We have therefore decided to withdraw Mr. Pickering from the game even at the risk of doing him and the Minnesota team an injustice, and thereafter to undertake a thorough investigation of the case at the earliest possible date. We also wish to add what we have received evidence tending to show that four members of the Wisconsin team, namely Moll, Mackmiller, Tandberg and Hoeffel, are guilty of professionalism under the conference rules, and we request the athletic authorities of Wisconsin to undertake immediately as thorough an investigation in these cases as they claim to have made in the case of Mr. Pickering. Signed: James Paige, E.V. Johnson, J.C. Litzenberg, David F. Jones, E.P. Harding.

On the Minnesota campus there was strong feeling that the game should be cancelled, but there were even stronger feelings in other quarters that it should be played but that athletic relations with Wisconsin should be severed after that.

The game was not cancelled, and relations with Wisconsin were not severed. Calmer heads prevailed in all the turmoil.

Wisconsin, with little time itself, did broadly investigate the charges against its four players, though it asked Minnesota for specific evidence and received only a telegram listing anonymous rumors. All four players swore in affadavits that they had lived up to conference and Wisconsin regulations, and all played. The rumors had charged all four with professionalism in summer baseball in northern Wisconsin, Minnesota, Indiana, and Missouri, and Mackmiller, additionally, with participating in a professional crew in St. Paul.

The 6-6 tie knocked Wisconsin out of the conference championship and let Minnesota, with a 3-0-1 record, make off with the undisputed title. A week after the Minnesota game Wisconsin lost, 5-0, to Chicago, which earlier in the season had lost to Minnesota. Chicago finished second in the race.

After such a fine though tumultuous first season, Richards

73

Quarterback Keckie Moll was called the "Bleacher's Pride" for his all-around play from 1909 through 1911.

looked ahead to 1912. But in the spring of that year he got into an argument with the university's military commandant, who refused to excuse freshman and sophomore football players from military drills for off-season practice. The result was that Richards resigned. Ohio State had just entered the conference (April 4, 1912), and Richards became head coach there, although he was destined to return to Wisconsin for a longer tenure in 1917.

Bill Juneau, star end on Wisconsin's teams at the turn of the century and former coach at Colorado College, South Dakota State, and Marquette, succeeded Richards in 1912. He inherited an outstanding squad and immediately produced the conference championship for Wisconsin denied by Minnesota in the 6-6 tie of 1911.

Juneau's team went through the season with seven straight victories, five of them in the conference and two outside. The team scored 246 points and allowed 29. The championship was Wisconsin's fifth since the conference's organization in 1896.

The season opened modestly enough with a 13-0 victory over Lawrence College. But there were signs that Wisconsin would develop into a formidable team. There was nothing

John Richards, star fullback in the nineties, came back to coach the Badgers in 1911 and 1917 and from 1919 through 1922.

Bill Juneau, star end at the turn of the century, returned as coach in 1912 and immediately produced an undefeated Big Ten champion.

modest about the next victories. The Badgers sank Northwestern, 56-0, then hammered Purdue, 41-0, and whipped Chicago, 30-12. In the fifth game they faced Arkansas in an intersectional battle, and if any doubt remained that they were truly one of the great teams in the country, it was dispelled then. Arkansas, coached by Hugh Bezdek, the old big league baseball outfielder, was smothered, 64-7. Bezdek had a scrappy bunch, and though hopelessly outclassed as the score mounted, they chanted in defiant unison, "Let's go, Arkansas," before every scrimmage. The Badgers liked such spirit and adopted the chant as their own, much to the bewilderment of the two conference teams they still had to play. They beat Minnesota at Minneapolis, 14-0, and Iowa at Iowa City, 28-10.

The game-by-game story of the team is the brilliant individual saga of quarterback Eddie Gillette, who had been a halfback the preceding year. He threw passes to Ofstie and Hoeffel for both touchdowns in the Lawrence victory; ran 90 yards for a touchdown in the Northwestern rout; and ran 60 and 50 yards for touchdowns and threw a 20-yard pass to Ofstie for another touchdown in the Purdue trouncing. He completed a half dozen passes to set up short scoring plunges in the Chicago trimming; did the same in the Arkansas game, in which he played only briefly; threw a touchdown pass to Hoeffel in the Minnesota game, which Juneau called the finest effort of the season; and then ran 50 yards for a touchdown and completed a short pass to Lange for another in the Iowa windup. Gillette got his greatest help from fullback Tandberg, halfbacks Van Riper, Bright, and Berger, and, of course, the strong line behind which they all operated. The Badgers used only 11 men against Minnesota.

The athletic board gave major "W's" to 19 men: Captain M.J. Hoeffel, Harold Ofstie, and Ray Lange, ends; Robert "Butts" Butler, Bill Breckenridge, and Edward Samp, tackles; Ed Gelein, Ray "Tubby" Keeler, and Tom Powell, guards; Walter Powell, center; Eddie Gillette and Frank Bellows, quarterbacks; Alvin Tandberg, Harold Moffett, and Arthur "Sheep" Alexander, fullbacks; and John Van Riper, George Bright, Al Tormey, and Louis Berger, halfbacks. Gene Van Gent, a fine tackle on the 1911 team, might have won a letter again. However, he broke his collarbone falling on a ball on the first day of practice and later, in the Arkansas game, suffered a broken nose. Although he played in some of the later games, technically he did not have enough playing time to get an award. John Wilce, who was captain of the 1909 team and later became Ohio State's highly successful coach, was student manager of the team as he pursued his medical studies. Joe Steinauer, swimming coach, intramural director, and "Langdon street windjammer," as he was affectionately known on the campus, was the team's trainer. Juneau had two assistants, Adolph "Germany" Schultz, center on Michigan's great "point-a-minute"

Eddie Gillette was the star quarterback of Wisconsin's undefeated Big Ten champions of 1912.

teams at the turn of the century, and Keg Driver, a Wisconsin fullback in Juneau's own playing days.

There was no question that Wisconsin was the best team in the West and truly one of the best in the nation. Walter Eckersall, a former Chicago quarterback and a highly respected football writer for the *Chicago Tribune* at the time, placed nine of the 19 Wisconsin letter winners on his annual all-conference team. They were Hoeffel and Ofstie at ends; Samp and Butler, tackles; Gelein and Keeler, guards; Gillette, quarterback; Tandberg, fullback; and Van Riper, halfback. The only outsiders on the team were Elmer Oliphant of Purdue at the other halfback slot and Pete DesJardien of Chicago at center. Eckersall also named five of the nine on his all-western team: Hoeffel, Keeler, Butler, Gillette, and Van Riper; M. H. Pontius of Michigan at end with Hoeffel; D. Barricklow of Ohio State at tackle with Butler; and Eberts of Wabash at guard with Keeler.

Eckersall's choices were more or less duplicated by other

well-established all-star pickers at that time. G. W. Axelson of the *Chicago Record Herald* had six Badgers on his all-conference team and six on his all-western. Art Schinner of the *Milwaukee Sentinel* picked seven Badgers—Hoeffel, Butler, Gelein, Keeler, Gillette, Tandberg, and Van Riper—and completed his team with DesJardien, Oliphant, Paul Tobin of Minnesota at end, and Jay Twickey of Iowa at tackle.

Never before or since has one school so dominated a Big Ten honor team as did Wisconsin in 1912. To top it all, Walter Camp named Butler at tackle on his prestigious All-American team, the first Badger to be so honored. Tug Wilson, former Big Ten commissioner, and Jerry Brondfield in their 1967 book, *The Big Ten*, called the team "one of the greatest clubs in Big Ten history." They added, "It probably deserves all-time national ranking as well."

The campus, the city of Madison, and the whole state exulted over Wisconsin's conference championship, and it was probably well they did. The championship was the last Wisconsin was to win for 40 years, and when it did win again in 1952, it was only to tie with Purdue. Between 1912 and 1952 every other conference team except Indiana won or tied for at

R.M. (Tubby) Keeler, a guard on the 1912 champions, was one of Wisconsin's first All-Americans.

*Wisconsin's 1912 team, coached by Bill Juneau, won seven
straight games and the undisputed Big Ten championship. Nine
of its men were named on the annual all conference team. M.J.
(Joe) Hoeffel, in middle holding ball, was captain. Front Row
(left to right): Louis S. Berger, Albert R. Tormey, Harold S.
Ofstie, E.A. (Max) Gelein. Second Row: Coach William J.
Juneau, Raymond C. Lange, Edmund S. Gillette, Captain*

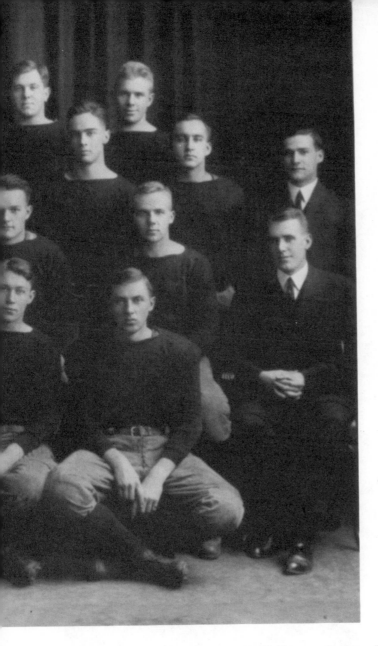

Merrill J. Hoeffel, Frank L. Bellows, Arthur H. Alexander, Inter-Collegiate Manager John W. Wilce. Third Row: Manager Benjamin R. Brindley, Walter D. Powell, Ray M. Keeler, George N. Bright, Alvin C. Tandberg, John Van Riper, Edward J. Samp, Trainer Joseph B. Steinauer. Fourth Row: William L. Breckenridge, Thomas C. Powell, Assistant Coach Earl S. Driver, Robert P. Butler, Harold L. Moffett.

least two championships, and Indiana won one outright.

The exultation in Madison apparently was something to behold. It was a drunken orgy of the first magnitude in which bars finally had to be closed. A Madison newspaper commented under the heading, "The Shame of the Game":

If decent and skill football cannot be played without being followed by a debasing drunken debauch then football must go. There is not a college in America that is large enough or strong enough, much less a commonwealth college, to long hold to a sport that inspires nothing better than shameful debauch.

It is a poor manifestation of sportsmanship to sprawl with clouded mind in the gutter. The saloon or the bar room is a poor sanctuary in which to honor and to praise a beautiful and beneficent alma mater. If there is no healthier and no happier way to honor and to love our college than by distressing our stomachs, souring our breaths, and befogging our brains, let us get something that is better than football, something that will inspire the happy and wholesome aspirations of manhood.

The athletics of the University of Wisconsin, here as elsewhere, are not clean and pure until the disorderly aftermath of the game is blotted out and so mulched that it cannot recur. The drunken carnival and the lawless smashing of glassware and furniture that compelled the Park Hotel to close its bar room in self defense early on Saturday night, is a reproach to the University of Wisconsin, for it is the University in the first and last analysis that governs and controls its athletics and if a well played and well won game of football can inspire those who profess to love this college with no better manifestation of their love and loyalty than the rotten drunkenness that was exhibited in every saloon and hotel bar room in this town Saturday night, then it is the duty of the regents of the University of Wisconsin, in the name of the state, to prohibit forever the recurring of such a game....

Wisconsin's first All-American, Robert (Butts) Butler, was picked as a tackle by Walter Camp in 1912.

The Slow Descent Begins

There was no Eddie Gillette around in 1913, and Wisconsin began the long, slow descent from the heights, accompanied by greater sobriety. Juneau's second team finished with a 3-3-1 record, his third with 4-2-1 in 1914, and his fourth with 4-3 in 1915. It was not a bad record, but it did not contain any victories over blood rivals Minnesota and Chicago. The Badgers lost all three games to Minnesota and two of three to Chicago. The other game with Chicago was a tie.

Juneau's last three years were not without a few high spots, however. In all three, 1913 through 1915, Juneau had a giant of a man at tackle—220-pound Howard (Cub) Buck. And in the last of these three years he had a quarterback who was second only to Pat O'Dea in kicking skill—Eber Simpson. Simpson also did the passing and much of the running.

Buck, who later played professional football with the Canton Bulldogs and Green Bay Packers, was a star on all three teams and was named to several All-American teams. He is a legendary figure in Wisconsin football history.

Simpson still holds the school record for extra points in a single game. In the 82-0 victory over Lawrence in 1915, Simpson kicked 10. The same year in the 85-0 victory over Marquette he kicked eight, all dropkicks.

Ring Lardner covered the Minnesota game of 1915, which happened to be homecoming and also Juneau's last game. He wrote one of his humorous and chatty letters to Harvey T.

84

Howard (Cub) Buck, a legendary tackle, won All-American honors in 1915.

Woodruff, then sports editor of the *Chicago Tribune*:

Friend Harvey—This fellow Ebenezar Simpson who plays quarterback for Wisconsin kicked the ball over the poles after they had marched down the field toward the Gofers' hole. That was the first score and the way them Wisconsin fellers did yell, and they was about 14,000 of 'em.

But maybe three minutes after that a guy by the name of Beerman grabbed the ball and made a touchdown.

Camp Randall Stadium as it looked in 1914 with permanent wooden seats.

Then them Minnesota Swedes yelled and both sides says, "We'll win sure now." But some of 'em were wrong, Harv, because this Beerman and a feller by the name of Wyman made two more touchdowns and the Gofers won, 20-3.

Say, Harv, them Wisconsins have got one demon, though. They call him Cub and he's a bear. His other name is Buck and he sure can. He's the best tackle I ever seen.

The "Beerman" Lardner mentioned was Bernie Bierman, destined to become one of college football's greatest coaches in his long tenure at Minnesota. He not only scored two touchdowns in the victory but also intercepted four passes.

The 1915 Minnesota game is remembered not only for what Bierman did but for a near tragedy.

A section of wooden stands on the north side of old Camp Randall collapsed in the third quarter, and a score of fans were hurt. Dr. Seth Cain of Brodhead, Wisconsin, one of those in the stands, recalled what happened. "The stands didn't collapse in a big way," he said. "They were rented circus seats and they just settled down slowly, which, as things turned out, was fortunate. Most of the injuries were to ankles or knees. After the injured were taken care of, we who weren't hurt watched the rest of the game along the sidelines. The most seriously injured as I recall was a woman who suffered a broken leg."

There were minimal medical claims, which the athletic department paid. Out of the collapse, however, came legislative help to build new Camp Randall. There was naturally criticism because the university did not have better than shaky wooden stands for its growing football crowds, and the state legislature shortly afterward appropriated $20,000 for 10,000 new concrete seats on an adjacent site. When an appeal to alumni for contributions to help in financing brought in only $2,079, the legislature approved another appropriation of $10,000 on July 2, 1917. Work on the new seats was begun March 16, 1916, and completed within a year. Expansion occurred periodically thereafter. The seating capacity was increased from 29,783 in 1925 to 77,280 in 1966. This made Camp Randall one of the largest college-owned football arenas in the country. Only Michigan, Ohio State, and Stanford have larger ones. As additions were built permanent dormitories were included, but these quarters are now used as athletic department offices or training and locker rooms.

Camp Randall's history involves more than football games. Before the Civil War the site was owned by the state agricultural society, which held its annual state fair there. With the outbreak of war the society turned everything over to the government, which used it as the state's major military training center. The display halls were transformed into whitewashed barracks, and the hall which had been used for flower shows became a hospital. Late in the Civil War the camp became a military prison where sick Confederates captured by General Pope at Island 10 in the Mississippi were brought. Many died in the drafty prison hospital and were buried in what is now Confederate Rest at Forest Hill Cemetery.

When peace returned the land again became the state's fairgrounds. When the state fair was moved to Milwaukee in 1892 and subsequently to suburban West Allis, it was proposed that the land be sold for building lots. Civil War veterans became aggressively incensed at such a proposal, calling it a "sordid sacrilege," and urged the state legislature to buy it. This the legislature did in 1893 and presented it to the university as a memorial athletic field. When the question arose as to what to call it, the war veterans carried the day again, and it was designated "Camp Randall," not "Randall field."

Juneau, who spent only his autumns in Madison, had a real estate business in Milwaukee and resigned as coach after the 1915 season.

With Juneau retired Wisconsin again went east for a successor and named as coach Dr. Paul Withington, who had learned football under famed Percy Haughton of Harvard. The good doctor assembled the largest staff of assistants of any Wisconsin coach up to this time: Dick King of Harvard, an All-American halfback; Ed Soucy, an All-American end; and Jack Doherty, a quarterback. He also obtained Cub Buck as line coach.

Withington, an eastern blueblood, started out well enough in 1916. Wisconsin won four of its first five games, beating Chicago, Purdue, Marquette, and Lawrence. The Badgers lost to Ohio State by only a point, 14-13, when Glenn Taylor dropped Simpson's kick out for position on the extra point. (Under the rules of the day a team punted out unmolested from the point of the goal line where the touchdown had been scored in order to get position for the kick on the extra point. If the punt out, always deliberately short, was dropped, the try for the extra point was forfeited.)

Ohio State's immortal Chick Harley first plagued the Badgers in this game. He passed to Captain Sorenson, who ran 22 yards for the Buckeyes' first touchdown, then ran back a punt 80 yards himself for the second. After both touchdowns he kicked the extra point. Simpson passed to Paulie Meyers for Wisconsin's first touchdown. Lou Kreuz scored the second on a short plunge after a long march.

After this good debut of four out of five, however, Dr. Withington made a fatal mistake. The vital Minnesota game was still to come. With an open date the week before, he elected to scout the Gophers himself against Illinois in a game which historically is still regarded as the Big Ten's biggest upset. Not accorded a chance in the public mind, the Illini won, 14-9.

Upon his return to Madison Dr. Withington publicly announced that Wisconsin would have no trouble beating Minnesota. How wrong he was! The score of the game played at Minneapolis was Minnesota 54, Wisconsin 0. It was the highest score run up by Minnesota against Wisconsin since the 63-0 shellacking in 1890 and the second highest in the history of the rivalry.

To the Badgers' credit, they tied Illinois, 0-0, a week later. However, Dr. Withington never fully recovered from the Minnesota disaster or the heartbreak imposed by Chick Harley in the Ohio State game and chose to retire.

John Richards was called to succeed him. At the time he was director of recreation in the Chicago south park system and

Dr. Paul Withington of Harvard served one year, 1916, as Wis-
consin coach.

accepted on the basis that he would spend only autumns in Madison. Working with only two assistants, Keg Driver and Guy Lowman, Richards immediately proceeded to reverse Wisconsin's descent from the heights of 1912 with a succession of winning teams. His 1917 team won four games, beating Beloit, Iowa, Chicago, and Minnesota; lost to Ohio State and Illinois; and tied Notre Dame. The game with Minnesota was the first Big Ten game in new Camp Randall after the wooden stands had been moved over to augment the new concrete seats. And the game with Ohio State again saw Harley personally destroy the Badgers. He passed to Bolens, who ran 38 yards for one touchdown; passed to Courtney on Wisconsin's two yard line from where Yerges scored a second touchdown; and kicked a 38-yard field goal for the final points. Simpson gave Wisconsin its only points with a dropkick.

The Illinois game of 1917, played at Champaign, produced one of football's rarest oddities: The football itself collapsed. George Halas, then an end under Bob Zuppke, still talks about that game (Illinois won, 7-0).

"I was back to take a kickoff and had started upfield," he recalls, "when suddenly the ball went flat. If I had been smart I'd have kept right on running, but I wasn't smart and stopped on the 25 yard line, waving the floppy casing over my head. The two teams naturally gathered around me. Nobody blocked and nobody tackled, and finally Referee John Schommer came up, and when he saw what had happened, he ordered the kickoff repeated. On the second one I didn't get up to the 25 yard line, which should be a lesson to young players. Keep going until the referee's whistle ends the play."

In 1918 Richards was excused for a year to work in the war effort in Washington, and Guy Lowman, who was also baseball coach, took over. Lowman's team in this war year is best remembered for the last victory to be scored over Ohio State in Columbus, 14-3. Fred Smith scored both touchdowns, one on a 68-yard run and the other on an 80-yard run. In all the years since, covering 19 games, Wisconsin has not been able to beat the Buckeyes on their home field, although they did tie them three times.

Richards returned in 1919 and immediately turned out another powerhouse, which lost only to Minnesota and Ohio

Coach Guy Lowman

State. In the Ohio State game it was Harley once more who starred. After passing to Pete Stinchcomb for a first down on Wisconsin's 15 yard line, he drop-kicked 15 yards for a 3-0 victory. The Badgers who suffered through this included the team's student manager, Fred Bickel, who later achieved movie stardom as Frederic March.

Such treatment at Ohio State's hands in those years was getting to be an irritation to the whole state of Wisconsin, especially since an old Wisconsin star, Jack Wilce, captain of the 1909 team and manager in 1912, was coaching the Buckeyes. But the end was not in sight.

In 1920 the Badgers had legitimate designs on the conference championship, which would have been their sixth. They missed it because of Ohio State. In the seven-game season, they beat Lawrence, Michigan State, Northwestern, Minnesota, Illinois, and Chicago and lost only to the Buckeyes at Columbus, 13-7.

Chick Harley was gone, but two new Ohio State villians appeared in scarlet and gray—Hoge Workman and Pete Stinchcomb. Between them they beat Wisconsin in a game that still stands as one of the biggest heartbreaks in Wisconsin history.

The Badgers had all the better of the early going in 80-degree temperature, but not until late in the second quarter did they finally take command with a touchdown. Harold Holmes scored it from the three yard line after he, Guy Sundt, and Alvah (Rowdy) Elliott running and Wallace (Shorty) Barr with a 20-yard pass to Elliott had carried the ball 75 yards down the field. Sundt added the extra point, giving Wisconsin a 7-0 half-time lead.

With Wisconsin dominating the play, the score stood up until only eight minutes in the fourth quarter remained. Then on a long drive Workman first passed to Slyker for 24 yards and then to Stinchcomb for 36 yards and a touchdown. Stinchcomb's kick for the extra point hit one of the uprights, bouncing back on the field. The Badgers still led, 7-6.

An exchange of punts left the Buckeyes on their own 10

Last Wisconsin coach to beat Ohio State at Columbus was Guy Lowman who took over as interim coach in 1918 while John Richards served in Washington in the war effort.

yard line, and with only three minutes to play they set sail for Wisconsin's goal 90 yards away. Workman passed to Slyker for 20 yards, and he and Stinchcomb ran to Wisconsin's 48 on two plays. It was third down, nine to go, with only a minute left when Workman started to his right on what looked like a wide sweep but ended up as a pass, while Stinchcomb deployed on the opposite side of the field behind Wisconsin's defensive backs and took the diagonally thrown ball on the dead run for the winning touchdown. The game and the conference championship went down the drain.

Undoubtedly this was one of Wisconsin's great teams with a line composed of Captain Frank (Red) Weston and Gus Tebell at ends; Ralph Scott and Howard Stark, tackles; Jim Brader and Harry Margoles or Marty Fladdoes, guards; George Bunge, Jr., center; and a backfield composed of Sundt at fullback; Holmes, Elliott, Gibson, or Rollie Williams at halfbacks; and Allan Davey or Wallace Barr at quarterback.

What balm the Badgers had for the Ohio State mistreatment in the years 1917 to 1920 came in two victories over Minnesota, 10-7 in 1917 and 3-0 in 1920, and three over Chicago, 18-0 in 1917, 10-3 in 1919, and 3-0 in 1920.

As the scores suggest, dropkicking played a big part, and Wisconsin had two men who could kick, Davey and Barr. Barr kicked a field goal, and Davey ran 60 yards for a touchdown in the 10-3 victory over Chicago in 1919. Davey also kicked the field goals that beat Chicago and Minnesota, each 3-0, in 1920.

Davey's 60-yard touchdown against Chicago in 1919 was scored in a dramatic situation. Davey was in Richards' doghouse for having used his own judgment over the coach's in the Minnesota game two weeks earlier which Wisconsin lost, 19-7. He did not start against the Maroons in this last game of the season.

It was a blow to him because his hometown of Freeport, Illinois, had decided to pay him tribute and had turned out en masse at Stagg Field in Chicago. On the bench he sat, however, while Barr directed the team through more than three quarters and with a 35-yard dropkick gained a temporary 3-3 tie. Only three minutes were left when Richards finally called Davey off the bench. Davey first helped pick up a first down on the 40 and then with a "weaving, twisting run," as one paper described it, ran 60 yards for the winning touchdown of the 10-3 victory.

Jack Wilce captained Wisconsin's 1909 team and served as Ohio State's very successful coach from 1913 through 1928.

Richards' 1921 team beat Lawrence, South Dakota State, Northwestern, Illinois, and Minnesota; tied Michigan; and lost only to Chicago. Ineligibilities all but ruined his team in 1922, in which Wisconsin finished 4-2-1. The Badgers lost to Michigan, 13-6, and Illinois, 3-0, and tied Chicago, 0-0.

As in 1911 when he left Wisconsin because the university commandant would not permit freshmen to skip military drill for off-season football practice, the feisty but likeable Richards again got into a hassle with the faculty. Dean George Sellery of Letters and Science remarked at a student rally that he would like to see more Phi Beta Kappas on the football squad, to which Richards retorted in effect, "I wish some of the faculty would have to take the acid test a coach takes every Saturday." Richards asked for a raise and resigned when he did not get it.

Several old Badgers, including Hod Ofstie of the 1912 team, were considered for the job as Richards' successor. However, Jack Ryan of Dartmouth was chosen. Ryan had been coaching at nearby Marquette. Wisconsin fans well remembered his Hilltoppers, as they were then known, for the 1919 game which Wisconsin won, 13-0, due to interceptions and fumbles on which Wisconsin capitalized.

With no great inheritance of material, Ryan still started out well enough in 1923. Wisconsin defeated Coe College, 7-3, and Michigan State, 21-0; walloped Indiana at Bloomington, 52-0; and tied Minnesota, 0-0, the next week (which was the first of more than 400 Wisconsin games this writer covered from 1923 through 1971). The last three games of the season were defeats. Illinois won, 10-0; Michigan, 6-3; and Chicago, 13-6. The Indiana game, in fact, was the only Big Ten game Ryan won in his two-year tenure. Oddly, for the first and only time in history, Wisconsin shed its cardinal that day and dressed in black. So completely did the Badgers dominate play that Indiana did not make a first down until the last three minutes of play.

The Michigan game was lost on a freak touchdown. The Badgers took the field a superbly drilled team that afternoon. At once they drove down the field to the five yard line, from where Captain Marty Below kicked a field goal for a 3-0 lead.

So it remained until well into the second quarter, when the freak touchdown was scored off a punt. Merrill Taft, Wisconsin's fine punter, first drilled a 45-yard kick to Tod Rockwell at safety for Michigan. Down fast on the kick, Below nailed Rockwell after a 10-yard return but loosened his grasp. Rockwell got up and started to run, only to be nailed again after a few steps by Russ Irish, a big end, and Adolph Bieberstein, a guard. They, too, loosened their grip when it seemed Rockwell was stopped, explaining later that the entire team had been warned earlier by the officials for piling on. Again Rockwell got up, however, and started to walk toward the goal. Once in the clear he began to run and, though two bewildered Wisconsin men gave pursuit, he easily reached the goal 50 yards away.

Pandemonium broke loose when Walter Eckersall allowed the touchdown which gave Michigan a 6-3 halftime lead which stood for the rest of the game.

Eckersall, the referee, was properly behind the punter as the play started, watching as he should have been for any roughing of the kicker. When he finally allowed the "touchdown," he merely supported his brother official, field judge Colonel Mumma. Mumma, an army man stationed in Iowa City, was on top of the play as Rockwell caught the ball and explained later that he firmly believed Rockwell's forward progress had never been stopped. He quoted rule six, paragraph A, which read: "The ball is dead when a player having the ball goes out of bounds, cries 'down' or is so held that his forward progress is stopped or when any portion of his person except his hands or feet touches the ground while in the grasp of an opponent."

The wildest scene in the history of Camp Randall ensued at the end of the game. Angry fans by the thousands rushed onto the field after Eckersall, and only the Wisconsin players who surrounded him saved him from harm. One fan did punch Eckersall's jaw and was arrested, but Eckersall himself asked that the man be released.

Not content with the demonstration on the field, hundreds of fans gathered at the door leading to the officials' dressing room and hundreds more at the railroad station where Eckersall ostensibly was to take a train for Chicago. The fans were in an ugly mood, but they never got to Eckersall again. Captain Below, a few other players, and Coach Ryan first led him to Ryan's car, which took him not to the station but to Milwaukee

Tackle Marty Below was captain of the team which lost to Michigan in the highly controversial game of 1923.

85 miles away. From there he took a train to Chicago.

Tom Jones, Wisconsin's acting athletic director, quickly answered rumors, announcing that there would be no break in relations with Michigan, to which Fielding Yost of Michigan said "Amen." The teams met again in 1924 when Michigan won, 21-0. In 1925 Michigan won by the same score and in 1926 by 37-0. Jones also said that Eckersall would never again officiate a Wisconsin game. (However, 10 years later Eckersall did again work a Wisconsin game.)

A few days after the Michigan game, Colonel Mumma in a letter to Frank Smith, sports editor of the *Chicago Tribune*, took sole responsibility for the decision which gave Michigan the touchdown. He wrote as follows:

> Departing from a fixed rule I have observed during more than 20 years as a football official, I desire to make a statement concerning the decision in the Wisconsin-Michigan game last Saturday. The referee, Walter Eckersall, has been subjected to unjust criticism and even mob violence for a decision for which I alone am responsible. He only gave finality to the decision upon my statement to him at the time the play occurred.
>
> In arriving at my judgement of what actually took place I had to use my own eyes and decide according to the dictates of my own conscience, and, having done so, I assume full responsibility for what proved to be an unfortunate defeat.
>
> The only question that ever entered my mind with reference to the play was, "Did the referee blow the whistle?" Not having heard one blown and being distant from the referee at the time I asked him as soon as he arrived at the spot if he had blown his whistle. Upon receiving a negative reply I gave him the facts on which he ruled.
>
> Signed, Morton C. Mumma.

The Badgers rallied nicely against Chicago in the 1923 season's last game but the Maroons, led by a great halfback, Jim Pyott, won, 13-6. Having one of his best days, Pyott scored both of Chicago's touchdowns. Taft took a pass from Schnieder for Wisconsin's consolation points.

100

Ryan's 1924 season was no better than 1923 and certainly not as tumultuous. His Badgers did tie Minnesota, 7-7, and Chicago, 0-0, in major games and beat North Dakota and Iowa State. They tied Coe but lost to Michigan, Iowa, and Notre Dame.

The Notre Dame game was against Knute Rockne's famous "Four Horsemen" of Elmer Layden, Jim Crowley, Don Miller, and Harry Stuhldreher, and not unexpectedly, it was a slaughter. The Irish won, 38-3.

As was his practice, Rockne started his shock troops and against them the Badgers held their own. Wisconsin even marched down to Notre Dame's three yard line in the first quarter from where, on fourth down, Doyle Harmon kicked a field goal for the first points of the game. The Notre Dame regulars entered the game here, though, and the rout was on. The individual Four Horsemen all had a hand in scoring, and a substitute halfback, John Roach, completed the job with a 15-yard touchdown run in the fourth quarter. Unfortunately, on his touchdown jaunt Roach thumbed his nose at his futile pursuers, and Rockne immediately thumbed him off the field.

The defeat did not help Ryan's security as coach, and when Iowa beat Wisconsin, 21-7, the next week the writing on the wall was clear. Ryan had won only one Big Ten game in his two years and only five of 15 overall.

The Wisconsin athletic program had been carried on for more than a decade under a plan which, when adopted, had been considered a temporary one. Professor J.F.A. (Sonny) Pyre, a star tackle in the nineties and chairman of the athletic council at this time, had been given supervisory authority, with track coach Tom Jones as acting director. In the winter of 1924-25, the council decided to hire a full-time director and in March 1925 picked George Little of Michigan for the job.

Track coach Tom Jones was acting athletic director from 1916 through 1924.

A Rally Under Little

George Little, who had been Fielding Yost's assistant in running the athletic department and in coaching at Michigan, chose to do both at Wisconsin. This, of course, meant Ryan's end.

Little, a burly, affable man, turned out a highly creditable team in 1925. The Badgers won six games, lost one (Michigan), and tied one (Minnesota).

One of Little's assistants in 1926, his second year, was Earl (Red) Blaik, who went on to become one of college football's greatest coaches at Army. Blaik handled the ends in his one year at Wisconsin, then moved on to Dartmouth and subsequently to West Point. At Wisconsin he worked with fellow assistants Tom Lieb of Notre Dame, Irv Uteritz of Michigan, and Guy Sundt of Wisconsin and was an important contributor to the success Little had in his brief tenure as coach.

The loss to Michigan, 21-0, in the third game of the 1925 season was probably the most stunning defeat Wisconsin ever suffered. The anticipation of a battle of coaching wits between Little and his former mentor, Yost, was so keen that the aura around the game became unreal.

The game was all but over in the first two minutes, in which the Wolverines took a 14-0 lead. Many in the capacity crowd of 30,000 had not yet settled in their seats when Benny Friedman, on the first play from scrimmage, hurled a 35-yard pass to halfback Bruce Gregory, who carried it 30 yards more across the goal.

George Little came from Michigan to be both Wisconsin's athletic director and football coach in 1925. He remained as coach through 1926 and as director through 1931.

Some of the crowd were still looking for their seats when Michigan scored again. Oddly, after the first touchdown Wisconsin elected to kick off. Friedman took the kick on his own 15 and on a darting run in and out among frustrated Badgers went 85 yards for a touchdown. Friedman added both extra points.

In spite of the demoralizing start, the Badgers held their own for the next 58 minutes, although only Michigan scored again. Friedman passed eight yards to Bennie Oosterbaan for another touchdown in the third quarter. Each team finished with seven first downs.

The 12-12 tie with Minnesota on a perfect football day in Minneapolis was one of those not-to-be forgotten team "highs" built largely around the exciting contributions of the Harmon brothers—Leo, a senior, and Doyle, a junior. The two had been highly sought-after South Dakota high school stars who had cast their lot with Wisconsin rather than their home state or nearby Minnesota.

Dr. Clarence Spears had a thundering herd of Gophers, and for three quarters they ran Wisconsin all over the field. So clear was Minnesota's superiority despite a rather meager 12-0 scoreboard lead as the fourth quarter started that Spears, looking ahead to his Iowa and Michigan games, withdrew most of his regulars. These included his devastating backfield of Herb Joesting, Shorty Almquist, Herman Asher, or John Murrell. Under the rules of the day they could not return to the field in this half.

To the end of his days Spears, who was destined to coach Wisconsin a few years later, rued his decision. Wisconsin suddenly exploded, and on the sidelines there was nothing Spears could do about it.

Not only had Minnesota built up a 12-0 lead in the first half but once had the ball on Wisconsin's three yard line where Wisconsin held, had it on the three yard line again as the half ended, and had outgained Wisconsin five to one. After the first touchdown Asher had kicked the extra point, but both sides were offside, and on the second attempt he missed.

The great Wisconsin comeback in the fourth quarter started when Doyle Harmon intercepted a pass on his own 13 yard line with eight minutes left. On the first play here, Pat McAndrews, a sprinter on the track team, swept around right end for 47 yards to Minnesota's 40, and on the next, Leo Harmon passed to Toad Crofoot for a first down on Minnesota's nine. In succession, Leo Harmon plunged for a yard; McAndrews lost four at end; and Leo's pass to Doyle picked up six, planting the ball on the six yard line, fourth down.

Here Leo, badly rushed, still managed to flip a short pass to Doyle on the goal line for a touchdown. Leo, however, missed the extra point, and Minnesota still led, 12-6, with four minutes left.

The Badgers kicked off, but they got the ball back almost immediately when one of Spears' subs, Borgendale, fumbled near midfield, and Don Cameron, a Wisconsin end, recovered. Again the Badgers swept right down the field.

The vital play in the drive was a long pass on which officials ruled interference, giving Wisconsin the ball on Minnesota's 26. Doyle picked up five yards, and Leo passed to Jeff Burrus for 20 and a first down on the one.

On the first down here Leo failed to gain, but on the second with time running out, he smashed into the end zone.

Everything, a tie or a victory, depended on Doyle Harmon's try for the extra point. The pass from center on a placement with Crofoot holding was a little low, and in the extra split second it took Crofoot to place the ball, the enraged Gophers swarmed in and blocked the kick. So the emotionally drained fans had a 12-12 tie to ponder on their way home.

Referee Jim Masker also had a lot to ponder. As he was about to flip a coin with the two captains to see which side would get the football for its trophy case, the still-furious Spears came up and uttered the insult supreme: "Why don't you keep the ball, Masker. You won it." He referred to the pass interference call on which Wisconsin built its second touchdown. Masker, dean of conference officials, later said he would never work a Spears game again. But he, too, relented and later officiated at quite a few more after Spears went to Wisconsin.

A week later, against Iowa at Iowa City, the Badgers had another harrowing day, although of a different kind. The game was played in what was unquestionably the worst weather conditions under which any Wisconsin team has ever played. Rain started falling in early morning; by mid-morning it had turned to sleet; and at game time it had turned into a real blizzard

Ed (Toad) Crofoot was quarterback from 1925 through 1927 and captain his last season.

blowing out of the north through the open end of Iowa's old stadium.

No tarpaulin covered the field, and workmen with brooms and shovels waged a losing battle all through the game to keep the sidelines and goal lines visible. So heavy was the swirling snow that the side of the stadium opposite from the press box was all but obliterated. Telegraph instruments in the open press box were totally fouled, and running copy had to be sent from hastily arranged communications in the nearby gym.

The game should never have been played. But it was, and Wisconsin won, 6-0.

Obviously, breaks were to decide it, principally breaks from kicks. Aided by the wind, kickers sent the ball booming; against it there was no telling where they would send it—out of bounds a few yards down the field or back over their heads. Players wore mittens, and simple ball handling was an art. Iowa fumbled 26 times, Wisconsin 14.

The big break occurred early in the fourth quarter when Wisconsin blocked an Iowa punt and recovered it in the end zone, but it did not count. Both sides were offside, and Don Graham, Iowa's punter, tried again. This time he sent it out of bounds on his own 11 yard line, and the stage was set for the winning points.

Here the succession of decisive plays occurred: Kruez gained two at center, and Doyle Harmon added three at tackle. Iowa was penalized five yards to the one yard line. Kruez went over center for the touchdown. Only a few thousand of the 15,000 in the stands at the start of the game remained for the finish.

So elated was Little after the win that in the gymnasium dressing room he kicked a dropkick through one of the windows.

Little's second season, 1926, was not quite as good as his first, although the Badgers did finish a respectable fifth in the conference race with a 3-2-1 record and overall in the season with 5-2-1. Again the Badgers were involved in an extraordinary game with Minnesota. Through the years of upsets, defeats, victories, oddities, and squabbles, it was usually Minnesota, it seemed, that was the party of the second part.

This was a game in Madison in which Wisconsin did not make a first down; Minnesota made 18; and Wisconsin was out-

End Jeff Burrus ran 84 yards with a fumble for Wisconsin's lone touchdown in the strange game with Minnesota in 1926.

gained in plays from scrimmage almost 10 to one, 289 yards to 31. But with four minutes left Wisconsin led, 10-9. Minnesota fumbled five times, and Wisconsin recovered four.

The odd pattern of the game began in the first quarter when Wisconsin's Jeff Burrus, an end who later became a Rhodes scholar, scooped up Herb Joesting's fumble and raced 84 yards across Minnesota's goal. The point was added, and Wisconsin led, 7-0.

The Gophers quickly ripped away at this lead, going from midfield across Wisconsin's goal in three plays. Herb Joesting tore away for 31 to the 19; Jim Peplaw went for nine to the 10; and Joesting smashed for 10 and the touchdown. The Badgers blocked Almquist's attempt for the extra point, and Wisconsin still led, 7-6. It was a short-lived lead, however. Late in the second quarter Peplaw kicked a field goal, and the Gophers moved out in front, 9-7.

Wisconsin regained the lead when Peplaw fumbled in the third quarter and Wallace Cole, a Wisconsin substitute, recovered. On three plays Wisconsin could not dent the tough Minnesota line. But on fourth down and from a difficult angle on the 30 yard line, Lester Leitl sent a place-kick over the bar for a 10-9 Wisconsin lead.

So it stood until only four minutes remained. Here Mally Nydahl took Rollie Barnum's punt in midfield and raced 55 yards for a Minnesota touchdown. Toad Crofoot had one last shot at Nydahl on Wisconsin's 15 but missed. And so another heartbreaking loss, 16-10, was written into Wisconsin history.

The writer early in the season got a lesson in journalism, or maybe horticulture, from his managing editor. Wisconsin beat an ordinary Kansas team, 13-0, on Crofoot's 80-yard run and Leitl's two field goals. The Jayhawkers reached midfield only once, late in the game, and the writer, in his Sunday story in the *Milwaukee Journal*, said: "Wisconsin cut down the Kansas sunflower to the size of a buttercup, 13-0."

Monday morning his managing editor gave his lesson. "Young man," he said, "the Kansas sunflower is never, but never, cut down to the size of a buttercup." He was a Kansas graduate.

As athletic director Little was busy all his years at Wisconsin promoting intramural sports. After the 1926 football season

Halfback Gene Rose caught three touchdown passes in home-coming victory over Iowa in 1926.

he decided to give up coaching, which interfered with his other athletic duties. In spite of the heartbreaks, he had given Wisconsin two good winners, finishing with a 16-game record of 11-3-2 and missing the championship in 1925 only because of the 21-0 loss to Michigan and the 12-12 tie with Minnesota.

At Northwestern at this time was Glenn Thistlethwaite, who had just finished the last year of his five-year contract as coach. He also had just tied Michigan for the conference championship with a 5-0 record. But for some unknown reason he was not happy with his situation, and when Little approached him about the Wisconsin job he accepted. "Gloomy Glenn," as he was known, remained for five eventful years—not Wisconsin's best five but certainly eventful and exciting. Overall he won 26 games, lost 16, and tied three. But in the conference he won only 10, lost 14, and tied three. Of the 10 he won, four were against relatively weak Chicago, then beginning its long slide into football oblivion. In his best years he finished 7-1-1 in 1928, 6-2-1 in 1930, and 5-4-1 in 1931.

In the 1928 season his team beat Notre Dame at Madison, 22-6, which was probably the high spot of his tenure. Also in 1928, he coached Wisconsin to the first victory over Michigan since 1899, but in 1929 he saw Wisconsin's first loss to Northwestern since 1890. A pass from Sammy Behr to Francis (Bo) Cuisinier gave Wisconsin the lone and winning touchdown against Michigan. Russ Bergham beat Wisconsin with a touchdown in the Northwestern game.

The victory over Notre Dame in 1928 has gone down in

Halfback Gene Rose races around end in Purdue game of 1927.

"Gloomy Glenn" Thistlethwaite
came from Northwestern, where
he had just tied for the Big Ten
championship, to coach Wisconsin from 1927 through 1931.

Wisconsin history as the "Victory in Tall Grass"—at least Knute Rockne of Notre Dame called it that. Arriving in Madison the day before the game, Rockne immediately took his team to the stadium for a workout. When he saw the length of the grass, he commented half jestingly, "What is Glenn trying to do, lose us in the grass? Get it cut." Thistlethwaite refused to let it be cut, however, and a fuming Rockne took his team to a large meeting room at the Park Hotel for signal practice.

The tall grass had little to do with the Notre Dame defeat the next day, however, for this was not one of the Fighting Irish's better teams. They also lost that year to Georgia Tech, Carnegie Tech, and Southern California.

Wisconsin had all the better of the play, scoring in every quarter except the second, in which the Irish got their consolation touchdown on John Niemiec's short plunge after a 73-yard march. The extra point was missed.

William (Whitey) Ketelaar, a big, blonde tackle, scored Wisconsin's first points in the first quarter when he blocked a punt that rolled out of the end zone for a safety.

Niemiec's touchdown gave the Irish the lead at the half, 6-2, but in the second half the Badgers poured it on, capitalizing on Notre Dame's mistakes. Jack Chevigny's fumble on his own 20 gave Wisconsin excellent field position early in the third quarter, and Sammy Behr's pass to Lewis Smith brought the ball home and put Wisconsin in front again, 9-6. Another break in the same period led to the next touchdown when Joe Morrissey of the Irish, back to punt on his own goal line, did not even touch the ball as he attempted to drop it on his foot. Milt Gantenbein fell on it as it rolled around on the two yard line, and Ken Bartholomew scored on the first play. In the fourth quarter a Behr-to-Cuisinier pass gave Wisconsin its final points, Cuisinier running 40 yards for the score. The game was loosely played. Notre Dame fumbled six times and Wisconsin five.

In that same year Wisconsin had another memorable game with Iowa at Iowa City, this one not in snow but in mud. A bit of coaching strategy by Thistlethwaite helped win it. As the Badgers took the field, he had them deliberately roll around in the mud while Iowa's players daintily stepped through it.

At game's start Thistlethwaite instructed Ernie Lusby at

safety not even to attempt to handle a punt, lulling Iowa men down on kicks into carelessness. Between halves, however, Thistlethwaite changed his instructions. "Handle the second or third punt they make," he told Lusby, and again Lusby dutifully did as told. On the second or third punt Lusby grabbed a rolling punt for the first time in the game and scooted away from loafing Iowa men down on the kick for 67 yards and a touchdown. It was the first of two the Badgers scored, but it was the only one they needed. George Casey fell on Mayes McLain's fumble in the end zone for the second in the 13-0 victory.

Lusby liked to relate the incident about his long run. "On the 20-yard line," he said, "I heard splashing footsteps behind me and for an instant I thought, 'Gosh, they're going to get me before I score.'" His fears were unnecessary, however, because the splashing footsteps were only those of Wisconsin men escorting him across the goal line.

The log for 1928 also included a 15-0 victory over Wallace Wade's Alabama Crimson Tide, which Gov. Bibb Graves of Alabama and a trainload of Bama rooters came up to see. It was a long ride home for them.

Zipp Newman of the *Birmingham News* was lavish in his praise of the Badgers. "Wisconsin was a better blocking team," he wrote a few days after the game, "than either Washington or Stanford. It will be almost impossible for the Crimson to face another team this season that blocks and tackles as hard as Wisconsin did Saturday. Alabama players coming back on the train stated that Bartholomew was the hardest back to stop they had ever played against."

It was a costly victory for Wisconsin, though. All-American tackle Milo Lubratovich suffered a broken leg. He remained in school and two years later played again.

The 1928 Big Ten championship was in Wisconsin's grasp when they took the field against Minnesota in the last game of the season. All they needed was a victory or tie against the Gophers. But superman Bronko Nagurski, that dreadnaught of all fullbacks, would have none of it. It is a convenient cliche to say that one man singlehandedly beat a team, but that is exactly what Nagurski did. Though his back was in a special brace to protect three ribs that had been torn in the Iowa game three

Quarterback Bo Cuisinier ran a kickoff back 63 yards for a touchdown against Alabama in 1928.

weeks before, he made this his personal game. When Russ Rebholz fumbled late in the second quarter on Wisconsin's 18 yard line, Nagurski recovered. Used largely as a decoy for Win

Brockmeyer and Fred Hovde up to this time because of his injuries, Nagurski came up with the touchdown that won the game, 6-0. On four successive plays he smashed for nine yards, three yards, two yards, and a touchdown. Then when Wisconsin threatened a little later, sending Cuisinier into the clear for what looked like the tying touchdown, the "Nag," who had the speed of a sprinter to go with his 225 pounds, cut diagonally across the field and saved Minnesota's victory.

It took only a year for Notre Dame to repay Wisconsin for the whipping inflicted in 1928. At Soldier Field, Chicago, in 1929, the Irish turned loose fullback Joe Savoldi and halfback Jack Elder, who buried Wisconsin under a 19-0 score. Savoldi scored two of the touchdowns, one on a run of 40 yards and the other on a run of 63. Elder scored the third on a 43-yard scamper.

In the Pennsylvania game in 1930 Wisconsin won easily, 27-0, after Penn coach Lud Wray for two weeks had belittled the Badgers in the eastern press. He told Philadelphia newsmen that the Wisconsin game was but a preliminary to the big games with Kansas and Notre Dame still to come. He further irritated newsmen in Madison the day he arrived with this comment: "Give me a dry field and we'll walk off with this game."

Wray got his wish on the weather. It was a sunny, warm day, bringing out a homecoming crowd of 40,000. But it was the only thing he got. Wisconsin scored in every quarter but the second. Sammy Behr ran back a punt 50 yards for Wisconsin's first touchdown, Lusby passed to Howard Jensen for the second, George Casey ran 45 yards with an intercepted lateral for the third, and Greg Kabat blocked a punt which Milo Lubratovich fell on in the end zone for the fourth.

Wray had started his shock troops as Rockne had been doing at Notre Dame, and he carried his indifference toward Wisconsin right to the field of play. While the Badgers lined up for the point after Behr's opening touchdown, Wray did not even bother to watch whether the point was made (which it was), but gathered his regulars about him and helped them peel off sweaters before sending them into the game.

Just for the record, Wray did beat Kansas later, 20-6, but lost to Notre Dame, 60-20.

Pennsylvania got its revenge the next year. At Philadelphia

Sophomore tackle Milo Lubratovich suffered broken leg in Alabama game of 1928 but came back two years later and won All-American honors.

in 1931 Pennsylvania beat Wisconsin, 27-13, largely on three long runs.

Many of Wisconsin's defeats in the era after World War I were genuine heartbreakers, and the 1930 season produced another. It happened in the Purdue game at Lafayette after the first Penn game, and this one Wisconsin lost, 7-6. Purdue scored first on a 50-yard pass play, Rich to Kissell, in the third quarter. But Wisconsin charged back in the closing minutes of the fourth quarter, smashing 90 yards down the field and capping the drive with a touchdown pass, Russ Rebholz to Behr. Only three minutes were left when Rebholz lined up to try for the extra point with Behr holding the ball. Rebholz was wide with his kick, and Purdue had the game. As Charles (Buckets) Goldenberg, a star blocking back who later had a distinguished career with the Green Bay Packers, recalled, it was the only point Rebholz missed all year.

Back home, Wisconsin fans listening to Quinn Ryan on Chicago's WGN radio station did not know about Wisconsin's defeat for a while, however. Ryan thought Rebholz's kick had been good and so announced it to his million listeners. Not until after the game was over did he realize his mistake and correct it as best he could.

Thistlethwaite's last game in 1931, and his last at Wisconsin, was a disaster. It was a postseason game with Michigan at Ann Arbor, arbitrarily arranged after the regular season as part of the Big Ten's plan to raise money for the unemployed of the depression years. Also as part of the fund-raising plan, undefeated Northwestern met once-defeated Purdue at Lafayette, Indiana; Ohio State played Minnesota at Minneapolis; and Chicago, Iowa, Illinois, and Indiana played a round-robin tripleheader of 30-minute games at Chicago.

Wisconsin and charity both took it on the chin at Ann Arbor on a cold, blustery day. Before a disappointing crowd of 8,000, Michigan won, 16-0, on touchdowns by Roy Hudson and Bill Hewitt and Hewitt's short field goal. Hewitt, a great end, was switched to fullback for this game. In his pro career later as an end with the Chicago Bears and Philadelphia Eagles, he was named to pro football's Hall of Fame.

In other games of the "unemployment" round, Purdue beat Northwestern, 7-0, and Minnesota dumped Ohio State,

118

Halfback Ernie Lusby shakes off a tackler in 1930 game with Minnesota.

10-7. Indiana won the round robin, winning its own first 30-minute game from Illinois and then beating Iowa in the second an hour later. Iowa reached the finals by defeating Chicago in the first game. All of the games except those in the tripleheader counted in the final standings. This meant that Michigan, Northwestern, and Purdue, each with 5-1-0 records, tied for the Big Ten championship. Wisconsin finished sixth with 3-3.

The Michigan game had fatal repercussions on Thistlethwaite's job. He had been coming under increasing alumni pressure for not winning more of the big games within the league, and probably only George Little's support the year before had saved his job. Two of the three alumni members on the athletic council, Jerry Riordan and Hy Marks of Chicago, were particularly loud in their demands for a coaching change. They were not without arguments either. The athletic department at season's end found itself with a deficit of $72,000. This was due not only to declining football receipts in the depression but partly to the expenditure of so much money on Little's program, which included a new field house to replace the "Little Red Gym." The field house quickly acquired the name of "Little's Folly" because it was not a field house in the true sense but a building suitable only for basketball. Little, a placid man, was criticized for building it and for letting himself be influenced by his basketball coach, Dr. Walter Meanwell, in its construction. The building cost roughly a half million dollars and seated 8,800.

The end of both Little and Thistlethwaite was inevitable. Not only the regents but also the state legislators studying the financial problems were disturbed. Little resigned first, and Thistlethwaite followed shortly after. The resignations were accepted by the regents December 28, 1931. It meant that Wisconsin had to look for both a new athletic director and a new coach.

Little went on to become athletic director at Rutgers University and Thistlethwaite football coach at Carroll College.

The athletic board dawdled for several months trying to decide on a coaching successor. They finally agreed on Ray Morrison of Southern Methodist. Scott Goodnight of the athletic council was reputed to have offered Morrison the job by telephone. "How much time do I have to decide?" Morrison is reported to have asked. "Three hours," said Goodnight, whose board had dawdled for months. Morrison called back in three hours with his decision: "No thank you. My wife doesn't want to move up among you northerners."

The alumni then took a more aggressive part in picking a coach, and because they could not forget the great teams Clarence (Doc) Spears had turned out at Minnesota in the middle and late twenties, they opted for him. Arlie Mucks, a Wisconsin All-American in 1917, was one of the great believers in Spears and his hard-nosed football. Although not a member of the board, he went to see Spears in Oregon, where Spears had gone after his last season at Minnesota in 1929. Spears had spent two great years as Oregon's coach when he accepted Wisconsin's offer. Behind him was an excellent 13-4-2 record, including important victories over UCLA and Washington both years.

At the same time that the athletic council accepted Muck's alumni recommendation on Spears, it also named Irv Uteritz, a Michigan football star in the early twenties and an assistant coach under Thistlethwaite, as athletic director. It acted under a new rule that henceforth no head coach of a major sport could also double as athletic director. Uteritz had no appetite for the job, however, and after a few weeks turned it back to the athletic board. The board decided on a triumvirate of Spears, track coach Tom Jones, and basketball coach Dr. Meanwell as advisors to J.D. Phillips, business manager of the university, who

120

would be acting athletic director.

Whether Spears had been promised the job as director or whether Mucks even had the authority to offer it to him as part of a package deal is not clear. Spears always claimed he had been offered the job; others said he had not. But the presence of two aggressive and ambitious personalities like Spears and Meanwell boded no good.

Meanwell, one of the greatest coaches in the history of basketball, and Spears, an All-American guard at Dartmouth in his undergraduate days and certainly a successful football coach, were like two fighting cocks ready to fly at each other. It was inevitable that they should clash.

In 1933, with Phillips claiming that the work of business manager and acting director was too much for one man and with intercollegiate athletics separated from intramurals in administration, the board offered Meanwell a choice under the new rules. He was to be basketball coach or athletic director, and he chose the latter. Spears' unhappiness was complete.

The Two Doctors
Feud In Public

"Doc" Spears had four eventful years as football coach aside from the internal department frictions. He started brilliantly in his first year, 1932, winning six, losing one, tying one, and finishing third in the Big Ten race behind Michigan and Purdue. Then he sloughed off badly. In 1933 the Badgers finished with a 2-5-1 record, in 1934 with 4-4, and in 1935, Spears' last year, with 1-7.

Today he is best remembered for his great first year in which his Badgers defeated Marquette, 7-2; Iowa, 34-0; and Coe, 39-0; lost to Purdue, 7-6; tied Ohio State, 7-7; and beat Illinois, 20-12; Minnesota, 20-13; and Chicago, 18-7.

The Marquette opener, involving what had become a bitter intrastate rivalry, was one of the most thrilling Camp Randall had seen in years. Marquette scored first in the early minutes when guard Ed Rozmarynoski, who later became a well-known trainer for the Chicago Bears, blocked Mickey McGuire's punt, which rolled into the end zone. McGuire was able to fall on it only because three Marquette men tried to outdo each other in reaching it. The safety gave Marquette a meager 2-0 lead, which stood until the first minute of the second half. Don Elliott of Marquette fumbled the third-quarter kickoff deep in his own territory, and Ray Davis of Wisconsin recovered. Three plays later Dick Haworth scooted 15 yards for a touchdown, giving Wisconsin a 7-2 lead.

On the last play of the game, however, Marquette threatened to take over again, and only a brilliant defensive move by

Halfback Joe Linfor breaks loose on a 60-yard touchdown run against Iowa in 1932.

McGuire, playing safety, saved the day for Wisconsin. It was Marquette's ball on its own 25 yard line with only five seconds left. Gene Ronzani, Marquette quarterback and later a coach of the Green Bay Packers, faded back to his own eight yard line and hurled a magnificent pass to substitute Dick Quirk. Quirk caught it in midfield near the north sideline and, with a clear field, headed for the goal line. For an instant it looked like a cinch touchdown, but out of nowhere came McGuire, gaining with every step, and he nailed Quirk on Wisconsin's five yard line. The final gun sounded as the two rolled on the ground.

Later in the year McGuire, a Honolulu boy, almost single-handedly beat Minnesota in another Hitchcock thriller, 20-13. He scored all three of Wisconsin's touchdowns. He ran the opening kickoff back 90 yards for a touchdown, then in the second quarter took a pass from Joe Linfor for the second. Less than a minute was left with the score 13-13 when he took another pass from Linfor for the winning touchdown. He wrestled the ball away from Captain Wallie Hass of Minnesota on the five yard line and wriggled into the end zone. The defeat was the last Minnesota coach Bernie Bierman was to suffer until 1936, when his Gophers lost to Northwestern, 7-0, on an official's disputed

Halfback Tom Fontaine follows good interference on 40-yard run against Marquette in 1932.

call.

McGuire was an outstanding all-around athlete. He came to Wisconsin as a walk-on who had worked his way to this country on a freighter from Honolulu with $200 tucked in his shoes for tuition. He had earned $200 working in a pineapple cannery all summer. In Hawaii he had been one of the island's greatest athletes, not only in football but also in track. In fact, it was because his Punahou High School of Honolulu had sent him to the Penn relays in 1929 that he had decided to go to Wisconsin. He met track coach Tom Jones there and liked him. "He was like a father to me," McGuire once recalled. "Several coast schools offered me tenders, but because of Jones I decided on Wisconsin." In football in Hawaii McGuire always kicked barefooted. At Wisconsin, after his freshman year, he kept his shoes on.

The Badgers were badly outplayed in the 7-7 tie with Ohio State, two first downs against 18. But they escaped with the tie on a spectacular 65-yard punt return by Marvin (Red) Petersen. Petersen, playing safety, took the kick on his own 35 yard line,

Mickey McGuire, who came to Wisconsin from Honolulu, scored all three touchdowns in 20-13 victory over Minnesota in 1932.

veered toward his right, then reversed his field, and finished down the opposite sideline. Linfor added the extra point.

Linfor was only atoning, however, for his failure to kick the point in the Purdue game at Lafayette two weeks before. There he missed the point and Wisconsin lost, 7-6. Paul Pardonner drop-kicked Purdue's big point, which hit the crossbar and flopped over the right way. Wisconsin had scored on one of "Doc" Spears' favorite plays—a forward pass followed by a lateral to a trailing lineman. Here the pass went from Harold Smith to George Thurber and the lateral to Milt Kummer.

Spears' personal troubles began to mount in the 1933 season. At the Illinois game, which Wisconsin lost, 21-0, he pushed a Chicago newspaper photographer who dared to walk in front of him on the sidelines. The incident had repercussions all over the league, aside from the furor in the papers the next day.

The photographers decided to set Spears up for a repeat of such an incident at the Chicago game a few weeks later. The plan was for one photographer to walk in front of Wisconsin's bench again and a second photographer a short distance away to take a picture of Spears' almost certain violent reaction. The plan never materialized, however. Bill Aspinwall, business manager of the athletic department, learned about it and sought special police protection on the sidelines. It was not fully granted. Only one extra policeman showed up, but Aspinwall was still ready, and with other help the photographers were kept away from the bench. The game ended in a scoreless tie.

The last game of the 1933 season saw another heartbreaker with Minnesota. It was played on a snowy, wet day in Minneapolis with a near gale blowing down the field through the open end of the stadium horseshoe. The team which had the strong wind had an enormous kicking advantage. Wisconsin had it in the first and fourth quarters and Minnesota in the second and third. The game might as well have been played on half a field; only half the field was cut up with cleat marks. Feeble kicks with the wind soared. Good kicks against the wind wobbled 15 or 20 yards. Players sloshed around or skidded, and it soon became clear that the breaks would be the decisive factors in the game.

A succession of poor punts by Pug Lund against the wind

Dr. Clarence Spears, football coach from 1932 through 1935, who was dismissed along with basketball coach Dr. Walter Meanwell after their acrimonious hearing before the regents in 1936.

gave Wisconsin good position in the first quarter, and Mario Pacetti managed a 30-yard field goal with the wind that gave Wisconsin a 3-0 lead at the half. It was obvious between halves that if the Badgers could hold in the third quarter they would be in excellent position to make Pacetti's three points stand up. But it was not to be. Lund's kick with the wind in the third quarter eventually pushed the Badgers into a deep hole on their own one yard line from which they could not escape. Hal Smith fumbled the wet ball, which Dick Smith of Minnesota recovered. It took only one play. Lund went over for the touchdown. The Badgers threatened with the wind in the fourth quarter, but could not score, and Minnesota had the victory, 6-3.

The 1933 season was not one to write home about, with only two victories (Marquette and West Virginia), five defeats (Illinois, Iowa, Purdue, Ohio State, and Minnesota), and one tie (Chicago).

Things picked up a little in 1934, a 4-4 season, but not enough to quiet the grumbling which followed the 1933 season. There were a few high spots, however. Marquette was beaten, 3-0, when Pacetti kicked a 23-yard field goal on the last play of the game; Michigan was defeated, 10-0, when Lyn Jordan ran back the opening kickoff 99 yards for a touchdown, and Pacetti added a field goal; and Illinois was beaten, 7-3, on an intercepted pass run back for a touchdown to the delight of Pat O'Dea, who had been brought back to Madison as honored guest after his long self-imposed exile.

In retrospect, Marquette put the noose around its own neck in the 3-0 loss by a bit of doubtful strategy. It was Marquette's ball, first down on its own 18 yard line with two minutes of a scoreless game left, when the Warriors elected to punt. The Badgers took the kick near midfield and, led by Jordan and John Fish, quickly worked it down to the 23 yard line, where Captain Jack Bender called time with one second left. In this situation Pacetti kicked his winning placement. Stan Ferris held the ball.

A big guard, Ed Christiansen, deserved billing with Jordan for the 10-0 victory over Michigan at Ann Arbor. It was he who helped clear the way for Jordan with an excellent block on the last man who had a chance to catch Jordan. And it was he who blocked a punt and recovered on Michigan's eight yard line for

Pacetti's field goal which completed the scoring. Except for these two plays, the Badgers could not score, although twice they had first down on Michigan's four yard line.

Christiansen also had a major hand in the 7-3 victory over Illinois the next week. He hit Lester Lindberg with a hard tackle on an attempted pass, causing the ball to pop in the air. Wisconsin center Allan Mahnke caught it and easily ran 25 yards across the goal for what proved to be the winning touchdown. Lindberg gave the Illini, undefeated at the time, their consolation points with a 16-yard field goal.

Spears was in deep trouble in the 1935 season. Everything went wrong, and Wisconsin managed to win only one of its eight games when the Badgers upset Purdue, 8-0, in the homecoming game. The touchdown was made on a pass from Emmett Mortell to Len Lovshin and a safety off a punt Christiansen blocked and which rolled out of the end zone.

The victory over Purdue was little solace. The team lost to South Dakota State, Marquette, Notre Dame, Michigan, Chicago, Northwestern, and Minnesota. The South Dakota State win so pleased Charlie Coughlin, a Milwaukee industrialist and South Dakota State graduate, that he rushed into the team's dressing room after the game and told Coach Threlfall to buy complete new outfits for the entire squad and to bill him. South Dakota State's stadium, to which he also contributed, bears his name.

The tension between Spears and Meanwell finally reached its explosive climax immediately after the 1935 season and reverberated throughout the state for months.

John Golemgeske, acting captain in 1935 after Captain Ray Davis was injured on the opening kickoff of the South Dakota game and captain-elect for the 1936 season, circulated a petition at a party for the football squad to have Spears removed as coach. When this news reached the papers, the Wisconsin athletic department was pushed into the nastiest episode in Wisconsin history.

The athletic council under Professor Andrew Weaver (father of today's university president) was directed by the board of regents to look into the matter and make a recommendation. Golemgeske admitted he had circulated such a petition. Then he dropped a bombshell: he said he had acted upon the

Mickey McGuire, Honolulu born halfback who scored all three touchdowns in 1932 victory over Minnesota, chats with band director Ray Dvorak during a campus visit in 1967.

suggestion of Athletic Director Meanwell, who had promised him a basketball letter and a coaching job upon graduation. What he did was described by Meanwell, Golemgeske said, as a "service to the university." One thing led to another in these revelations, all published in the papers, and other bombshells followed.

Bill Fallon, team trainer, said in an affidavit that Spears had ordered that whiskey be put in the coffee served players between halves of the Minnesota game on a cold day in Minneapolis. The university hospital pharmacist, Ernest Kuenzli, was said to have provided the whiskey and entered the sale in his records as "special stimulating liniment" because, as he explained, he did not think it would look good to provide whiskey for the football team.

Red Smith, one of Spears' assistants, refuted Fallon's testimony. He then added that he had seen Meanwell give whiskey to Golemgeske and another big tackle, Jim Nellen, after the Northwestern game on a cold day in Evanston.

It was further revealed that when Meanwell had been forced to choose between the job as basketball coach and athletic director, he had named Bud Foster, a former star of his, as the new basketball coach with the written stipulation that if Meanwell ever asked Foster to resign, it would be done without "publicity or objection." A similar "memo," as Meanwell called it, was also exacted from Bobby Poser, who at the same time had replaced Uteritz as baseball coach.

It was also brought out that the faculty-dominated athletic council had held out against Spears' selection as coach as long as possible before capitulating to alumni demands as represented by Arlie Muck's recommendation after his trip to see Spears in Oregon.

Quite a bit was made of Meanwell's practice of buying basketballs and basketball shoes only from companies which gave him royalties for using his name. In the case of the "Meanwell basketball," it was revealed that the special valve which made the ball distinctive was actually the invention of Irl Tubbs of Superior Normal who sued the manufacturer, won the case, and also received royalties. Meanwell denied that he knew Tubbs had invented the valve.

Finally, the university regents decided that the charges,

Tackle John Golemgeske captained the 1936 team and was a pivotal character in the bitter Meanwell-Spears departmental controversy after the 1935 season.

denials, and countercharges in the newspapers had gone far enough. They decided to investigate the matter themselves through a committee composed of Dan Grady, a Portage lawyer; Harold Wilkie, a Madison lawyer; Clough Gates, a Superior newspaperman; John R. Callahan, state superintendent of schools; and A. C. Backus, a Milwaukee judge. University president Glenn Frank and business manager J. D. Phillips served as ex-officio members.

The regents never received the recommendation from the athletic council as asked for earlier in the controversy—only a confusing 700-page report. Between lines of the report, it was clear, however, that the council was determined to save Meanwell at all costs.

The regents publicly censured the athletic council for neglecting to come up with a recommendation and for its imperious attitude of "after us you come first." But the faculty-dominated council declared that the regents' intervention might jeopardize Wisconsin's position in the Big Ten, which insisted upon strict faculty control—and the regents, of course, were not members of the faculty. Professor Weaver also irritated the regents in the midst of the turmoil by declaring in an address in Janesville, "I would take the word of Meanwell against Golemgeske's any day of the week anywhere."

Excerpts from the transcript of the regents' public hearings on the matter revealed how fully they explored every facet of the problem. The jaunty Meanwell appeared on the stand with a bulging briefcase which included a set of 30 mimeographed questions which he passed out to the quizzing regents, with the suggestion that these might help in getting the facts. The regents ignored this help and questioned as they wished.

Before the regents opened their hearings, Golemgeske made a statement which appeared in the *Milwaukee Journal*: "I was misled, and that's all there is to it. It now looks as though I'm going to be the goat...I'm for Doc (Spears) 100 percent, and I've called him up and told him so. I'd like to forget the whole thing, but it doesn't seem as though that will be possible."

Most of the questioning was handled by Grady, and he made Meanwell squirm when he touched on the matter of memos exacted from Foster and Poser:

Q — When you became director is it correct that you

exacted in writing from them (Foster and Poser) as part of their contracts the right to select assistant coaches?

A — No, I did not exact this.

Here Grady introduced the two agreements and read them to the committee. The agreement signed by Foster on the day of his recommendation by Meanwell to the athletic council stated: "Bud and I agree that I may suggest his retirement if I deem it best and secure it without publicity or objection; that I suggest the basketball staff in all respects for a few years. Agreed to by Bud Foster (signature)."

Poser's agreement was the same kind: "Agreement between Bob Poser and W.E. Meanwell by which the conduct of the baseball team will always be in conformity with the plans of the director for the best interests of the department as a whole. Further that Bob render loyal support to the director in all ways possible to this end. Bob Poser (signature)."

Meanwell could not very well deny existence of the memos, but he had an explanation:

> I've had basketball at the university here for 20 years. It was a small thing at first but I nursed it along and at the end of 20 years built it up to where it stands now. I am proud of it. It is everything to me and when I was forced to give it up it was like giving up my right arm. And more, I gave it up to a young man—a young man who had my complete confidence, understand, but was still untried. His failure or success meant much to me and I felt that for a few years at least I should advise him, not on matters of technique for he is very competent. I have set foot on the basketball floor only once in two years. In matters of coaching personnel, however, I think I can help him. I feel I did no wrong.

Foster himself felt the memo he signed was a good thing, and even went so far as to say it might be a good idea for all coaches to sign something like this if they felt about the director as he did.

Questioned about statements that he had given whiskey to football players, Meanwell admitted he had given some to Jim Nellen on the train back from the Northwestern game because

Dr. Walter Meanwell, basketball coach and later athletic director whose differences with football coach Dr. Clarence Spears led to the dismissal of both by the university regents.

the boy "seemed depressed and needed cheering up." (Northwestern had won, 32-13.) He also said he had given Golemgeske what was left in the bottle (a medicine bottle) when trainer Bill Fallon asked if he had a stimulant for the player. He denied he had ever given any of his basketball players whiskey in his 20 years as coach at Wisconsin.

Fallon's statement that he had put whiskey in coffee for the players between halves of the Minnesota game, as ordered by Spears, appeared in an affidavit but was flatly denied by Spears himself. The idea of an affidavit, Fallon later admitted, was inspired by Professor Weaver.

"Alcohol is a depressant," Spears testified, "and I have never permitted its use with any team with which I was connected."

Spears also revealed how he had happened to come to Wisconsin, first explaining why he had left Minnesota for Oregon. "I left Minnesota because I was offered more money," he said, "and because I was to have charge of a new health service there. My salary was $11,500 a year. Arlie Mucks of the Wisconsin alumni approached me about the Wisconsin job; then-president of the regents Fred Clausin spoke to me about it; and later President Glenn Frank called me and told me he thought the directorship could also be arranged. He said that Irv Uteritz would probably remain as director for the time, but that when and if the position opened up he, Mr. Frank, would give me his support. He even told me to draw up plans for the department such as a director might draw up, and I was assured that the athletic board would be with me to a man."

President Frank bristled at this and interrupted the questioning to have his denial read into the record.

"I called Dr. Spears and asked him to draw up plans," Frank admitted, "but I did not assure him that the athletic board was with him to the man."

Meanwell, who had squirmed when confronted with the Foster and Poser memos he had first denied, squirmed again when questioned about royalties he received from equipment manufacturers. He first denied he knew anything about the Irl Tubbs basketball valve but then admitted that he knew that Tubbs also received royalties from the manufacturer.

The harassed athletic director was miffed that the matter

was ever brought up.

"It rankles me," he said, according to the transcript. "I don't think it's quite the sporting thing to do. I am ready to answer all questions pertaining to my department but I do think it would be better taste to leave my personal affairs alone...."

Meanwell flatly denied that, because he had an interest in the Meanwell shoe, he would not even let other salesmen show him their basketball shoes. "I wouldn't be that discourteous," he said. "The Meanwell shoe naturally had features I liked, and I bought it."

Dean Scott Goodnight testified that the faculty had been loath to have Spears as coach and had tried to hold out against him as long as possible. When asked whether it had been his understanding that Spears would be fairly considered for the job as athletic director, he said he understood that the alumni had promised Spears this but that the athletic board had not.

Goodnight's testimony appears in the transcript as follows:

Q — Did you ever say you didn't like the way Spears was selected and you smarted under it ever since?

A — Yes.

Q — Did you ever say that there was a definite feeling of prejudice among faculty men against Spears?

A — I don't recall that I ever said this, but it was true, although Spears in his first year did much to win the faculty over to him. He ruined this feeling, however, when he spoke over the radio one day and compared unfavorably Wisconsin's eligibility requirements with those at other schools. That created a bad feeling in the faculty.

Q — Is that the reason for the prejudice?

A — Yes, that and the many defeats.

The hearing produced a few light moments, too, as when Meanwell was asked whether he had written any letters to friends telling them he was "assured" of exoneration. He said he used the word "assured" only to convey his own feelings on his ethical conduct. He was also asked whether he had sent a picture of himself to Professor Weaver when the athletic board was considering the selection of a director. He said he did not remember but added he might have as he would have sent one to any friend.

Regents Clean House

After all this there was nothing the regents could do but clean house. They dismissed Dr. Meanwell, which ended 20 years of winning service to the university (four Big Ten basketball championships, four ties for the Big Ten title, two undefeated teams). They dismissed the trainer, Bill Fallon, and dismissed Dr. Spears, although toward the end of the hearings Regent Wilkie had said that Spears need have no worries about his job. He would be back. The athletic board of Andrew Weaver, Asher Hobson, Robert Aurner, Gustave Nohstadt, Walter Hyman, and Howard Huen resigned as a body.

University president Glenn Frank immediately named a new board of Dr. William Lorenz, Edwin Witte, Dr. Harold Bradley, Oliver Rundell, Dr. James Dean, Howard Potter, and Harold Huen, the student representative, and charged it with finding a new coach at once.

The board first set its sights on Clark Shaughnessy, then at the University of Chicago, and invited him to a meeting at the Union League Club in Chicago, where the job was offered. All but Rundell of the new board attended the meeting. Dr. Jack Wilce, a Badger star shortly after the turn of the century and Ohio State coach for 16 years up through 1928, also attended as an invited alumni consultant. Shaughnessy at the time was getting $9,000 a year on the Midway, where football was on its last legs, and Wisconsin was ready to pay this to get him. But he also had a $300-a-month university pension plan when and if Chicago gave up football, which already had been rumored, and

138

Harry Stuhldreher, quarterback of Notre Dame's famous Four Horsemen, came from Villanova in 1936 as Wisconsin's athletic director and coach and remained as coach through 1948 and as director through 1949.

this Wisconsin could not match, or would not. Shaughnessy turned down the offer. At the same meeting the board then proceeded to discuss other possibilities and finally narrowed the field down to two Notre Dame men active in coaching, Harry Stuhldreher at Villanova and Marchy Schwartz at Stanford. Shaughnessy recommended both as possibilities, and Dr. Wilce concurred.

Stuhldreher, who had been quarterback of Notre Dame's famous "Four Horsemen" of the mid-twenties, was agreed upon and was immediately telephoned in Philadelphia. Yes, he would take the job; yes, he expected he could get his release from Villanova. But he mentioned one other matter: he also would like the vacant athletic directorship. The board's rule not to have the coach of a major sport also as athletic director was suspended, and he was offered and accepted both jobs. In April 1936 he arrived in Madison for spring practice and what was supposed to be a new era of winning football at Wisconsin. As it turned out, it was more of the old.

Stuhldreher, a dapper, charming little man whose appearance belied his reputation as a great Notre Dame quarterback, was hailed throughout the state as the Moses who would finally return the Badgers to the glory they once knew on the football field. Actually, he took the state's fans on a roller coaster of ups and downs for 13 years.

The "downs" started early. In his first year Stuhldreher's team beat only Cincinnati and South Dakota State and lost Big Ten games to Purdue, Chicago, Northwestern, and Minnesota and outside games to Marquette and Notre Dame. The fans remained patient, however, and learned to echo those famous old words Wisconsin got to know so well, "Wait till next year."

The ups included one of Wisconsin's greatest teams in 1942, which just missed both the Big Ten and national championships by inches in the one game it lost in an 8-1-1 season. Iowa won the vital game at Iowa City, a major 6-0 upset, by stopping Wisconsin on the six inch line as the first half ended. As it was, Wisconsin was hailed by the Helms Foundation of Los Angeles as the national champion.

Other than this one great Stuhldreher team, however, there were major disappointments. Overall in his 13 years, Wisconsin won only 45 of 113 games and only 26 of the 75 in the Big

140

Fullback Pat Harder roars through a big hole over tackle against Marquette in 1942.

Ten. As criticism mounted, he was booed by part of the crowd at the 1948 game with Yale at Madison and heard a small group of students sing "Goodbye Harry" to the tune of "Goodnight Ladies."

It was a crushing experience for a man with all the success he had had in football and who was burdened with dual jobs in the athletic department, but his players remained intensely loyal. T.A. Cox, a good punter whom Stuhldreher always inserted in kicking situations (though such substitution always cost Wisconsin five yards under the rules of the day) returned to the bench after one of his punts in the Yale game shaking his fist at the chanting crowd.

It was only because of consistent success against Marquette over his 13 years, which meant so much to recruiting in the state, that Stuhldreher finished with as good a record as he did. Of 13 games with the Milwaukee rival from 1936 through 1948, Wisconsin won 10 and lost only three.

Big Ten teams were Stuhldreher's major stumbling blocks. He did not have an edge on any of them except almost perennially weak Iowa, with only a slim 7-5 margin.

In Big Ten games his Badgers lost nine of 13 games with

Northwestern, 11 of 13 with Minnesota, four of six with Ohio State, and all four with Michigan. They also finished 5-5-2 in 12 games with Purdue, 3-3-1 in seven with Indiana, and 1-1-0 in two with Chicago. Chicago's 7-6 victory in 1936 was its last in the Big Ten before dropping football after the 1939 season.

The losses to traditional rival Minnesota especially stung and did not help stem the criticism which was slowly building up and which engulfed Stuhldreher after the 1948 season.

In major games outside the league, Stuhldreher lost three and tied one with Notre Dame; lost two to Pittsburgh; dropped single games to Columbia, Texas, and Navy; split even with Camp Grant, a wartime collection of football stars from all over the country; lost two of three with California; split even in two with Yale, and split two and tied one in three games with Great Lakes, another wartime collection of college stars. His only outside victories of note without corresponding defeats were over Missouri and UCLA.

Stuhldreher's career as coach at Wisconsin is best remembered for his great 1942 team—and also for the heartbreak of its only loss that year at Iowa. It was a team that clearly belongs in school history among Wisconsin's greatest. It defeated Camp Grant, 7-0; Marquette, 35-7; Missouri, 17-9; Great Lakes, 13-7; Purdue, 13-0; Ohio State, 17-7; Northwestern, 20-19; and Minnesota, 20-6; tied Notre Dame, 7-7, and lost to Iowa, 6-0. The Northwestern game was won when Bud Seelinger threw a touchdown pass to Mark Hoskins in the last minute.

Angelo Bertelli, quarterback in Notre Dame's T-formation which Leahy had introduced only that season, engineered the

Halfback Elroy Hirsch breaks away with blocking by Pat Harder for the touchdown that tied Notre Dame in 1942.

drive in the second quarter which gave Notre Dame its tie. Jim Mello scored the touchdown which offset Elroy Hirsch's earlier one scored after a 60-yard run.

The vital game with Iowa ruined what would have given the Badgers their first championship season since 1912. With an undefeated team on that gray, dull November 7, 1942, in Iowa City, Wisconsin was an overwhelming favorite. The Badgers only a week before had beaten Ohio State, which, by itself, was an event. The Iowa Hawkeyes in earlier games had been whipped by Great Lakes, 25-0, and Illinois, 12-7.

It was Iowa's homecoming, and the Hawkeyes came out on the field in high spirits. The Badgers, who had spent the night in nearby Cedar Rapids, loafed out as though all they had to do was put in an appearance. They quickly found out differently.

Iowa scored in the second quarter. Tom Farmer, a senior quarterback, threw a long wounded duck pass which Bill Burkett, a junior end, had to come back for but which he caught and carried across the goal. Jack Wink blocked the attempt for the extra point.

Enraged Wisconsin immediately stormed back. One first down, two, three, four, and then the fifth (it was a screen pass from Elroy Hirsch to Pat Harder for 14 yards) which planted the ball on the one foot line. Twenty seconds of the half were left, and hurriedly the Badgers lined up. The battering Harder, who the year before had led the Big Ten in scoring with 58 points and in rushing with a 5.6-yard average and who was well on the way to duplicating those feats, was stopped without gain. Again the Badgers quickly lined up, and again Harder got the ball. But he picked up only six inches, or so the head linesman ruled, although Bob Duncan, a Wisconsin man at one end of the sticks, maintained to his dying day that Harder had scored. Harder himself in later years always refused to say, probably because he is now a National Professional League official.

So the Iowa game was lost, and Stuhldreher suffered what was undoubtedly one of the biggest coaching disappointments of his life. Those who knew him best have always felt that if his Badgers had won that Iowa game, he would have retired then as coach and remained as director.

There were even more tough breaks ahead immediately

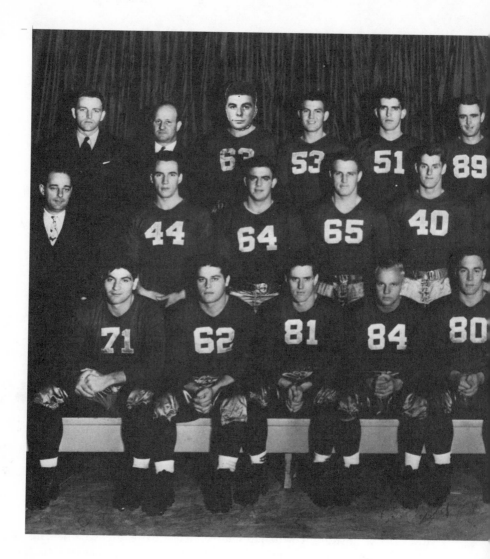

The 1942 team with an 8-1-1 record was Harry Stuhldreher's greatest in his 13 years as coach. It was hailed as national champion by the Helms Foundation of Los Angeles. Front row, left to right: Paul Hirsbrunner, George Makris, Pat Lyons, Bob Stupka, Co-Captain David Schreiner, Co-Captain Mark Hoskins, Leonard Calligaro, Robert Ray, John Roberts, and James McFadzean. Second Row: Head Coach Harry

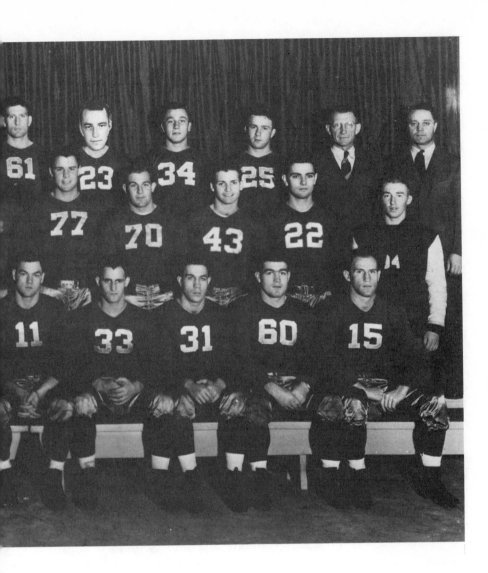

Stuhldreher, James Regan, Kenneth Currier, Jerry Frei, Elroy Hirsch, Robert Baumann, Richard Thornally, Lloyd Wasserbach, Leonard Seelinger, Ashley Anderson, senior Manager Eldon Fischer. Third Row: Assistant Coach George Fox, Assistant Coach Guy Sundt, Evan Vogds, Robert McKay, Fred Negus, Franham Johnson, Patrick Boyle, Robert Dierks, Pat Harder, Jack Wink, Trainer Walter Bakke, and Assistant Coach Russ Rippe.

after the 1942 season. The war was on, and though Stuhldreher might well have had another good team if 1943 had been a normal year, the Marines took 11 of his best men, seniors and underclassmen alike, and sent them to Michigan for officer's training. There they helped wallop their old Wisconsin mates, 27-0, and gave Michigan a tie with Purdue for the Big Ten championship with a 6-0 record.

Most of these players, both major and minor lettermen, would have been back in 1943 in normal times. The only senior key men who would not have returned were Mark Hoskins, a halfback; Lloyd Wasserbach, Richard Thornally, and Robert Baumann, tackles; and Dave Schreiner, an end.

Elroy Hirsch, who got the nickname "Crazy Legs" on the day he ran 60 yards for the touchdown that tied Notre Dame, 7-7, in the 1942 season, led the forced flight to Michigan after that season.

Hirsch also won letters in basketball, baseball, and track. He is the only man in Michigan history to win awards in four different sports.

Unfortunately, only some of these players returned to Wisconsin after their military tour, aside from graduating seniors. Hirsch signed a pro contract with the Chicago Rockets of the old All-America League. Pat Harder, after a service stint with the Marines, signed with the Chicago Cardinals of the National Professional League. And Bob Hanzlik, who had received a letter in 1941 but not in 1942, enrolled at Minnesota. He became the only man in Big Ten history to win varsity letters at three different Big Ten schools—Wisconsin, Michigan, and Minnesota—at three different positions—end, tackle, and guard.

The 1942 team was an ill-fated group. Schreiner and Baumann, who had enlisted immediately upon graduation in June 1943, were killed in action in Okinawa. Wasserbach died in a hotel fire in Ripon, Wisconsin.

Schreiner, one of the greatest ends in Wisconsin history, won All-American honors in both 1941 and 1942. Harder won them in 1942. And Harder, Schreiner, and Fred Negus won All-Conference honors in 1942.

Schreiner was an exceptional pass catcher and an outstanding defensive end who was posthumously named to both the Wisconsin state Hall of Fame and college football's Hall of

Elroy (Crazy Legs) Hirsch, star halfback on 1942 team, is now Wisconsin's athletic director.

Fame. He scored touchdowns on long passes against both Ohio State and Minnesota in the great 1942 season. A memorial scholarship helps keep his name fresh in Wisconsin memory.

While Stuhldreher could never forget the 1942 season and the heartbreak of the Iowa game, he did find a little balm in what happened in a few other seasons.

In 1937 Wisconsin got a 7-7 tie with Purdue when tackle Al Dorsch fell on Cecil Isbell's fumble in the end zone for the tying touchdown. In 1938 Wisconsin beat Indiana, 6-0, when Wisconsin drove 72 yards for a touchdown on a short end run by quarterback Vince Gavre just before the end of the half. Also in 1938, Howie Weiss, one of Wisconsin's long line of fine fullbacks, unravelled a long touchdown run against Northwestern, which all who saw it recall as one of the greatest they had ever seen. He reversed his field from one sideline to the other at least twice until he was able to straighten out and, behind Blackie O'Brien's final block, cross the goal. He covered only 39 yards to the goal, although actually he covered a total of more than 100 yards in his run. The touchdown was the decisive difference in the 20-13 upset victory.

It was also in 1938 that the Badgers beat UCLA, 14-7, on a memorable trip west. They had as a fellow traveler Father Flanagan of Boys' Town, who joined their party on the train at Omaha. They were met at the station in Los Angeles by John Richards, Wisconsin coach of 20 years earlier, and Herbert Stothart, a former University of Wisconsin professor and then musical director at MGM studios. Stothart arranged a tour of the studio, where the squad saw the filming of *Idiot's Delight* with Clark Gable and Norma Shearer and the *Wizard of Oz* with Judy Garland.

In 1939 Wisconsin scored only one victory, beating Marquette, 14-13, in a bitterly fought contest that was decided by an odd play. Tony Gradisnik passed 25 yards to Fred Gage for Wisconsin's first touchdown, and Billy Schmitz passed eight yards to Billy Cone for the second. The oddity occurred after Cone's touchdown. Bob Eckl's attempt for the extra point was blocked, and the ball rolled dead off to one side, where it lay

Dave Schreiner, All-American end on the 1942 team, was killed in the Okinawa invasion.

149

unnoticed until Schmitz picked it up and easily ran it across the goal. Marquette scored early when Jimmy Richardson ran back a punt 83 yards and scored again in the last two minutes when he passed 25 yards to Dick Vosburg. Bob Kemnitz, who kicked the extra point after the first touchdown, missed the vital second, which let Wisconsin make off with the victory.

As a kind of prelude to the bitter frustration of the Iowa game in 1942, the Badgers in 1939 lost to Illinois at Champaign, 7-0, in a game in which they outdowned their rivals—17 first downs to three—and even worse, had the ball on Illinois' one yard line as time ran out. Illinois scored the winning touchdown on Jimmy Smith's 82-yard run with three minutes left in the first half. In midfield Wisconsin players always claimed that Smith, running down their side of the field, had stepped out of bounds. The officials did not see it that way, however, and the touchdown stood. Wisconsin's futility was probably epitomized in the first quarter when the Badgers reached Illinois' six yard line, and Ted Damos missed a field goal from directly in front of the uprights.

In the second game of that season Wisconsin lost a bitter game to Texas at Madison, 17-7—bitter because Stuhldreher's father died the morning of the game and because the Texans left little doubt about their superiority. They also left remembrances of their visit—at least so Bill Aspinwall, business manager of the athletic department, always maintained. The dressing room Texas occupied was infested with tiny horned frogs, which had Aspinwall and his workers hopping around for almost a week to clean up.

The 1940 season had one great game that momentarily made up for a lot of disappointments. The Badgers were trailing Purdue, 13-0, with five minutes left when they rallied with two touchdowns and actually won the game 14-13, on an extra point after time was up. On seven straight first downs Wisconsin first marched down the field to Purdue's one, from where Bob Ray, substituting for starter George Paskvan at fullback, went over for the first touchdown. Two and one-half minutes were left when Fred Gage kicked the extra point.

When Purdue a little questionably went for first down in its own territory a minute later and failed, the Badgers got the ball back in scoring position. Only five seconds were left when

Howie Weiss, another in a long line of great Wisconsin fullbacks, won All-American recognition in 1938.

John Tennant passed to Ray Kreick, who ran 10 yards into the end zone as time expired. Kreick kicked the vital extra point with Tennant holding. Earlier Wisconsin had blocked the attempt for the extra point after Purdue's second touchdown which really opened the way for the Badger victory.

In 1941 a defeat at Syracuse's hands in Madison, 27-20, produced new fodder for Stuhldreher's critics and also helped lead to a change in the rules. Wisconsin was outgained two to one in a not particularly well-played game. Syracuse, coached by Ossie Solem, came to Camp Randall with a reverse center, a deployment on offense in which the center tossed the ball facing his own backfield rather than between his legs facing the opponents. The rule permitting this was changed the next year. Touchdowns by Pat Harder, Tom Farris, and Frank Riewer gave Wisconsin its consolation points.

The same men played key roles a week later when the Badgers righted themselves and fought Ohio State to a near standstill in Columbus before losing, 46-34. The game was a spectacular offensive show in which Ohio State scored seven touchdowns and Wisconsin five. On the second of Wisconsin's touchdowns, the Badgers had the help of a fifth down. On

Head Coach Harry Stuhldreher and his assistant coaches of the once defeated 1942 team. Left to right: Stuhldreher, George Fox, Russ Rippe, Guy Sundt.

In the pantheon of great Wisconsin fullbacks, Marlin (Pat) Harder, an All-American in 1942, is one of the greatest.

fourth down Tom Farris had failed to score, but Referee Jim Masker became confused and gave Wisconsin another down from the one yard line. Bud Seelinger then passed to Farris for the tally.

All universities contributed to the war effort, but while Michigan got those 11 football-playing Badgers for Marine officer training, Wisconsin as a naval radio training base got almost nothing as far as football talent was concerned. The results in the next few years were inevitable.

In the wartime years of 1943-45 after Wisconsin lost players to the Marines and other enlistments, the Badgers won 7 games, lost 19, and tied 2.

The 1943 season was a disaster. The team won one and lost nine, beating only Iowa, 7-5, and losing by such scores as 50-0 to Notre Dame, 41-0 to Northwestern, 33-7 to Marquette, and by double figures to every other opponent. In one stretch starting with the Notre Dame trouncing, the Badgers went five straight games without a point. In 10 games, the Badgers scored only 41 points and allowed 282.

153

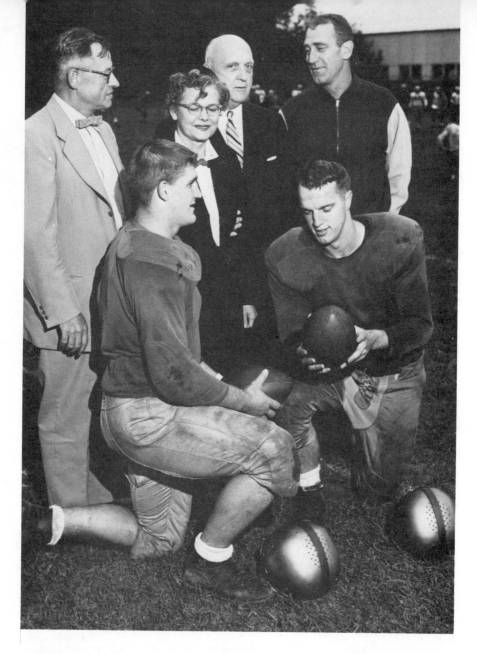

From left to right: Mr. and Mrs. Allan Shafer (parents of Allan Jr.,), university president E. B. Fred, and Coach Ivy Williamson (all standing) with 1953 recipients of Allan Shafer memorial scholarships, John Dittrich and Ron Locklin (kneeling left to right). Allan Shafer, Jr., died of injuries suffered in Iowa game of 1944.

Stuhldreher had a moment of outside glory in 1943 when he was chosen as coach of the College All-Stars against the Washington Redskins, champions of the National Professional League, in the annual *Chicago Tribune* charity game.

Stuhldreher's team, with players like Pat Harder, Gil Dobbs, and Bob Steuber, won in a romp, 27-7, taking full command after the Redskins, with Sammy Baugh at quarterback, scored the first touchdown. Harder scored two of the College All-Stars' touchdowns and Steuber and Graham, one each.

Things got little better in 1944 and 1945, in each of which seasons Wisconsin won three games in a nine-game schedule. The Badgers defeated Marquette, Iowa, and Northwestern in 1944 and Marquette, Iowa, and Minnesota in 1945. The 1944 season had a tragic note when Allan Shafer, Jr., died of injuries suffered in the Iowa game at Madison. Even an All-American quarterback, Earl (Jug) Girard, an excellent runner and good passer and punter, and Don Kindt, back from military service, could not stem the tide of defeats in 1945.

Ten of the men who had won letters on the great 1942 team returned after the war for the 1946 season, their eligibility not affected by their military service. And so the season began with high hopes.

The key returnees among the major and minor letter-

Workhorse halfback Jerry Thompson dives over for a touchdown in 1944 game with Iowa.

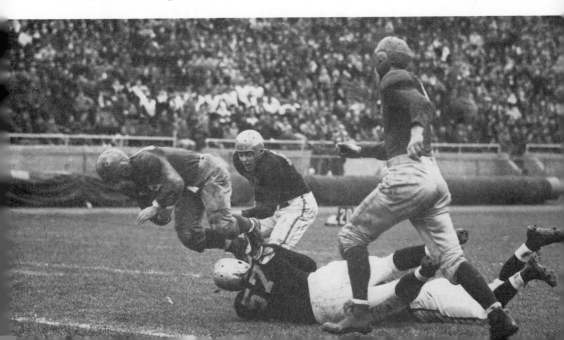

men of 1942 included Ashley Anderson, Ken Currier, Jerry Frei, Ralph Davis, Fred Negus, Jack Wink, Earl Maves, Bob Rennebohm, Hank Olshanski, and Dave Donnellan.

But success was still out of reach. Wisconsin won four and lost five in 1946. The victories were over Marquette, 34-0; California, 28-7; Ohio State, 20-7; and Purdue, 24-20. In the 21-7 defeat by Iowa in 1946, Wisconsin made only one first down. The Badgers won five, lost three, and tied one in 1947, a good season. But they sloughed off badly again in 1948, Stuhldreher's last year. The team won only two of nine games, downing Marquette, 26-0, and Illinois, 20-16.

Stuhldreher had a disciplinary problem with the 1946 team when Farnham Johnson and Hank Olshanski disobeyed the coach's orders and stayed over in Ann Arbor after the Michigan game to visit friends of their Marine training days. They were dropped from the squad for the windup Minnesota game the next week. They reported for practice on Monday as usual but found their lockers had been emptied. Stuhldreher first said he would explain their absence by announcing they had been injured, but neither player would accept this, and the real story of their absence soon became known.

The 1947 team delighted fans with long runs. Jug Girard, just returned from military service, ran back punts of 65 and 85 yards for touchdowns in the 46-14 victory over Iowa. Lisle Blackbourn, Jr., whose father was an assistant coach, made a

Earl Maves (35) looks for an opening with the help of a block by Clarence Self (18) in the Indiana game of 1947.

Halfback Clarence Self sees an opening at end against Iowa in 1948.

65-yard punt return for a touchdown in the same game. Girard also ran 64 yards for a touchdown in the 35-12 victory over Marquette. Clarence Self ran 78 yards for a touchdown as Wisconsin beat Purdue, 32-14, and dashed 67 yards for the consolation points in the 48-7 trouncing at California's hands.

In December 1948, with growing discontent and "Goodbye Harry" signs painted on campus walls, Stuhldreher resigned. The athletic board told him at its December meeting that as athletic director alone he could retain his salary of $12,000 a year, and he stepped down as coach but remained as director. In that role he participated in the search for a new coach. (He was later succeeded as athletic director by Guy Sundt.)

Stuhldreher was a crushed young man when he gave up football. Among other things, he had encountered almost open rebellion on his squad. Richard Leonard, now editor of the *Milwaukee Journal* and then editor of the *Daily Cardinal*, the student newspaper, tells of the situation.

"The disgruntled players would come up to see me in my *Cardinal* office and even come up to my room late at night to discuss their discontent. Mostly they felt Stuhldreher's football lacked imagination. Among other things they were mostly men who had been in the service and didn't like the discipline that the coach sought to maintain. They had had enough of that in

157

the service. The *Cardinal* editorially generally sided with them."

Bob Teague, a halfback on the football team and a sportswriter on the *Cardinal*, writing under the pseudonym of "Spartacus," added fuel to the burning situation with revelations of squad happenings that ordinarily would not have been publicized, and that probably helped hasten Stuhldreher's end.

Suggestions covering a successor to Stuhldreher poured in, and the athletic board in the next month interviewed a dozen men. Among them were Bud Wilkinson of Oklahoma, Rip Engle of Brown, Ivy Williamson of Lafayette, Liz Blackbourn, and three or four well-known state high school coaches.

Williamson, a star end at Michigan in the early thirties, who among other campus achievements, had won various scholastic honors, was finally chosen. Because of the similarity in Wilkinson's and Williamson's names, some fans for a while thought they were getting the great Oklahoma coach. When corrected, they naturally asked, "Who is Williamson?"

Yet Williamson had served a thorough and successful apprenticeship. Upon graduation in 1933 from Michigan, where his coaches, Harry Kipke and Fielding Yost, had hailed him as one of the greatest ends in Michigan history, he turned to football and basketball coaching at Roseville, Michigan, high school. There he immediately produced an unbeaten football team and in 1934 moved on to Yale as an assistant to Ducky Pond. In 1942 he enlisted in the navy and put in a season of coaching under Potsy Clark at the Pensacola navy base. His wartime service also included stints at Hollywood, Florida, on the Cadet selection board at Detroit, and on the training carrier, *Wolverine*, in Chicago.

In 1945 he resumed his former duties at Yale, this time under Howie Odell. In 1947 he moved on to Lafayette as head coach. There Williamson's teams in two years won 13 games and lost five, beating such teams as Fordham and Syracuse and losing only to such major powerhouses of the day as Army and Pennsylvania.

Halfback Earl Girard, one of the most versatile backs in school history as a passer, kicker, and runner, played on Coach Stuhldreher's last teams in the late forties.

Coach Harry Stuhldreher watches the action from the sidelines with Assistant Coach Russ Rippe on the telephone to his left in the 1942 season.

If some Wisconsin folks first confused him with Wilkinson, they quickly learned who Williamson was. Almost miraculously Wisconsin's football fortunes changed. In Williamson's seven years at Wisconsin, which Bill Aspinwall, then business manager of the athletic department, still refers to as the "seven years of plenty," his teams won 41 games, lost 19, and tied four. In 1952 the Badgers tied Purdue for the Big Ten title and were chosen to go the Rose Bowl.

Ivy's Ivy-Covered Record

Williamson's record for his seven years from 1949 through 1955 is still the finest in the school's modern history. In the Big Ten family only Ohio State, with Wesley Fesler and Woody Hayes as coaches in this period, had a better mark (46-15-4). Williamson had the Badgers in title contention through the final Saturday of the season in all but his last year. Marquette, Northwestern, Purdue, and Indiana could not win a game from him. Iowa could win only one in seven and Illinois only two of seven. Against Michigan State the Badgers split two games. Even against traditional opponent Minnesota, they had a 3-2-2 record.

Games outside the Big Ten, aside from Marquette, gave Williamson the most trouble. It was his philosophy that only games within the Big Ten were truly important, and he never particularly emphasized outside games. His teams beat Rice twice, Navy and Penn State each once, and split evenly with Pennsylvania. But they lost twice to Southern California and UCLA and once to California, to the annoyance of Wisconsin graduates on the coast, who wrote him scathing letters about the failures.

Williamson had an exceptionally keen football mind and was a tremendous organizer, who understood that any coach in a league as tough as the Big Ten needed a staff of good assistants. And he got them. He brought in Milt Bruhn, a Minnesota star under Bernie Bierman in the thirties, as line coach; Paul Shaw, a Pittsburgh star under Jock Sutherland in the same era,

161

Center and 1954 captain Gary Messner with Coach Ivy William-son.

as end coach; Bob Odell of Pennsylvania as backfield coach; and Fred Marsh of Bowling Green and George Lanphear of Wisconsin as general assistants. Bruhn and Shaw had been Williamson's assistants at Lafayette. Odell, a Maxwell trophy winner in his undergraduate days at Penn and a brother of the Odell who Williamson had worked with at Yale, was an assistant at Temple. Marsh was a boyhood pal who had starred at Bowling Green and had won all-state honors. Lanphear had played all sports at Wisconsin in the thirties and had coached at Ripon College in the forties. All but Odell remained with Williamson throughout his seven years.

The crowds which had started to fall off in Stuhldreher's last years picked up at once with Williamson. Sellouts were the rule in the stadium, whose capacity was increased from 45,000 to 51,000 in 1951.

In his first year, 1949, Williamson worked largely with material inherited from Stuhldreher and brought the team into the last game of the season, against Minnesota, with title hopes alive. There the Badgers lost, 14-6, although Gene Evans, a reckless little runner, gave Wisconsin a 6-0 halftime lead with a 62-yard punt return. The team threatened several times to score again, even reaching Minnesota's four yard line as the game ended. This was a Minnesota team that had men like Bud Grant, Clay Tonnemaker, Lee Nomellini, and Gordon Soltau, all of whom went on to outstanding careers in professional football.

Wisconsin finished fourth in the Big Ten in 1949 with a 3-2-1 Big Ten record and 5-3-1 overall. Ohio State and Michigan tied for the championship with 4-1-1 marks. A year earlier, with many of the same men, the Badgers had won only two of nine games and one of five in the Big Ten.

Williamson himself summed up the season with one of his rare accolades: "This team played closer to potential than any other I have ever had."

What Williamson achieved that year excited the whole state. Captain Bob (Red) Wilson was converted from center into an All-American end. Bob Teague, a 170-pound halfback who had received only indifferent attention from Stuhldreher, began to run wild. In the 30-14 rout of Indiana he scored touchdowns on runs of 46, 20, and 43 yards. In the 48-13 victory over Navy he dashed 64 yards across the goal, and in the 14-6 victory over

Halfback Gene Evans breaks off a 35-yard run against California in 1949.

Northwestern he ran 94 yards, only to have the touchdown called back. Assistant Coach Milt Bruhn called the line of Wilson, Joe Kelly, Don Knauff, Hal Otterback, Ken Huxhold, and Bill Gable the best he ever had at Wisconsin.

Williamson's record after his first season got progressively better, going to 6-3 in 1950, to 7-1-1 in 1951, and to 6-3-1 and the Rose Bowl in 1952.

The 1950 team followed the 1949 with a slightly different but still very successful cast of players. John Coatta, destined to become Wisconsin's coach 17 years later, took over as quarterback in the latter part of the season, and the veteran Bob Petruska, whom Coatta replaced, remained in the lineup as right halfback. With two such passers the Badgers posed a double threat in the air and made good use of it. Both men threw touchdown passes along the way to Gene Felker, Roy Burks, Tilden Meyers, Bob Mansfield, or Hal Faverty. Burks, a fleet, chunky little halfback ran 80 yards for a touchdown in the 33-7 victory over Purdue.

It was always Williamson's thinking that a team that passes well naturally defends well against passes. Wisconsin in this 1950 season did. Bob Radcliffe intercepted a pass which he ran back 31 yards for the winning touchdown as the Badgers beat Illinois in the rain at Champaign, 7-6. Ed Withers intercepted three passes for 103 yards as the team beat Iowa, 14-0, carrying

164

one of the three 30 yards for a touchdown. Burks ran back another against Iowa for a touchdown.

Through his first two years Williamson escaped the bitter frustrations which so often bedeviled other Wisconsin coaches in moments of apparent triumph as in the Ohio State game of 1920, the Illinois game of 1939, and the Iowa game of 1942. But with the 1951 season he, too, suffered some frustrations, and the whole state with him.

This was the team known as the "Hard Rocks" because of their superb defensive play. A Madison sports editor, Hank McCormick, came up with the name. The Badgers missed an undefeated season and probable Rose Bowl bid because they could not score on four downs from the one yard line against Illinois at Champaign, losing 14-10. They outdowned the Illini, 20-8, and outgained them, 274 yards to 142. The Badgers finished the season with a 7-1-1 record against Illinois' 9-0-1, Illinois going to the Rose Bowl.

The 1951 defense was not only the best in the Big Ten but the best in the nation, allowing only 40 points in seven Big Ten

Captain Bob Wilson, end on offense and linebacker on defense, was named the Big Ten's most valuable player in 1949. Here he catches a pass against Navy.

Bob Teague, Wisconsin's rushing leader in 1949, follows his blocking well against Iowa.

games and 53 in nine games overall and yielding only 68.9 yards a game. More than that, with its defensive brilliance, the team coupled a high scoring punch of its own. It led the Big Ten in points scored with 158, 42 more than Purdue, the second best scoring team.

The "Hard Rocks" were a collection of 17 seniors, 15 of whom had won varsity letters the previous year; 18 juniors, eight of whom had won such letters; 16 sophomores, two of whom had won varsity letters; and four outstanding freshmen: Clarence Stensby, a guard; Don Ursin and Don Voss, ends; and Alan ("The Horse") Ameche, destined to become the greatest fullback in Wisconsin history.

The varsity-letter winners of the previous season, of course, provided most of the muscle by which the "Hard Rocks" forged their way into Wisconsin history: ends Hal Faverty, Gene Felker, and Pat O'Donahue; tackles Jerry Smith, Bob Leu, Art Prchlik, Charlie Berndt, and Dave Suminski; guards Harry Gilbert, George O'Brien, and George Steinmetz; centers Dave Hansen and George Simkowski; linebacker Deral Teteak; defensive backs Bill Lane, Ed Withers, and Burt Hable; running backs Harland Carl, Rollie Strehlow, Jerry Witt, and

All-American end Pat O'Donahue was a defensive mainstay on the 1951 "Hard Rocks."

166

Fullback Alan Ameche won every honor collegiate football has to offer in a four-year career from 1951 through 1954.

Bill Hutchinson; fullbacks Jim Hammond and Tom Schleisner; and quarterback John Coatta. And, of course, the freshmen, who were great contributors.

A few sophomores who had won only freshman numerals the year before complemented this group: ends Norb Esser and Gerald Wuhrman; halfbacks Roger Dornburg, Tom Canny, Ron Hoenisch, Gerald Witt, and Tom Rendler; tackle Mike Cwayna; linebacker Cary Bachman; guard Wendell Gulseth; and fullbacks John Dixon and Bob Lamphere.

Coatta, a senior, had had a league-leading passing percentage of .642 in 1950 and came back in this year with .521. In one stretch of the Ohio State game, he completed 10 in a row. He was also an excellent place kicker. Witt, a late bloomer, scored four touchdowns in the victory over Northwestern and led the Big Ten in scoring with 48 points. Carl, a track team sprinter with fine moves on the football field, unfortunately had a career of injuries or surgery—knees, hand, ankles. When healthy he was a touchdown threat every time he laid hands on the ball.

With the 1951 season, Ameche also began the four-year career unmatched in modern Wisconsin history. In his collegiate years Wisconsin won 26 games, lost eight, and tied three, and in virtually every victory his rushing was the top factor. Coach Red Sanders of UCLA once publicly stated that "Ameche is the strongest runner in football history, not excepting Bronko Nagurski."

In his four years Ameche carried the ball 701 times for a net of 3,345 yards, 25 touchdowns, and 4.8-yard average per carry. Not until late in his career was he ever seriously hurt. He suffered an ankle injury against Northwestern in 1954 and tailed off in the last two games against Illinois and Minnesota.

Ameche started as a 205-pounder but grew into a 212-pounder in his junior and senior years, when he needed special shoulder pads.

His honors as a collegian included about everything ever given to any player, including the Heisman award in 1954. In his last three years he was named on one or more All-American teams, including the most prestigious every year. He was the No. 1 draft choice of the Baltimore Colts in 1955, and on his very first play in his first pro league game, he ran 79 yards for a

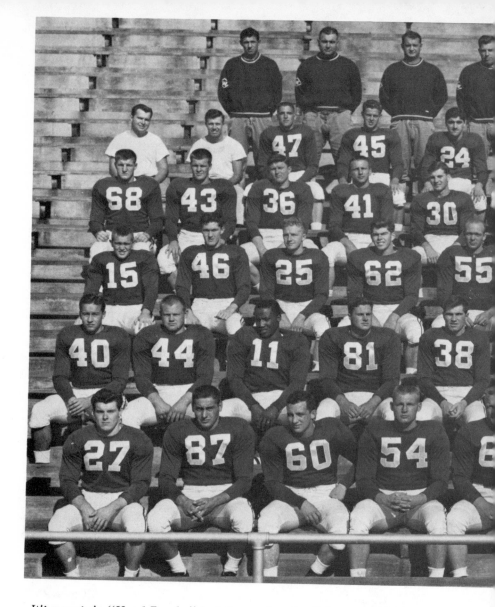

Wisconsin's "Hard Rocks" led the nation in defense in 1951 but missed an undefeated season by losing to Illinois. Front row, left to right: John Coatta, Gene Felker, Harry Gilbert, Dave Hansen, Bill Gable, Captain Jim Hammond, Bill Lane, Bob Leu, Pat O'Donahue, and Jerry Smith. Second Row: Rollie Strehlow, Deral Teteak, Ed Withers, Harold Faverty, Bill Schleisner, Charles Berndt, Bob Kennedy, George Simkowski, George Steinmetz, and George Suminski. Third Row: Archie Roy Burks, Bill Hutchinson, Norris Ace, George O'Brien, J. Cary Bachman, Burt Hable, Carl Martin, Bill Miller, Kent Peters, and Bob Lamphere. Fourth Row: Art Prchlik, Tom Proctor, Ervin

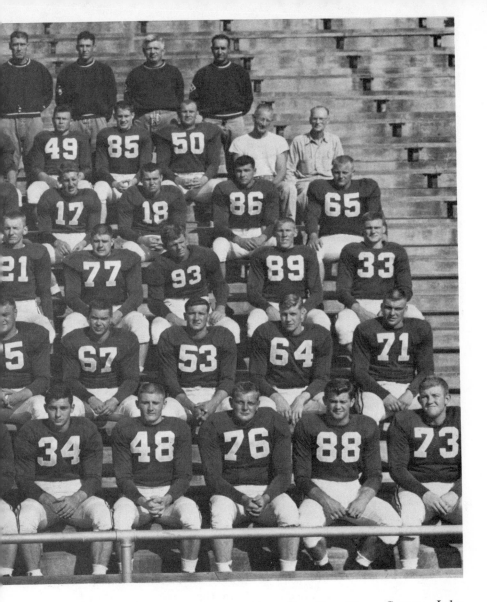

Andrykowski, Harland Carl, Tom Rendler, Tom Canny, John Dixon, Roger Dornburg, Norbert Esser, and Wendell Gulseth. *Fifth Row:* Senior Managers Gordon Becker and John Freidel; Ron Hoenisch, Wayne Hansen, Gust Vergetis, Glen Wilson, Gerald Witt, Jerald Wuhrman, Jim Craine, Trainer Walter Bakke, and Equipment Manager Gene Roberts; *Top Row:* Assistant Coaches Tom Bennett, George Lanphear, Paul Shaw, Milt Bruhn; Head Coach Ivy Williamson; Assistant Coaches Bob Odell, Fred Marsh, and LaVern Van Dyke. *Not Pictured:* Alan "The Horse" Ameche, Clarence Stensby, Don Voss.

Halfback Jerry Witt scores the second of his four touchdowns against Northwestern in 1951.

touchdown against the Chicago Bears. He scored the winning touchdown for the Colts in overtime of their memorable 23-17 victory over the New York Giants in the 1958 championship game. He is now the millionaire owner of a chain of drive-in restaurants in the East.

The Illinois game of 1951 which Wisconsin lost, 14-10, may live as the worst of all the frustrations the Badgers suffered. Wisconsin not only led, 10-7, at the end of the first half but also took the kickoff in the second half and strung together six straight first downs to Illinois' one yard line in a 10-minute excursion. A clinching touchdown looked like a cinch, but Illinois had other ideas.

On first down Wisconsin's Rollie Strehlow lost three yards, although his mates always maintained that he had not been given his forward progress by the officials and at worst had been held without gain. On second down Wisconsin was penalized five yards for motion. On a repeated second down Coatta got the five back around end, and on third down Ameche failed to gain. At this point it was fourth down on the four, goal to go, and the battering Ameche was given the ball again. No gain, and Illinois took over.

Wisconsin still led, 10-7, after these failures, but the Illini quickly took over. Johnny Karras, who had scored their first touchdown on a seven-yard run in the first quarter, broke away

173

for 30 yards to pull out of danger on the first play and then led an uninterrupted march down the field for the winning Illinois touchdown. He scored it from two yards out in the fourth quarter.

Jim Hammond had given Wisconsin its first points by falling on Karras' fumble in the end zone in the second quarter, and Coatta had kicked a 25-yard field goal a few minutes later for the 10-7 halftime lead. Hammond's touchdown was typical of Wisconsin's defensive efforts all season long. All told, the defense accounted for 31 points. Roger Dornburg ran back an interception 53 yards for a touchdown against Marquette, and Bob Leu ran back one for 39 yards against Penn. Deral Teteak fell on a fumble in the end zone against Penn. And the aggressive defensive play up front accounted for three safeties, two against Purdue and one against Marquette.

If the Badgers lost a dramatic game to Illinois, however, they redeemed themselves when they beat Indiana in a blizzard in Madison, 6-0. So bad was the snow that only 40,000 of the 50,000 homecoming celebrants could make it to the stadium. Cars had to be abandoned on highways. One side of the field was almost obliterated from the other. It was a scoreless game until only 48 seconds remaining, when Coatta hurled a 36-yard pass through swirling snow to Bill Hutchinson for the winning touchdown.

The season had one other high spot. Ohio State, the traditional nemesis, was tied, 6-6, in a game at Madison a week after the Illinois heartbreak. Coatta threw a touchdown pass to Hal Faverty to match one Vic Janowicz threw to Jim Armstrong. It was a game the Badgers could well have won, for they had all the better of the statistics. Coatta and Janowicz each missed the extra point.

Pat O'Dea, the great Wisconsin kicker and captain at the turn of the century, called this 1951 team the greatest in Wisconsin history. It may well have been, because it set Big Ten records in five divisions of departmental play, and no fewer than four of its number won All-American recognition of one kind or another—Ed Withers, Pat O'Donahue, Hal Faverty, and John Coatta.

Art Lentz, then the university's director of athletic publicity and later executive director of the United States Olympic

174

committee, once wrote: "I don't know when a team so captured the interest of the state, alumni, and students as this one with its ability and tremendous spirit after the early season loss to Illinois and the tie with Ohio State. Though it won all of the other games, it ironically finished only third in the Big Ten race behind Illinois and Purdue." He wrote what most Wisconsin followers still feel—that this was certainly one of Wisconsin's greatest teams, if not the greatest.

Williamson Goes
To The Rose Bowl

The Badgers did not have to wait long for the Rose Bowl bid which had eluded them in 1951. They got it in 1952 after tying with Purdue for the championship with a 4-1-1 Big Ten record. The bowl selection was made by vote of the league's athletic directors, who favored the Badgers because of their better overall record of 6-2-1 to Purdue's 4-3-2.

The offense was every bit as potent as the 1951 team's, with a ballcarrier like Alan Ameche around, plus a very good passing successor to John Coatta at quarterback in Jim Haluska. But the defense was not as good. Statistically these Badgers of 1952 scored exactly as many points as the 1951 team (158 in six Big Ten games) but gave up 97 points as compared with the 1951 team's 40. The difference was understandable, because the principal defensive sinews of the "Hard Rocks" had graduated.

The Badgers beat Marquette, Illinois, Iowa, Rice, Northwestern, and Indiana, tied Minnesota, and lost to Ohio State and UCLA. The Iowa and Minnesota games are best remembered. Against Iowa the Badgers had the help of the longest punt in their modern history. George O'Brien, standing on his own goal line, booted the ball 96 yards, including the roll, to Iowa's three yard line, where the ball rolled dead. In the Minnesota game, upon which a share of the title and the Rose Bowl trip depended, the team was pushed to the very limit to preserve a 21-21 tie. Paul Giel, Minnesota quarterback, operating off the shotgun offense, drove the Badgers a little crazy with his passing and running. On the very last play he tossed a pass up for grabs in Wisconsin's end zone, which Burt Hable intercepted with a leaping effort. It was Hable's third interception of the game. Earlier, Giel had thrown touchdown passes to Bob McNamara and to Dale Quist and himself had scored from the two yard line after gaining this scoring position with his deadly passes. So wild was the finish that the ball changed hands six times in the fourth quarter through interceptions or fumbles. Paul Shwaiko of Wisconsin and Tom Cappellitta of Minnesota each intercepted two passes, in addition to the one that Hable intercepted to end the game. Witt and Giel each lost the ball once on a fumble.

So Wisconsin won the Rose Bowl trip to meet Southern California.

Up to this point the Big Ten, in six modern-day trips to the bowl, had never been beaten. But Wisconsin lost, 7-0, on a 22-yard pass, Rudy Bukich to Al Carmichael, on the fag end of a 73-yard drive by the Trojans in the third quarter. Bukich, a transfer from the University of Iowa, was a substitute quarterback who had replaced All-American Jimmy Sears after Sears had suffered a broken leg on the ninth play of the game.

Sears' early loss was a tremendous blow to the Trojans but no more than Wisconsin's in practice at Brookside Park before the game. At that time Harland Carl twisted his knee and did not get to play until the last three minutes of the game, when he finally got in on the tail end of Wisconsin's last desperate drive.

Ameche spearheaded Wisconsin's attack, carrying 28 times for 133 yards. On the first play of the third quarter, he broke off tackle for 54 yards and with a five-yard lead on all pursuers in midfield seemed headed for a certain touchdown. But Frank Clayton, a substitute halfback with very little playing time in the regular season, hauled him down from behind.

With first down on Southern California's 33 yard line after the run, the Badgers met frustration again. Haluska's nine-yard pass to Erv Andrykowski and a two-yard run by Jerry Witt carried them to Southern California's 22 yard line. But on second down Roy Burks fumbled when tackled by Bob Van Doren, and Hooks of the Trojans recovered on his own 27.

The Trojan touchdown drive on which Bukich completed five of six passes, topped by the touchdown pass to Carmichael,

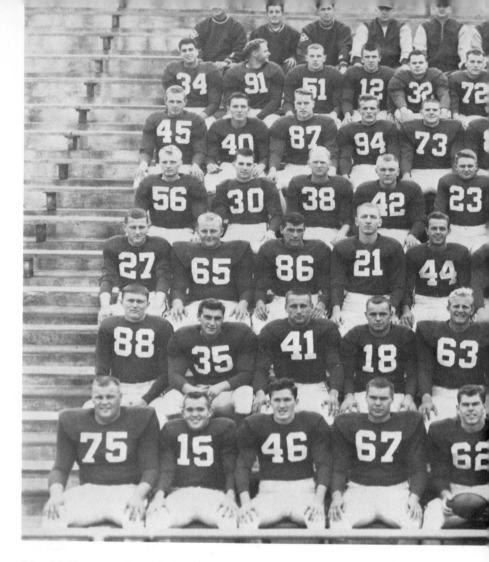

The 1952 team shared the Big Ten title with Purdue but lost to Southern California in the Rose Bowl. Front row, left to right: Charles Berndt, Archie Roy Burks, Bill Hutchinson, Bob Kennedy, Captain George O'Brien, Kent Peters, Art Prchlik, George Simkowski, George Steinmetz, and George Suminski. Second Row: Ervin Andrykowski, Alan ("The Horse") Ameche, Harland Carl, Roger Dornburg, Clarence Stensby, Don Voss, Gerald Witt, Tom Canny, Mike Cwayna, John Dixon, and Joseph Terry Durkin. Third Row: Don Schaefer, Wendell Gulseth, Norbert Esser, Burt Hable, Wayne Hansen, Mark Hoegh, Robert Jacobsen, Bob Lamphere, Carl Martin, Bill Miller, and Tom Proctor. Fourth Row: Harold Rebholz, Tom Rendler, Bill Rutenberg, Bernhard Schmidt, Jack Torresani, Gust Vergetis, Glen Wilson, Hugo Wimmer, Jerald Wuhrman,

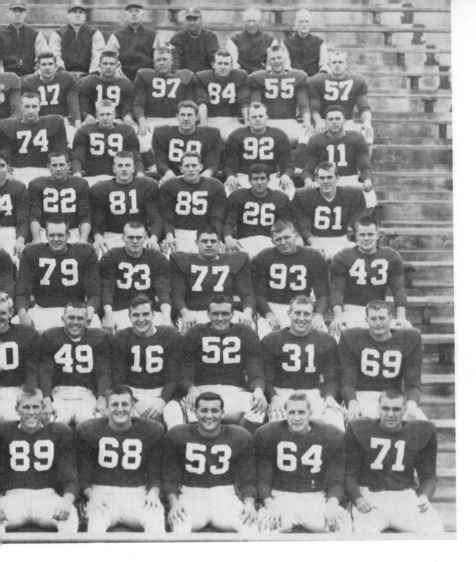

Mario Bonofiglio, and William Brandt. *Fifth Row:* Clarence Bratt, Bob Gingrass, Ron Locklin, Keith Lundin, Ed Ronzia, Jim Temp, Don Ursin, Richard Wohlleber, Norm Amundsen, William Barney, and Darwin Destache. *Sixth Row:* Michael Gitlitz, George Drewry, Wells Gray, Jim Haluska, David La-Duke, Herdis McCrary, Donald Pierce, Bernard Schencker, Paul Shwaiko, Robert Sternat, Jack Walker, Gerald Walsdorf, and Watson Woodruff. *Seventh Row:* Senior Manager John Eldredge; Manager Laurenzi; Assistant Coaches Tom Bennett, George Lanphear, Paul Shaw, Milt Bruhn, Head Coach Ivy Williamson; Assistant Coaches Bob Odell, Fred Marsh, LaVern Van Dyke; Trainer Walter Bakke; and Equipment Manager Gene Roberts.

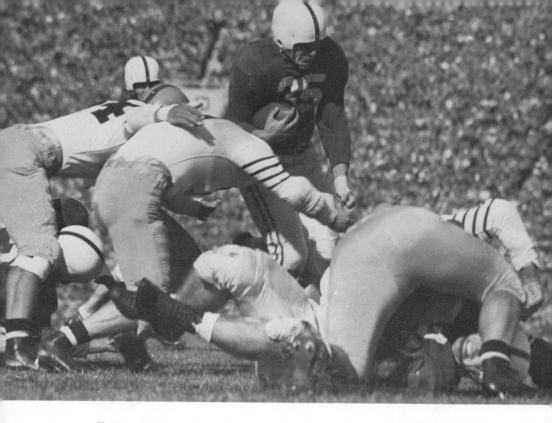

*Fullback Alan Ameche is stopped just short of the goal in 1951
Illinois game.*

began at once. Sam Tsagalakis kicked the extra point. Earlier his
attempted field goal from the 23 had hit the crossbar and
bounced back harmlessly.

In most of the statistics, the Badgers had all the better of
the game, and this was one of Southern California's finest
teams. Eleven of them went into professional football—
Carmichael, Lindon Crow, Jim Psaltis, George Timberlake,
Charlie Ane, Al Barry, Jim Sears, Aramis Dandoy, Des Koch,
Elmer Wilhoite, and Ron Miller.

The Badgers outrushed their rivals, 211 yards to 48; outdowned them 19 to 16; controlled the ball on 76 plays against
60, exclusive of punts; and had the game's outstanding ballcarrier in Ameche. But they could not match the Trojans in
passing or kicking. Southern California completed 18 of 27
passes for 185 yards against Wisconsin's 11 of 26 for 142, and
they averaged 51 yards on eight punts against Wisconsin's 39
yards on five. One of Koch's punts sailed 72 yards—still the

Rose Bowl record.

Wisconsin's most bitter frustration occurred in the last three minutes when the team put together four first downs to Southern California's 24 yard line. With 90 seconds left and Carl in the game for the first time, Haluska's second-down pass was ticked by safety Harry Welch just as Carl, in the end zone, was about to pull it in. On fourth down with the same yardage to gain, another pass intended for Roger Dornburg was overthrown. That was the game.

As the possession statistics suggest, the Badgers moved the ball well. They went 66 yards in the first quarter and gave up the ball on downs on Southern California's 13, then went 41 yards in the second quarter but had to punt. They went 66 yards to start the third quarter and lost the ball on Burk's fum-

Wisconsin players autographed footballs in a drive to raise funds for the Los Angeles Children's Hospital during their Rose Bowl visit in 1953. More than $1,000 was raised at an auction. Left to right are guard Bob Kennedy, guard and captain George O'Brien, quarterback Burt Hable, Coach Ivy Williamson, and tackle Charlie Berndt.

Tackle Dave Suminski, an All-American, was one of the main-stays in Wisconsin's line in the Rose Bowl game of 1953.

ble and drove 79 yards a few minutes later inside the Trojan's 10. But they lost the ball on downs again when a clipping penalty nullified Witt's five-yard dash to the two yard line. They went 57 yards to Southern California's 23 in the fourth quarter but gave up the ball on downs and came right back 47 yards to Southern California's 24 a few minutes later when the pass to Carl in the end zone was ticked.

Don Voss, a truly great defensive end and one of the best Wisconsin ever had, was injured in the second quarter of the game and never returned.

The defeat, yet another in the long list of frustrations that had bedeviled Wisconsin in football through the years, did not stop these Williamson teams, however, from continuing their drive to eminence in the league. "Be a Spartan," Williamson used to say, "keep coming whatever the odds or adversity." His Badgers did.

From the very beginning at Wisconsin Williamson had said that his first job was to get rid of what had become a losing campus complex, and so far as a coach could destroy this, he did.

In 1953, the year after the Bowl game, his Badgers had a 6-2-1 record, losing only to Ohio State and UCLA, and in 1954 a 7-2 record, losing only to Ohio State and Iowa.

If ever a team had a nemesis, it was Wisconsin with Ohio State and specifically with one man—Howard (Hopalong) Cassady. Cassady an All-American, a Heisman trophy winner, and one of the greatest athletes in Ohio State history, was the principal architect of every defeat the Buckeyes slapped on Wisconsin in his four years (1952-55). He usually did it with high drama, too: as in 1953, when he caught a pass from Dave Leggett with two minutes and 31 seconds left and covered 60 yards for the winning touchdown of a 20-19 victory, and as in 1952, when he caught a pass from John Borton for 44 yards and a vital touchdown in the 23-14 victory. In every year it was Cassady's running, pass catching, interceptions, and even his passing on option plays that made life miserable for the Badgers. The whole state breathed a sigh of relief when he was graduated, although Ohio State has continued to dominate the series. To this day Wisconsin has not defeated Ohio State at Columbus since 1918 and in 45 games going back to 1913 has

Quarterback Jimmy Miller sets himself before lofting a scoring pass to Norb Esser (not shown) in 1953 game against Minnesota.

won only seven and tied four.

Williamson was a coaching genius when he shot for the Illinois game in 1953. He took dead aim at the Illini for what they had done to the "Hard Rocks" in 1951, and though Illinois had a very good team, with backs like J.C. Caroline and Mickey Bates, the Badgers crushed them, 34-7.

Williamson's last year as coach, 1955, was his only losing season. The Badgers won four and lost five. When Guy Sundt, athletic director who had succeeded Stuhldreher, died unexpectedly the Monday after the Ohio State game, Williamson was offered and accepted the job as director.

Williamson left a lasting memorial not only as a winning coach but as athletic director. It was he who increased the stadium capacity to 76,000 and installed artificial turf; built a new natatorium, a new baseball field, and a new football press box; expanded intramural activities and restored hockey as an intercollegiate sport. As the new director after giving up coaching to succeed Sundt, Williamson naturally had to pick a successor coach.

184

Coach Milt Bruhn (left) receives congratulations from Athletic Director Ivy Williamson whom he succeeded in 1956.

Head Coach Ivy Williamson watches his last team in 1955 before stepping down to become athletic director. At far right, also standing, is his successor, Line Coach Milt Bruhn.

It was not an easy choice for him, but a trend in having successful coaches become athletic directors only was developing all over the country, and Williamson was caught up in it. Biggie Munn had stepped down as coach at Michigan State to become director there, and Bud Wilkinson had done so at Oklahoma. Stu Holcomb, at the same time, had left Purdue as coach to become director at Northwestern. Forest Evashevski a few years later took the same step at Iowa.

As Sundt's successor it was Williamson's job to recommend a successor coach, and he pondered his choice carefully. Should he go outside his immediate coaching family for the new coach, who might insist on bringing in an entirely new staff of assistants? Or should he select a coach from "family" and thus very probably protect the jobs of the other assistants, all of whom had come with him from Lafayette? He chose the latter course and selected the man who had been his own right-hand man, line coach Milt Bruhn.

Bruhn, recognized as one of the finest line coaches in the country, got off to a bad start in 1956, winning only from Marquette, 41-0, and tying Purdue, 6-6; Illinois, 13-13; and

Minnesota, 13-13, for a 1-5-3 season. He corrected this start quickly, however, adding Perry Moss to his coaching staff for two years and later Clark Van Galder and Deral Teteak, and ambitiously setting his sights on the Rose Bowl.

He had a 6-3 record in 1957 and a 7-1-1 in 1958. In 1959 he won seven of nine games (5-2-0 in the Big Ten) to take the undisputed conference title and the trip to Pasadena.

Though it occasionally faltered, the 1959 team did several things few Wisconsin teams have ever done. In one and the same year it beat its most stubborn rivals, Ohio State, Minnesota, and Michigan, along with Iowa and Northwestern. Yet it lost to Purdue, 21-0, and to Illinois, 9-6.

The 1959 drive to the Rose Bowl had team followers in a sweat from beginning to end. It started with the Stanford game in a hard rain. The Badgers were thoroughly bamboozled by Dick Norman, who completed 17 of 25 passes, but they still sneaked by, 16-14. They had an easy time with Marquette the next week, 44-6.

The first Big Ten game, against Purdue, was played in a torrential downpour, and Wisconsin collapsed, 21-0, Purdue taking a 14-0 lead in the first seven minutes. They recovered against Iowa the next week, 25-16, though Olen Treadway of the Hawkeyes completed 26 of 41 passes for 304 yards.

The Ohio State game was probably the high spot of the season. On a wet, slippery field, the Badgers did everything right

Halfback Danny Lewis follows his blocking against Illinois in 1957 homecoming game against Illinois.

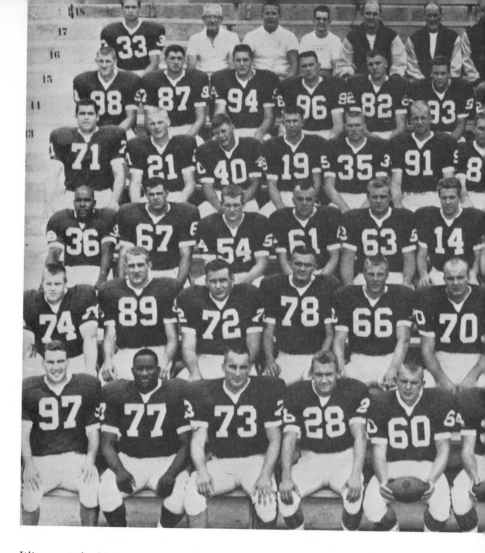

Wisconsin's 1959 Big Ten champions took a lacing from Washington in 1960 Rose Bowl game. *Front row, left to right:* Jim Holmes, Lowell Jenkins, Dan Lanphear, Dale Hackbart, Co-Captain Jerry Stalcup, Co-Captain Bob Zeman, Jim Heineke, Ron Steiner, Billy Hobbs, Eddie Hart, and Bob Altmann. *Second Row:* John Allen, Henry Derleth, Karl Holzwarth, Terry Huxhold, Gerald Kulcinski, Bob Nelson, Ron Perkins, Jim Rogers, Alan Schoonover, Charles Sprague, Tom Wiesner, and Pete Zouvas. *Third Row:* Tom Anthony, Tom Genda, John Gotta, Tom Grantham, Alex Muszytowski, Bob Hudson, Milton Lambert, Gary Harms, Bill Kellog, Francis "Shorty" Young, Dave Bichler, Ron Adamson, and Otto Peucker. *Fourth Row:*

188

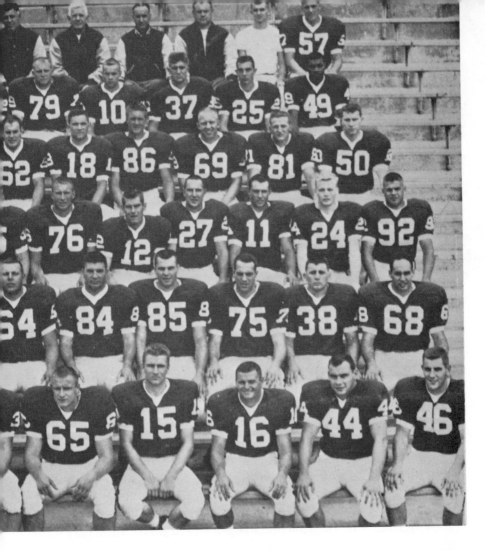

Barry Armstrong, Jim Bakken, Stu Clark, Billy Hess, Tom Neumann, Carlton Olson, Dick Pauley, Don Schade, Ron Staley, Mike Stanki, Bill Suits, Chuck Vesel, and Richard Wittig. *Fifth Row:* Ed Dolly, Dick Grimm, John Grossenbacher, Richard Kilger, Daniel Klinkhammer, Richard Lane, Tom Mettlach, Brian Moore, Neil Nelson, Phil Pisani, Ron Vander-Kelen, and Alvin Whitaker. *Sixth Row:* John Rensch; Trainer Walter Bakke; Assistant Trainer George Wastila; Equipment Manager Art Lamboley; Assistant Coaches Fred Jacoby, Clark Van Galder, Paul Shaw; Head Coach Milt Bruhn; Assistant Coaches Fred Marsh, LaVern Van Dyke, and Deral Teteak; Manager Lee VanderVelden; Bill Pidcoe.

189

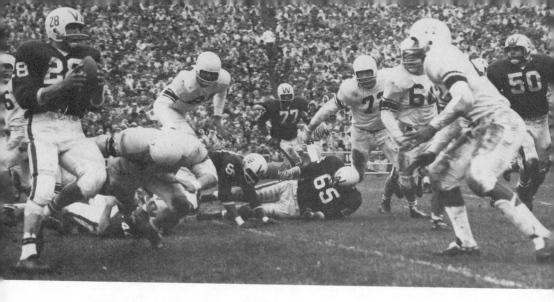

Quarterback Dale Hackbart (28) is badly rushed as he attempts to pass against Minnesota in 1958.

to win, 12-3.

Wisconsin had to hang on for dear life against Michigan, a team which was not going anywhere in particular. The Badgers won, 19-10, but led by a scant 16-10 until the last minute of play.

The Badgers beat Northwestern, 24-19, although they twice had to protect their lead with their backs against the wall.

In a season of sweating like this, there had to be a heartbreak, and it occurred in the Illinois game. The Illini, trailing 6-2, scored the winning touchdown of a 9-6 victory on the very last play of the game. The electric scoreboard clock showed a big, red "zero" as fullback Bill Brown smashed into the end zone from one yard out. Jim Bakken's fumble in the end zone had given Illinois a safety and two points in the first quarter.

At this point, as the race had developed, everything depended on the closing Minnesota game, and the Badgers had to sweat this one out as no other. Minnesota took a 7-0 lead with a 57-yard touchdown pass on the fourth play of the game and led by this score at the half.

A pass intercepted by Bob Altman late in the third quarter gave the Badgers position on Minnesota's eight yard line, and after three plunges had carried to the four, Karl Holzwarth kicked a field goal, which cut the deficit to 7-3. It was just the spark the Badgers needed to flare up, and the next time they got the ball they drove 80 yards across the goal, Hackbart scoring the touchdown on a sneak from the one. The decision was made to go for a two-point conversion and it was good. The Badgers, with an 11-7 lead, still were not home free. But the defense did the rest, stopping the Gophers once inside the 10 and intercepting a pass in the end zone a little later. The final score stood at 11-7.

Wisconsin was a 6½ point favorite against Washington in the Rose Bowl at Pasadena, but never was a team so brutally humiliated. Jim Owens' Huskies won easily, 44-8. The Badgers were never really in the game, as the Huskies' quarterback Bob Shloredt, halfback George Fleming, and the rest of their pack had more fun than on a Tuesday afternoon practice. The pattern of the game was almost set before play began. The Badgers were obviously in California for a good time. The married players had been permitted to take their wives. The players set the curfew they wanted, 10:30 p.m., but they did not always observe it. They graciously accepted Pasadena's hospitality. The Huskies, in turn, were a sullenly dedicated bunch, even down to their practices, which were held with military precision. And they played with crackling snap.

When the Badgers won the toss and chose to kick off instead of receive because of a gusty wind, the rout was on. Fleming returned the kickoff to midfield, and while the Huskies did not go much farther on this first possession, they were able to throw the play deep into Wisconsin territory.

The annihilation thereafter was complete. Washington went 48 yards on 10 plays for the first touchdown, which Don McKeta scored from six yards out. As soon as they got the ball again they went 29 yards on seven plays for Fleming's 26-yard field goal. A few minutes later Fleming returned a punt 53 yards for their second touchdown. The Huskies flew 27 yards on three plays for their third touchdown on Shloredt's pass to Lee Folkins. The score at the half was 24-8. They went 66 yards on 10 plays for their fourth touchdown early in the third quarter, Ray Jackson scoring from five yards out, and smashed 93 yards on 10 plays for their fifth. Shloredt himself scored this one from the three.

Substitutes took over here and accounted for the final

Jubilant teammates carry Alan "The Horse" Ameche off the field following the final game of his career against Minnesota in a 27-0 win in Camp Randall Stadium. Badgers identifiable are Clarence Bratt (22), left; Jim Miller (21), center; and Bill Mc-Namara (51), right.

points. Bob Hivener passed to Don Millich for 12 yards.

Shloredt, Associated Press All-American, who had only 10 percent vision in his left eye, ran the quarterback option roll-outs to perfection, darting inside and outside Wisconsin's ends or tackles as he wished or passing with 55 percent accuracy to Folkins, Fleming, McKeta, Jackson, or John Meyers.

Wisconsin got its consolation points immediately after Fleming's field goal. On nine plays, most of them passes, the Badgers went 69 yards. Dale Hackbart's pass to Allan Schoonover was good for 24 yards, to Hank Derleth for 13, and to Bob Zeman for 20. With the ball on the four, Tom Wiesner smashed home. A pass, Hackbart to Schoonover, gave Wisconsin a two-point conversion. It was only a brief interruption, however, in Washington's irresistible assault.

Typical of the Badgers' woes were four fumbles, all of which they lost. Bill Hobbs made two and Ron Steiner and Hackbart each one. Considering the score, the Badgers did not fare too badly in statistics. They got 13 first downs to Washington's 16, 123 yards running against 215, and 153 yards passing against 127. Hackbart completed 14 of 32 passes, Shloredt seven of 13.

Los Angeles newspapers had fun with Wisconsin's poor showing. Melvin Durslag of the *Los Angeles Examiner* put it this way the day after the game: "Welcome Badgers—the pride of America's dairyland. Wisconsin proved itself a cheese champion yesterday. Here you had the combination of a horrible performance on the part of one team, Wisconsin, and an absolutely magnificent showing by the other, Washington. The men from Wisconsin couldn't play football for sour apples, or, for that matter, saurbraten."

Bruhn had tears in his eyes as he tried to explain in the post mortems what had happened. "They gave us a good going over and that's all there was to it," was as far as he would go.

Athletic Director Ivy Williamson, whose own Badgers had lost to Southern California seven years before, had salt rubbed into the wounds. Leaving the hotel for a Wisconsin reception after the game, he took a cab whose driver did not recognize him.

"What a bunch of bums," the cab driver innocently remarked as he drove away.

"Why?" Williamson asked.

"Why?" the indignant driver retorted. "I lost $100 on them Wisconsin guys seven years ago, and I lost another $100 on them today. They can keep Wisconsin."

Wisconsin used only 28 of the 44 men who made the bowl trip, but all shared in the gloom on the trip home.

VanderKelen To Richter

Milt Bruhn was to bring another Wisconsin team to the huge Arroyo Seco bowl in Pasadena on January 1, 1963, this one also an undisputed Big Ten champion and the best Wisconsin ever sent west.

Like its predecessors it, too, lost. But only after one of the greatest games in Rose Bowl history, one usually referred to as the "VanderKelen game" because of the heroics of that Wisconsin quarterback in the fourth quarter.

Before this bowl game, however, there were two rebuilding seasons. The 1959 team had been largely a veteran bunch. In 1960 the Badgers had a record of four and five, and in 1961, six and three, giving an inkling of what they were prepared to do in 1962.

The great team of 1962 lost only one game in nine, bowing to Ohio State, 14-7, in the fourth quarter. Through three quarters it was a toss-up game. Ohio State scored first on a nine-yard pass from Joe Sparma to Paul Warfield in the first quarter, and the Badgers matched this in the second quarter on a short pass from Ron VanderKelen to Ron Smith, who ran 47 yards down the sidelines for the touchdown. Dick Van Raaphorst kicked Ohio State's conversion and Gary Kroner, Wisconsin's.

Woody Hayes' "three yards and a cloud of dust" decided the game in the fourth quarter. Starting in midfield, the Buckeyes pounded 43 yards across the goal. Quarterback John Mummey sneaked the last yard.

The game was really a battle between Ohio State's pulver-

Star end Pat Richter (88) goes high for a pass against Indiana in 1962 game.

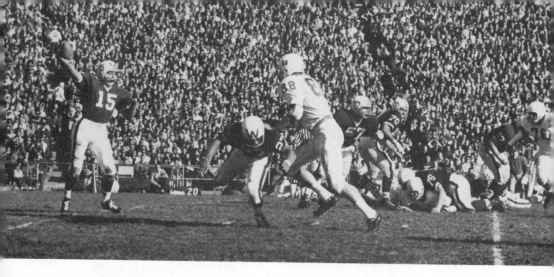

Quarterback Ron VanderKelen gets good protection as he cocks his arm to pass against Minnesota in 1962.

izing ground attack and Wisconsin's mixture of passing and running. The Buckeyes rushed for 213 yards and the Badgers for 106. The Badgers passed for 111 yards, the Buckeyes for 33.

The 1962 season included three particularly notable victories. In the first, the Badgers beat Notre Dame at Madison, 17-8, jumping off to a 10-0 lead in the first quarter; in the second they mauled Michigan at Ann Arbor 34-12; and in the third beat Minnesota 14-9 for the championship. VanderKelen was the principal executioner in each, completing nine of 14 passes against the Irish, 19 of 30 against the Wolverines, and 10 of 24 against the Gophers.

VanderKelen was a remarkable young man. He had only seconds of varsity experience behind him at season's start, all as a third-string substitute behind Dale Hackbart and Jim Bakken in 1959. In 1960 he had suffered a broken leg on a summer construction job and needed immediate surgery, so he did not play that year. In 1961 he was ineligible because of tardy progression in the technicality required for eligibility.

In all, through this exceptional 1962 season, VanderKelen completed 91 of 168 passes for 1,181 yards and 12 touchdowns (77 of 146 for 1,009 yards and 10 touchdowns in Big Ten play). His favorite receiver, end Pat Richter, caught 38 for 531 yards and five touchdowns. The combination was destined to make history in the Rose Bowl.

As so often in the past, the championship, and in this case

196

the trip to Pasadena, hinged on the last game of the season. It matched the league's best offensive team, Wisconsin, against the league's best defensive squad, Minnesota. The rivals were tied with 5-1 records going into the game. The Badgers won, but only after a furious battle in which penalties played a vital, if not decisive, role.

The Gophers scored first on a pass from Duane Blaska to Jim Cairnes but missed the conversion. The Badgers came right back on Ralph Kurek's 11-yard touchdown run and made the conversion. At the half Wisconsin led, 7-6.

Minnesota twice threatened with a touchdown in the third quarter but was thwarted each time by a penalty. The first time, with first down on Wisconsin's two yard line, the Gophers were penalized 15 yards for holding. The second time, after completing a pass from Blaska to Bill Munsey inside the five yard

Halfback Ron Smith scores the third of his three touchdowns against Iowa in 1962.

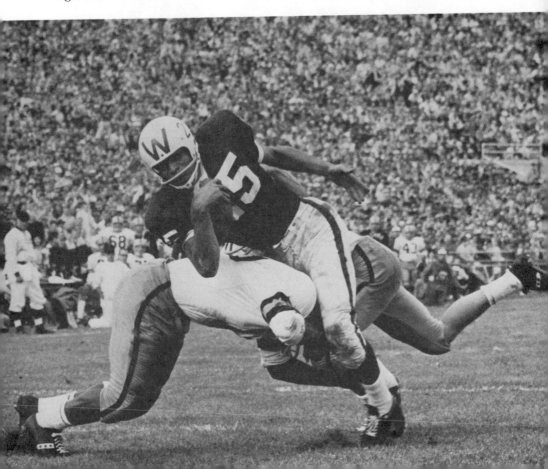

All-American end Don Voss was hurt in the second quarter of the 1963 Rose Bowl game, and his entire career was over.

line, they were penalized 15 yards again when an overzealous teammate tried to push Munsey over the goal. Instead of a touchdown, the Gophers got a 32-yard field goal from Jim Versich and took the lead, 9-7.

Versich's three-pointer loomed larger and larger going into the fourth quarter. But with only four minutes left, the Badgers, with the help of two more penalties against Minnesota, settled everything. Starting on their own 20, they quickly moved to midfield on VanderKelen's passes to Richter of 12, 18, and 12 yards.

Here occurred the most vital penalty of all. Back to pass again, VanderKelen was roughed by All-American tackle Bobby Bell. His feeble toss was intercepted by Jack Perkovich, but the entire play was nullified by the roughing penalty, and Wisconsin retained the ball. Coach Murray Warmath of Minnesota protested so loudly about the roughing call that the referee

Coach Milt Bruhn with his staff in championship years of 1959 and 1962. No other Wisconsin coach in this century won two championships. Kneeling, left to right: Deral Teteak, Milt Bruhn, LaVern Van Dyke. Standing: Clark Van Galder, Fred Jacoby, Paul Shaw, and Fred Marsh.

marched off another 15 yards for unsportsmanlike conduct while the largest crowd ever to see a football game in Madison howled.

It was almost inevitable after all this that the Badgers should win. With the ball now on Minnesota's 13, Lou Holland picked up five, VanderKelen added three on a keeper, and Kurek ploughed the last five into the end zone.

The victory gave Wisconsin its finest season in 50 years and its third chance to do something at Pasadena's Rose Bowl. For the second time the opponent was Southern California.

Although the Badgers went west seeking redress for the Rose Bowl beating of 1953 and the humiliation of 1960, they were defeated again, 42-37. But only after one of the most sensational rallies in the history of football. Down 42-14 as the fourth quarter began and apparently headed for another crushing defeat, the Badgers came up with three touchdowns and a safety and just missed another touchdown and victory by a hair on the last play.

The Badgers started their furious counter charge after Southern California had moved out in front, 42-14, in the first minute of the fourth quarter. Once under way there was no stopping the men in cardinal. They had scored two touchdowns earlier, one by Kurek in the first quarter and the other by VanderKelen early in the third quarter. They had also had a touchdown pass to Holland called back in the second quarter because of clipping.

In the fourth period with the score now 42-14, they exploded. For the first touchdown of the counter charge, the Badgers went 80 yards on 12 plays. VanderKelen completed eight of 10 passes for 63 yards. Kurek plunged for four, and Holland took a pitchout around right end for 13 across the goal. Eleven minutes and 51 seconds of the fourth period still remained.

The Trojan rooters must have sensed what was about to happen. They had been yelling, "We want the Packers," but they suddenly grew quiet. Ben Wilson, a 225-pound Trojan juggernaut at fullback, conveniently fumbled on the first play after the subsequent kickoff, and Elmars Ezerins recovered on Southern California's 29 yard line. On five plays the Badgers drove home again. VanderKelen's pass to Richter was good for

19. Holland and Jim Purnell added six on the ground, and VanderKelen's four-yard pass to Kroner in the end zone cut the deficit to 42-28. Eight minutes, 42 seconds remained.

Briefly the Trojans started to control the ball again, but they produced nothing. They finally gave up the ball on downs on Wisconsin's 32. Once more the Badgers flew goalward, but after they reached Southern California's four, the Trojans' Willie Brown intercepted a pass in the end zone.

However, the Trojans could not advance, and on an attempted fourth-down punt from their own 25 yard line, the pass from substitute center Pete Lubisich sailed over punter Ernie Jones' head into the end zone, where Jones fell on it with Badger Ernie Von Heimburg on top of him. It was a safety, and the score became 42-30 with two minutes and 40 seconds left.

Badger Ron Smith, who later distinguished himself as a kick returner in professional football, ran back Southern California's punt out 21 yards to the Trojans' 43, and Wisconsin was in a position to hang up points. Again VanderKelen went to work. He passed to Holland for six, to Richter for 18, and to Richter again for 19 and a touchdown. The score was now 42-37. One minute and 29 seconds remained.

The Badgers tried an onside kick, but Lubisich recovered on his own 41. On three plays the Trojans lost 12 yards, and on fourth down they had to punt from their own 29. Here occurred perhaps the most vital play of the game. Ezerins, inserted into Wisconsin's lineup at right end, rushed in fast on the punt and barely missed blocking it. From the press box it looked as though the kick had sailed through his outstretched arms. Head Coach Milt Bruhn and End Coach Paul Shaw later said he had just missed the ball.

In midfield Holland awaited the kick and tried to run it straight ahead but fumbled when tackled. Jim Schenk of Wisconsin recovered on his own 40. The game ended on this play—final score 42-37—and the capacity crowd went home limp.

Wisconsin fans have always speculated about what might have happened if Holland had not fumbled and had run out of bounds, stopping the clock, instead of straight ahead. The Badgers were out of time outs at this point. On an out-of-bounds they might have had a few precious seconds left, and no one knows what might have happened. So the best of the three

Coach Milt Bruhn anxiously watches action in 1963 Rose Bowl game as Jim Jax (74), Jim Purnell (38), Roger Jacobazzi (79), Pete Bruhn, coach's son (55), Ron Henrici (56), and Duncan Hoffman (84) wait to get into game.

teams Wisconsin sent to the Rose Bowl will always be in the records as a magnificent team which lost.

VanderKelen was outstanding. He completed 33 of 48 passes for 401 yards and two touchdowns, ran 17 for another touchdown, and after subtracting 30 yards of losses on several option plays, finished the day with a total offense mark of 406 yards.

Next to VanderKelen was Pat Richter, who caught 11 passes for 163 yards and one touchdown. Between them they set bowl records that may never be broken in passes attempted and passes completed. Richter also averaged better than 40 yards on four punts.

While several of the Badgers, including Ken Bowman, Richter, and Kroner, were picked by the pros in their draft a few weeks before the game, VanderKelen was not, although he had led the Big Ten in passing, touchdown passes, and total

Quarterback Ron VanderKelen set all-time Rose Bowl records for passes attempted (48), passes completed (33), yards gained passing (401), and total offense yards (406) in 1963 game.

Pat Richter, star end who caught 11 passes in 1963 Rose Bowl game.

offense. As a free agent after his spectacular game, he had pro clubs pounding on his door all through January and had his choice of team and bonus. He finally signed with the Minnesota Vikings.

The Badgers had no running game to match their passing. They gained only 67 yards on the ground, with Holland contributing 27 and Kurek 26. The Trojans were no great shakes themselves, rushing with only 114 yards. Their great reliance, too, was in the air, where quarterback Pete Beathard completed eight of 12 passes for 190 yards and four touchdowns, one on a tackle-eligible play. Hal Bedsole caught two of the touchdown passes.

The team statistics emphasized what a remarkable offensive show the game was. Wisconsin had 32 first downs, 23 of them on passes, and Southern California had 15, nine of them in the air. Both teams drew frequent penalties, Wisconsin seven for a loss of 77 yards and Southern California 12 for 93 yards.

Trojans coach John McKay, who won his first Rose Bowl victory, became a little irritated with the praise heaped on the Badgers and VanderKelen and later asked, "Say, who won this game anyway?"

Delayed at the start for 12 minutes because of television commitments, the game lasted three hours and eight minutes and wound up in semidarkness. Lights were turned on in the second half, but they were totally inadequate. Jim Murray observed in the *Los Angeles Times* the next day that a man standing in the end zone with a cigarette lighter would have provided more light. In 1969 the Rose Bowl committee did install new lights.

The game was poorly officiated, and this was not Wisconsin's complaint alone. Not only did the officials not hurry things along at the start while the Badgers, first on the field, fidgeted around, but they also let the scoreboard clock get out of hand in the fourth quarter. With four minutes left, the timer had to rush out to tell the referee the clock was wrong, and play was suspended while it was corrected. The Badgers always maintained that the time taken to correct it cost them 25 seconds.

It was a game that sent every West Coast writer except Melvin Durslag into rhapsodies.

"You can be charitable and call it exciting," Durslag wrote

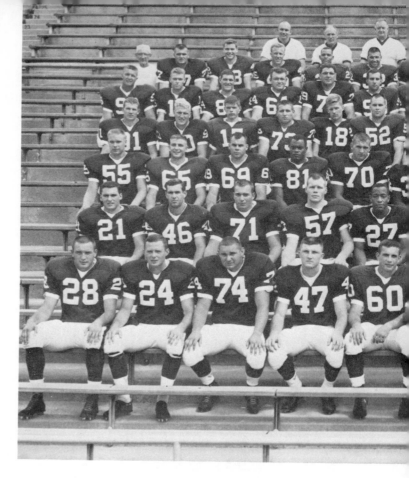

Wisconsin's last Big Ten title team lost to Southern California in 1963 Rose Bowl game. Front Row, left to right: *(28) Ron Carlson; **(24) John Fabry; *(74) James Jax; *(47) Gary Kroner; *(60) Co-Captain Steve Underwood; *(88) Co-Captain Pat Richter; *(44) Merritt Norvell; *(66) Jim Schenk; **(56) Ron Henrici; *(82) Elmars Ezerins. Second Row: (21) Brad Armstrong; (46) Bill Barnett; (71) John Fox; *(57) Ken Bowman; *(27) Louis Holland; *(40) Bill Smith; *(26) Jim Nettles; (67) Dion Kempthorne; **(41) Ken Montgomery; (50) Jim McMillan; (15) Ron Vanderkelen. Third Row: (55) Pete Bruhn; *(65) Mike Gross; (69) Joe Heckl; **(81) Larry Howard; *(70) Roger Pillath; *(33) Gerald McKinney; *(38) Jim Purnell; *(61) Andy Wojdula; (12) Greg Howey; (85) Steve Oleson; *(63) Ron Paar; (10) Arnie Quaerna. Fourth Row: (91) Dale Paddock; (90) Kurt Abraham; (17) Bob Allison; *(73) Lee Bernet; *(18) Harold Brandt; (52) Charles Brooke; (95) Mike Cox; (89) Ralph Farmer; (14) Lee Fawbush; (42) Ron Frain;

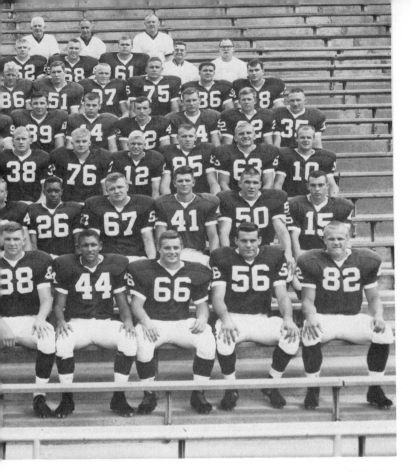

(94) Bob Freimuth; (22) Pete Heebink; (35) Tom Posewitz. Fifth Row: (96) Don Hendrickson; (16) Jim Hennig; (84) Duncan Hoffman; (64) Jon Hohman; *(79) Roger Jacobazzi; (93) Joel Jenson; (34) Ralph Kurek; (86) Ron Leafblad; (51) Ken Luthy; (97) Mike McCoy; (75) Niles McMaster; (36) Joe Milek; (78) Bob Monk. Sixth Row: Walter Bakke, Trainer; (77) Albert Piraino; (48) Rick Reichardt; (45) Carl Silvestri; (25) Ron Smith; (32) Stan Andrews; (53) Duane Stremlau; (62) Ernest von Heimburg; (68) William Weisendanger; (61) Steve Young; Art Lamboley, equipment manager; Jim Manteufel, senior manager. Seventh Row: Assistant Coaches Fred Jacoby, Clark Van Galder, and Paul Shaw; Head Coach Milt Bruhn; Assistant Coaches Fred Marsh, LaVern Van Dyke, and Deral Teteak. Absent when picture was taken: (87) Jim Jones, and (19) Bob Johnson.

*Major "W" Award winner; **Junior "W" Award winner.

in the *Herald Examiner*. "But it was in truth pretty sloppy stuff, hardly becoming the No. 1 and No. 2 teams in the United States which Southern California and Wisconsin happened to be. The two spent the afternoon flooring each other with sucker punches."

Durslag was alone in this appraisal, however. Paul Zimmerman of the *Los Angeles Times* wrote: "The most magnificent offensive battle in the 49 game history of the Rose Bowl." Jim Murray of the *Times* added, "In the longest, wildest Rose Bowl game in history, the Trojans beat Ron Vanderkelen. They may be No. 1 as their rooting section constantly reminded them but if so, Vanderkelen is No. 2. In a rematch I wouldn't make him worse than even money. He completed more passes than a sailor on leave in Tahiti."

Maxwell Stiles, sports editor of the *Hollywood Citizen-News*, said, "Wisconsin was as true blue a No. 2 team as ever graced the wire service poll." Rube Samuels of the *Pasadena News* added: "Whew, please pass the aspirin, also the tranquilizers. They just don't come any better than Tuesday's Rose Bowl football game and that goes for all football." Joe Hendrickson of the *Pasadena News* chipped in: "Ron Vanderkelen put on the greatest exhibition of passing and eluding defenders ever seen in the Rose Bowl."

With 16 sophomores and 18 juniors of the Rose Bowl team coming back—26 of them letter winners—there were high hopes that the next few seasons would be great Wisconsin years. But it did not turn out that way. The men who had manned the skill positions on the bowl team, especially Vanderkelen and Richter, were graduated, and without them Wisconsin was just another team.

The 1963 team opened with a rush, beating Western Michigan, Notre Dame, Purdue, and Iowa in the first four games, apparently confirming early hopes. But they won only one other game, against Northwestern, and finished with a 5-4 record.

As had happened so often before, Ohio State started them on their slide with a 13-10 licking at Madison. The Buckeyes won the game in the last two minutes of play when Matt Snell smashed the last two yards of a crunching 80-yard drive. The decisive march started immediately after Don Hendrickson's

Dan Lanphear of 1957-1959 teams was named a lineman on all-time Wisconsin team picked by fans in late sixties.

attempt for a field goal from the 34 had hit the crossbar and bounced back on the field of play. If good, it would have given Wisconsin a 13-6 lead.

Ohio State had scored earlier on two field goals by Dick Van Raaphorst, one of 26 yards and the other of 45. However, Wisconsin still had a 10-6 lead going into the fourth quarter on Dave Fronek's 20-yard field goal in the first quarter and Carl Silvestri's 13-yard run for a touchdown in the third quarter.

Wisconsin had outdowned Ohio State, 19 to 12, and outgained them, 263 yards to 147, but typical of this series, Wisconsin still lost.

Fronek's 27-yard field goal accounted for Wisconsin's victory over Northwestern, 17-14. With the score tied 14-14 in the fourth quarter, he came off the bench and booted the vital points. He almost did not get to kick it, however. When the kicking situation finally presented itself, he could not find his kicking shoe on the sidelines, and Wisconsin had to take time out while a hurried search was made.

The 1964 season was worse, though the Badgers still had a fine all-around back in Carl Silvestri. The team beat only Kansas State, Iowa, and Minnesota and finished with a 3-6 mark. The Minnesota game, played in near-zero weather, was won in spite of nine fumbles, six of which Wisconsin lost. In the losing effort against Illinois the week before (29-0), the Badgers got only 23 yards rushing and gave up 332. Jim Grabowski alone rolled up 239, a Big Ten record at the time.

Bruhn himself summed up, "This was a season with the frustrations and injuries of two or three all rolled into one. We need help. Things could get worse before they get better."

Bruhn was right. They did get worse. The 1965 team beat only Iowa and Northwestern; tied Colorado, 0-0; and suffered a succession of shellackings down the stretch. They lost the last five games, giving up in this period 208 points and scoring only 38.

The 1966 season was Bruhn's last. Criticism had been building up ever since the shoddy performance against Washington in the Rose Bowl game of 1960: poor recruiting, unimaginative offense—all the customary charges critics hurl at a coach they want to see ousted. Only university president Fred Harrington's recommendation to the regents that Bruhn be retained

Fullback Ralph Kurek (34) scores winning touchdown against Minnesota in 1964.

had saved his job the previous year when the athletic board voted 4-4 on the question of his retention.

Bruhn, a very decent and sensitive man, suffered through the first eight games of the 1966 season, which produced only two victories and a tie. Then on the Thursday before the closing Minnesota game, he took matters into his own hands and resigned. In accepting the resignation, the athletic board voted to retain him in the athletic department, with his duties to be determined later. These turned out to be as assistant to Athletic Director Williamson.

Bruhn's resignation two days before the Minnesota game shocked the football team, which responded the way a team usually does when it loses a well-liked coach. It beat Minnesota, 7-6.

The point after touchdown which provided the margin of victory was kicked by Tom Schinke after Wisconsin had scored in the fourth quarter on a pass from sophomore John Ryan to sophomore Tom McCauley. Minnesota had scored in the last 30 seconds of the first half on a six-yard pass from Larry Carlson to Kenny Last but had failed on the conversion when the pass from center was high.

211

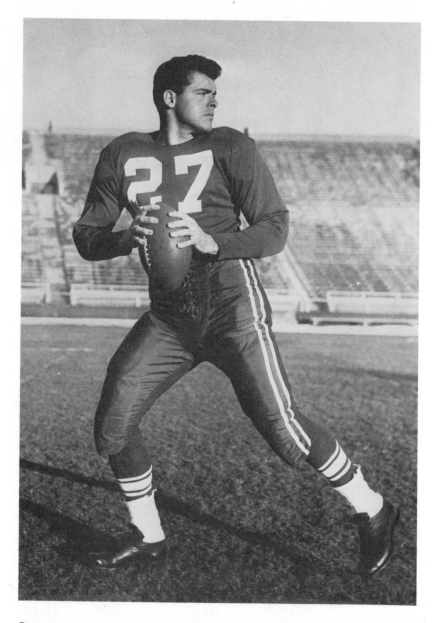

Quarterback John Coatta of Wisconsin's "Hard Rocks" of 1951 returned as coach from 1967 through 1969.

Actually, Bruhn's record for the 11 years he coached was not as bad as some of the criticism suggested. Overall he had won 52 games, lost 45, and tied five.

In the Big Ten he finished with a 35-37-5 record. The only Big Ten teams to have an edge on his Badgers were Ohio State with a 9-1-1 record, Michigan State with 5-1-0, and Illinois with 6-4-1. Against Minnesota in the traditional rivalry, Bruhn had a winning 7-3-1 record; against Michigan, 3-2-0; against Northwestern, 7-3-1; against Iowa, 6-5-0; against Purdue, 4-3-1; and against Indiana, 2-0-0. He won all five games against Marquette and two of three from Notre Dame.

In searching for a coaching successor to Bruhn, Williamson interviewed a score of men. These included Bo Schembechler of Miami of Ohio, now of Michigan; Frank Navarro, an assistant at Williams; Buck McPhail, an assistant at Illinois; Dan White, an assistant at Washington; Mike Lude, head coach at Colorado State; and John Ray, one of Ara Parseghian's assistants at Notre Dame. Williamson wanted Ray, but Ray asked for $25,000, and university president Harrington felt that the athletic department, then in a financial pinch, could not afford to pay that much. The search then turned to Bruhn's own staff of assistants. All who applied were interviewed as though they were outsiders: LaVern Van Dyke, Deral Teteak, Mike McGee, and John Coatta.

Coatta, a star quarterback and passer on Wisconsin's strong teams of the late forties and early fifties, was finally selected. Bruhn had received $20,228. Coatta accepted $19,500.

As assistant athletic director under Williamson after his resignation as coach, Bruhn, normally in line to succeed to the position of director after Williamson died, was acting director for a short while. But he was passed over in the final selection. The alumni, led by alumni secretary Arlie Mucks, Jr., whose father had been so instrumental through the alumni association in obtaining Doc Spears as coach in 1932, had settled on Elroy Hirsch as the man to head the athletic department, and they had their way. The athletic board finally hired Hirsch, with Bruhn still assistant.

At about this time the State Audit Bureau suggested that the university's board review the financial situation in athletics with an eye to cutting down costs. The board decided to dismiss an assistant director as one step and to dismiss George Lanphear, well-known throughout the state as an assistant coach, recruiter, athletic public relations director, and equipment manager at various times, as another.

There was no formal public announcement of the personnel changes and no formal notification to Bruhn. And when the story broke on how the matter had been handled, the university had an exceedingly cardinal face.

Bruhn, returning from a one-day trip to St. Louis a week after the board action, drove up to a gas station on his way home and was told by the attendant, "Tough luck, Milt."

"What do you mean, tough luck?" Bruhn inquired.

"They got rid of you," the attendant, who had read about it in the afternoon paper, told him. Vice Chancellor Robert Atwell had confirmed a rumor of the change earlier in the day.

That was how Bruhn learned of his dismissal as assistant athletic director.

University president Fred Harrington called Bruhn the next day to apologize personally. Professor Arno Lenz, former chairman of the athletic board, and Fred Haberman, new chairman, issued a joint statement deploring the way the story had been handled and also apologized. The next day a meeting was held of all parties who might have had a hand in the matter in order to get to the bottom of it, if possible, and to see that nothing like it ever happened again. Hirsch did not attend; he had left a week before for Hawaii. He had told Lanphear of his dismissal before he left, but in his haste to get away he had neglected to notify Bruhn. No public announcement of this change was ever made, and it became known only when Lanphear himself announced it.

The Bittersweet
Coatta Years

John Coatta, who had been a coaching assistant at Florida State University before joining Bruhn's staff in 1965, inherited a deteriorating situation in 1967. He was just beginning to turn it around when his record and alumni pressure caught up with him.

His three years at the helm, through 1969, were the worst in Wisconsin history. In 1967 the Badgers lost nine games and tied Iowa. In 1968 they lost 10 straight. And in 1969 they won three and lost seven. In recapitulation, they suffered 18 straight defeats, the longest losing streak in the school history, and went 23 games without a victory. Most discouraging was Wisconsin's defense. Every opponent the Badgers met in the 30 games played scored in double figures.

The height of frustration was reached in the Indiana game of 1968 when Wisconsin missed six field goals and lost 21-20.

Yet in Coatta's third year his team scored two notable victories. In the fourth game of the season against Iowa, the Badgers won, 23-17, finally ending the long losing streak with a fourth-quarter explosion as great as the 1962 team's against Southern California in the Rose Bowl. And five games later, after having just lost to Ohio State, 62-7, they mauled Illinois, 55-14.

The Iowa victory was unquestionably one of the greatest Wisconsin ever scored. A crowd of 53,000 nearly went berserk. As the fourth quarter got under way, the Hawkeyes led, 17-0, and everything indicated they would have an easy time down

215

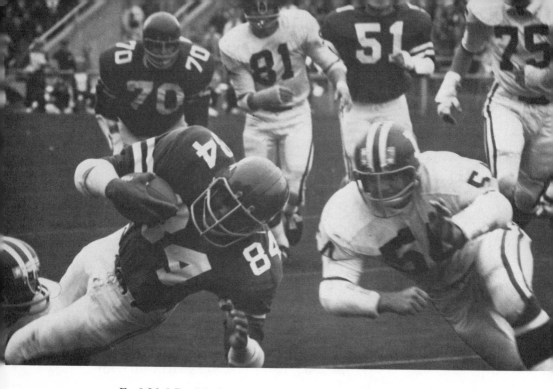

End Mel Reddick scores on a pass against Indiana in 1968.

the stretch. Allan Schuette had given them a field goal in the first quarter, Mike Cilek had passed to Jerry Reardon for a touchdown in the second quarter, and the two had collaborated for another touchdown in the third.

It was all Wisconsin in the fourth quarter as the Badgers turned the game around completely. On their first touchdown they went 74 yards on 16 plays, Alan Thompson going the last two yards. On their second they went 56 yards on eight plays, Thompson going over from six yards out. And on their third, with 11 yards to go on fourth down on Iowa's 17 yard line and with two minutes left, Neil Graff went the distance with a pass to Randy Marks down the middle. When Dennis Green fumbled the subsequent kickoff trying to run it out of the end zone, the Badgers added a safety. Roger Jaeger kicked all three of Wisconsin's extra points.

After such heroics there was no containing the crowd, and with 1:10 left, hundreds swarmed onto the field, halting the play. It took almost four minutes to clear them back. However, Iowa could do nothing in the remaining time, and the great

216

Cardinal drought was ended.

The Illinois game, next to last of the season, was an easy 55-14 Wisconsin victory. This was not a good Illinois team, and Wisconsin scored at will. Thompson ran two yards for the first touchdown, and Gary Losse passed 15 yards to Stu Voigt for the second and then seven yards to him for the third. Dan Crooks ran back the kickoff 87 yards in the third quarter for the fourth touchdown, Losse sneaked one yard for the fifth, Neil Graff passed 25 yards to Al Hannah for the sixth, and Greg Johnson ran 20 yards for the seventh. Jaeger added all seven extra points and also chipped in with two field goals, one from 35 yards out and the other from 26.

The two big victories in 1969, plus another over Indiana, 36-34, were not enough to save Coatta's job, however. Under extreme pressure, particularly from Chicago and Milwaukee alumni, Elroy Hirsch, who had succeeded to the Wisconsin athletic directorship after Ivy Williamson's death the previous January, had little choice except to dismiss Coatta after the 1969 season.

Hirsch, a star halfback on the great 1942 Wisconsin team and later an even greater end with the Los Angeles Rams (whom he also served as general manager and assistant to the president after his playing days), narrowed the field of coaching prospects to two men, John Jardine, offensive line coach under Doc Prothro at UCLA, and Ron Ehrhardt, head coach at North Dakota State. In his days at Los Angeles Hirsch had gotten to know Jardine, and in the end he selected him.

Jardine, a guard at Purdue in the middle fifties, aggressively went after the job, which probably was also a factor in his selection. He himself said after his appointment, "I actively sought this position at the University of Wisconsin. I went after it with reckless abandon. I wanted it and I don't care if I was the first choice or the ninth choice. I'm not the least bit interested in the past. I'm interested only in how things are going to be. I said we'd win. I didn't say how many games but I sure hope I never go into a season thinking it's going to be a losing season."

Yet in six of his first seven years, through 1976, he had losing seasons. His only winning season was in 1974, when the Badgers won seven games and lost four overall and won five and

217

Quarterback Neil Graff directed winning 23-point fourth quarter rally against Iowa in 1969 that ended 18-game losing streak extending back to 1967.

lost three in the Big Ten. Even the winning record had a built-in penalty, however, because it sent championship and bowl hopes for the 1975 season ridiculously high. And 1975 became one of the most deflating seasons in the school's history.

Jardine's Badgers had a 4-5-1 record in 1970, 4-6-1 in 1971, and 4-7 in 1972 and the same in 1973 before they finished 7-4 in 1974. In 1975 they slumped to 4-6-1 again and in 1976 gained only slightly to 5-6. Ohio State and Michigan, always tough ones for Wisconsin, have been particular thorns to Jardine. The Buckeyes have won all seven games and the Wolverines all five. Overall in his seven years, Jardine's teams have won 32 games, lost 41, and tied three.

Only in playing teams which Wisconsin traditionally does well against have his teams at least held their own. They have a 4-2-1 record against Indiana, 5-2-0 against Northwestern, 2-3-0 against Illinois, and 4-3-0 against Iowa. Against Minnesota they have 3-4-0 and against Michigan State, 1-3-0.

In most years Jardine's Badgers have had exciting personnel, and their play has been reflected in attendance, which has consistently hovered around 70,000 or more a game. The games with Ohio State drew 72,758 in 1970; 78,713 in 1972; 77,413 in 1973; and 79,579 in 1976. The Michigan contests drew 72,389 in 1970; 78,911 in 1974; and 79,022 in 1975. The 1976 attendance at the Ohio State game is the record.

Wisconsin's exciting personnel has made for exciting games in the past few years, whatever the won-lost record. Jardine has had men like Rufus (Road Runner) Ferguson, Alan ("A" Train) Thompson, Bill Marek, Ken Starch, and Selvie Washington to run with the ball; quarterbacks like Neil Graff, Rudy Steiner, or Gregg Bohlig to throw it behind a line, which at different times has had men like Mike Webster, Joe Norwick, Dennis Lick, Keith Nosbusch, Terry Stieve, or Bob Braun; kickers like Roger Jaeger, Ken Simmons, or Vince Lamia; and defensive backs like

Fullback Alan (A-Train) Thompson gained 220 yards in the opening game against Oklahoma in 1969.

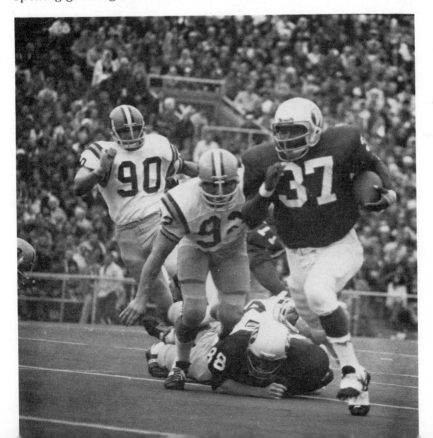

Quarterback Neil Graff (12) piled up 4,134 yards in total offense as a three-year starter.

Dave Lokanc, Chuck Winfrey, Dave Anderson, Danny Crooks, Ken Criter, Jim DeLisle, Neovia Greyer, Rick Jakious, Mark Zakula, Jim Schymanski, Bob Storck, Mike Seifert, Chris Davis, Steve Wagner, and Ron Buss.

Marek broke every school rushing and scoring record which Ameche, Ferguson, or Thompson had held earlier. In his four years (actually only three years since as a freshman he carried the ball only once) he rushed for 3,709 yards, an average of 5.2 a carry, and scored 278 points. Against Minnesota in 1974 he rushed for 304 yards and scored five touchdowns.

Graff set records in passing and total offense which Coatta, Haluska, or VanderKelen had previously held. He passed for 3,699 yards and 23 touchdowns and ran for 565 yards. Greyer holds the school record for interceptions in a career (18) and interception yards (285).

Selvie Washington ran back a kickoff 96 yards for a touchdown against Nebraska in 1973, and Greg Johnson ran one back 88 yards for a touchdown against Indiana in 1971. He also returned a punt 85 yards against Northern Illinois in 1971.

Crooks holds the school record of 87 yards on a punt return against Michigan in 1970. He also ran back a kick of 87 yards against Illinois in 1969 and 84 yards against Northwestern in 1970. Jaeger kicked a 48-yard placement against UCLA in 1969 and one of 42 yards against Penn State in 1970. Simmons averaged 42 yards a punt.

Lokanc, Criter, and Winfrey rate with the greatest line-backers Wisconsin has ever had in total tackles and solo tackles. Webster, an All-Big-Ten center, was an early draft choice of the Pittsburgh Steelers and played outstanding ball in both his super bowl appearances.

Jardine clearly has had talent in his squads, but he also had some of the toughest schedules Wisconsin has ever played. In 1970 the Badgers opened with Oklahoma, Texas Christian, and Penn State in that order before going into the customarily tough Big Ten schedule. In both 1971 and 1972 they had a relatively soft opener with Northern Illinios but then had to play Syracuse and Louisiana State before heading into an eight-game Big Ten series.

The tough schedule only added spice to the performances, however. The Badgers gave Oklahoma a tough battle in the 1970 opener before bowing, 21-7. They led the Sooners 7-0, at the end of the first half on Ferguson's 11-yard run but wilted in the second half. Jack Mildred drove the Sooners 80 yards the first time they had the ball in the third quarter and scored the tying touchdown on a one-yard run. Greg Pruitt's 46-yard punt return gave Oklahoma position on Wisconsin's 28 to get the lead touchdown a few minutes later. Oklahoma's Roy Bell ran the last four yards. On a 62-yard drive in the fourth quarter, Bell completed the scoring from 11 yards out.

Two weeks later the Penn State game gave Jardine his first victory at Wisconsin, 29-16. The Nittany Lions came to Madison as the No. 2 team in the polls but were crushed in the fourth quarter by Graff's passing. With the score tied at 16 in the final period, Graff first passed 27 yards to Terry Whittaker for the lead touchdown and then to Larry Mialik on a 52-yard play for the clincher.

Jardine's first Big Ten victory came in the Indiana game three weeks later when the Badgers whipped the Hoosiers,

30-12. Illinois and Minnesota in the last two games of the 1970 season gave him his other Big Ten triumphs.

The Syracuse game of 1971 was one of the most exciting of Jardine's years. Wisconsin took the lead, 20-14, on a 15-yard pass, Graff to Mialik, with two and one-half minutes left. Next, however, occurred a crushing play. Trying for a two-point conversion, Alan Thompson, all alone in the end zone, caught a pass but dropped it, and the door was open for Syracuse in the last two minutes. Starting on their own 13 yard line with exactly 2:24 left, the Orangemen smashed 87 yards for a touchdown. A pass, Woodruff to Brian Hambleton, carried into the end zone. The conversion kick would have given Syracuse the game. But they had their own frustration here. Ed Albright, rushing in from left linebacker, blocked Eric Baugher's attempt, and the game ended in a 20-20 tie.

The rest of the 1971 season was up and down. Louisiana State, led by Bert Jones, won a wild offensive show at Madison, 38-28, and Northwestern, Ohio State, Iowa, Illinois, and Minnesota added to Wisconsin's defeats. The only victories, in addition to the one over Northern Illinois in the opener, were over Indiana in another wild contest, 35-29; Michigan State, 31-28; and Purdue, 14-10.

Defensive weaknesses were obviously Wisconsin's primary problems under Jardine up to this point, and they continued to be so in both 1972 and 1973. After beating both Northern Illinois and Syracuse in 1972 by identical scores of 31-7, the Badgers allowed 215 points in their last nine games while scoring 90 and won only from Northwestern, 21-14, and Iowa, 16-14, the rest of the season.

The 1973 season included bitter defeats. Purdue won, 14-13, Nebraska, 20-16, and Minnesota, 19-17. Wyoming, Iowa, Indiana and Northwestern gave the Badgers their only victories of the 4-7 season.

The dawn was not far behind, however, and it occurred in 1974, when the Badgers had their first winning season under Jardine (7-4). The team beat Purdue, 28-14; Nebraska, 21-20; Missouri, 59-20; Indiana, 35-25; Iowa, 28-15; Northwestern, 52-7; and Minnesota, 49-14, in that order. It lost to Colorado, 24-21; Ohio State, 52-7; Michigan, 24-20; and Michigan State, 28-21.

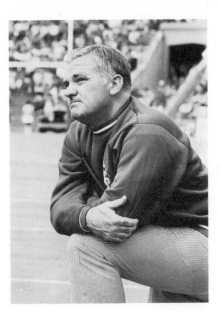

In 1977 Coach John Jardine, former UCLA offensive line coach, began his eighth year as Wisconsin's head football coach.

In 1977 Director of Athletics Elroy Hirsch, former Badger grid immortal, began his ninth year as head of one of the nation's top university athletic programs.

The Nebraska victory had one of the most dramatic finishes Camp Randall has ever seen. The Cornhuskers, then No. 4 in the press polls, led, 20-14, with four minutes left and apparently had the game well in hand, as the statistics showed. They had lost their ace passer and quarterback, Dave Humm, in the first quarter, but that had not stopped them. In getting Nebraska's 20 points, Don Westbrook had run 22 yards for one touchdown, John O'Leary six yards for another, and Mike Coyle had kicked field goals of 30 and 22 yards after Wisconsin's stubborn defense had twice saved the goal, once on the two yard line.

Through all this the Badgers had remained within hailing distance on Gregg Bohlig's nine-yard pass to Ron Egloff for a touchdown in the first quarter and Marek's one-yard scoring plunge early in the fourth.

On one brilliant play, however, with four minutes left, the Badgers finally moved out in front. They took the kickoff on their own 23 after the second of Coyle's field goals and on second down dramatically struck for the victory. Bohlig, who had played an outstanding game at quarterback all afternoon, rolled out to his right, while flanker Jeff Mack sped down the west sidelines unmolested and pulled in a long pass on his own 45. He easily sped the remaining 55 yards across the goal while a capacity crowd howled. Vince Lamia added the vital extra point, as he had two earlier ones, and Wisconsin had the game, 21-20.

Statistically, even without Humm, who had received early All-American mention, the Cornhuskers generally had the better of the day except in passing and the score. They outdowned Wisconsin 19 to 14 and outrushed them, 258 yards to 77. Wisconsin, however, had a marked edge in passing, 242 yards to 47. The Bohlig-Mack combination hurt Nebraska all afternoon. Bohlig completed 14 of 21 passes, and Mack caught four for 132 yards.

Wisconsin's defense had never looked better. Aside from protecting the goal in close twice, it saved the day as the Cornhuskers desperately charged back after losing the lead. They reached midfield, but here Steve Wagner intercepted a pass, and Wisconsin ran out the clock.

"We're finally over the hump," an elated Jardine, not

unaware of earlier defensive deficiencies, commented after the game. For the moment, though, the observation was a little premature. A week later the Badgers lost to Colorado, 24-21, on a fourth-quarter touchdown. The Badgers fell behind early, 10-0, then charged back for a 21-10 lead which the defense could not protect in the third and fourth quarters.

So the 1974 season ended with a 7-4 record, Jardine's best in his five years, and hopes soared for 1975. In fact, they got out of hand with talk all summer about a championship and the Rose Bowl.

Through a quirk in schedulemaking after the league had gone to an 11-game schedule, the Badgers opened the 1975 season against Michigan at Madison, and that was fatal. Everyone remembered the thrilling victory over Nebraska and the mauling of Missouri, Northwestern, and Minnesota the year before and forgot that over the years Michigan had won 26 and tied one of 34 games with Wisconsin going back to 1892. Michigan had scored 682 points to Wisconsin's 298, and now had bowl hopes of its own.

A record crowd of 79,002 was in the stands at the kickoff. Jardine was optimistic, although he no longer had Bohlig at quarterback, the fleet Mack at flanker, Jack Novak at tight end, and defensive men like Mark Zakula, Mike Vesperman, Rick

Halfback Rufus (Road Runner) Ferguson ranks third in Wisconsin's all-time rushing list with 2,814 yards and second in all-time scoring list with 158 points.

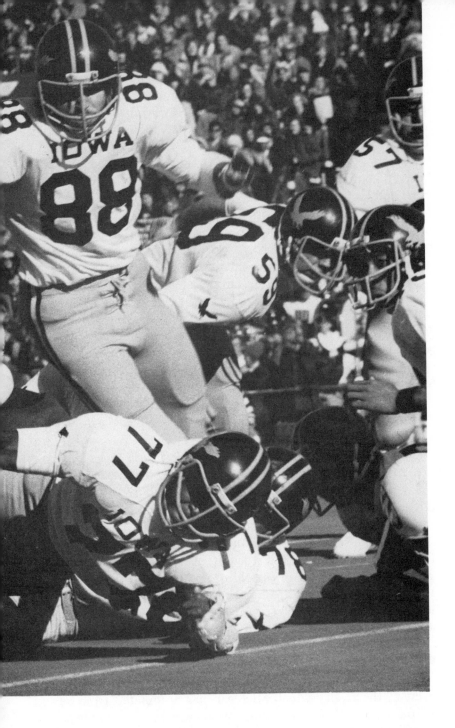

Halfback Billy Marek, all-time scoring leader during 1972-76 career, breaks away around end against Iowa in 1973.

Jakious, Randy Frokjer, and Mike Jenkins. The problem at quarterback was particularly pressing. Jardine started with four principal candidates—senior Dan Kopina, who had been an understudy to Bohlig but who had rarely played; Tony Dudley, a freshman from Detroit; Mike Carroll, a transfer from Lakewood Junior College; and Charlie Green, a freshman from Mobile, Alabama, whom Henry Aaron of baseball's Milwaukee Brewers helped recruit.

Kopina, the only man with any varsity experience, started, although he never started again. In fact, he appeared in only one more play the rest of the season. Carroll eventually became the No. 1 man. Jardine clearly had encountered trouble settling on his No. 1 man in spring and early fall practices.

It was not the quarterback, or lack of one, which lost the game, however. It was Michigan's line which won it. The Wolverines smothered Wisconsin up front where, oddly, the Badgers consistently centered their attack. Wisconsin had the ball inside Michigan's 15 yard line three times and came out of such position with only two field goals, their only points of the day. Once with four to go on fourth down on Michigan's 12, they ignored another field goal and gave up the ball on downs with a futile dig at Michigan's tough line.

The Badgers led early in the game, 3-0. Lamia kicked the first of his two field goals from 22 yards out. The rest of the way it became Michigan's game. In order, Bob Lytle ran 15 yards for a touchdown, and after Lamia had given Wisconsin three more points with his second field goal in the second quarter—this one from 31 yards out—Dick Wood kicked three field goals. One was from 22 yards out, also in the second quarter, another was from 25 in the third, and the third from 22 in the fourth period. A pass, freshmen Rick Leach to Gordon Bell in the fourth quarter, completed the scoring. Leach, a great high school athlete, started and played the whole game. His quarterback option "killed" Wisconsin. The final score was Michigan, 23, Wisconsin, 6.

The Michigan defeat was more than just one game lost, however, in the rivalry which Michigan has dominated from its inception. With all the high hopes Wisconsin had felt entering the game, the defeat was a demoralizer for the season as a whole, and the Badgers never really recovered. They did beat South Dakota, Purdue, Northwestern, and Illinois and tied Indiana, but they took lickings, some of them bad ones, from Missouri, Kansas, Ohio State, Iowa, and Minnesota. They finished with a season record of 4-6-1 and a Big Ten record of 3-4-1.

There was only small solace in the individual recognition some of the Wisconsin players received. Halfback Billy Marek wound up his three-year career with 3,705 yards, second best in Big Ten history behind Archie Griffin of Ohio State and best in Wisconsin history. He also scored 278 points, which established both Big Ten and Wisconsin marks. Dennis Lick, 262-pound offensive tackle, received Big Ten and All-American honors, and Terry Stieve, 260-pound offensive guard, earned All-Big-Ten distinction.

In setting his records, Marek played no favorites, rushing for 198 yards against Northwestern, 189 against Illinois, 182 against Indiana, and 152 against Purdue. Marek had only little help, however, and a porous defense and the demoralizing Michigan opener dampened a season that Coach Jardine and followers had felt would be a winner.

As a team the Badgers led the league in pass defense in the 1975 season, yielding only 61 yards a game, and finished third nationally in that category of play with an average of 65.2 yards.

There were no such high hopes in 1976, and through another quirk in scheduling, Michigan again was the opener and once more dealt Wisconsin a crushing defeat. The Wolverines, destined to win the Big Ten title and go on to the Rose Bowl, won in a canter, 40-27. Against Michigan's 455 yards from scrimmage, Wisconsin got 425, and against their 62 total plays, Wisconsin had 85, indicating excellent ball control by the Badgers. The scoring punch, however, was Michigan's.

Returning to easier fare after the Ann Arbor game, the Badgers beat North Dakota, 45-9, and Washington State, 35-26, but then lost three in a row—to Kansas, 34-24; Purdue, 18-16; and Ohio State, 30-20. In each of these defeats, however, Wisconsin outgained its opponents: Kansas, 477 yards to 444; Purdue, 382 to 276; and even Ohio State, 416 to 364.

The three defeats in a row could well have been extended to four in the next game, which was against Northwestern. Only a late rally saved the day. Wisconsin trailed, 25-21, until, with only 12 seconds left, Larry Canada, who had replaced Marek as Wisconsin's big running threat, plunged one yard for the winning touchdown. His touchdown capped a 74-yard march in 12 plays. The drive started immediately after Northwestern had taken the lead on Jim Whim's one-yard plunge. The Wildcats outdowned the Badgers, 26 to 14.

Wisconsin next made a game run at Illinois, coming back from a 31-12 deficit before bowing, 31-25.

Winding up the season, the Badgers walloped Iowa, 38-21; lost a tough one to Indiana, 15-14, and beat Minnesota, 26-17, in the final game.

The bitterest defeat for the Badgers occurred at Bloomington in the game with Indiana. The Hoosiers went for and made two points after their fourth-quarter touchdown. The Badgers had led at the half, 14-0, on Ira Mathews' two touchdowns, but then could not hold the Hoosiers in the second half, losing in the closing minutes. Keith Calvin scored Indiana's first touchdown on a pass from Scott Arnett and Dick Ennis the second on a one-yard sweep. Tim McKay then ran for the two-point conversion.

Though the season was a loser with a record of five victories and six defeats overall (three and five in the Big Ten), it had a lot of fine moments. Ira Matthews, a fleet halfback, ran back a kickoff 100 yards against Iowa, equalling Eddie Cochems' record set against Chicago in 1901; ran another 97 yards against Northwestern; and carried a punt back 56 yards for a touchdown against Indiana. He led the nation in kickoff returns with his 29.6 average.

Quarterback Mike Carroll finished third in league passing with an average of 157.2 yards a game. He completed two touchdown passes each against Michigan, Kansas, and Purdue. Twice against both Purdue and Northwestern he completed five passes in succession. He led the league in yards gained passing with 1,171, but unfortunately also led in interceptions thrown with 12. In total offense he finished second with 1,260 yards. His favorite receivers were David Charles, who caught 28 passes, and Ira Matthews, who pulled down 16.

Some of the team's brightest moments occurred as a result of senior Vince Lamia's kicking. In Big Ten games only, old "Surefoot" booted 19 of 20 extra points and 11 of 18 field-goal attempts. Dick Milaeger, a walk-on, gave the Badgers excellent punting all season with a 41-yard average.

In Retrospect

Through the years various men intimately close to Wisconsin football have picked all-time Wisconsin teams. Thus in 1927 George Downer, a track athlete at the university in the late nineties, graduate manager of the athletic department shortly after the turn of the century, football coach briefly at Milwaukee Normal, sports editor of the *Milwaukee Sentinel*, and publicity director of the university athletic department, with advice from coaches he knew well, picked his all-time Wisconsin team up to that time. He chose to cover the years from 1906 through 1926 because modern football, with legalized passing and other fundamental rule changes, actually started in 1906.

On his first team Downer named Gus Tebell (1922) and Paul Meyers (1919) at ends, Cub Buck (1915) and Robert (Butts) Butler (1913) at tackles, Howard Hancock (1918) and R.M. (Tubby) Keeler (1912) at guards, Howard Carpenter (1919) at center, Eddie Gillette (1912) at quarterback, Rollie Williams (1922) and John Van Riper (1912) at halfback, and Merrill Taft (1923) at fullback.

On the second team which, Downer said, was probably just as good, he picked Merrill (Joe) Hoeffel (1912) and Harlan (Biddy) Rogers (1908) at ends, Ralph Scott (1920) and Marty Below (1923) at tackles, Adolph Bieberstein (1924) and Jimmy Brader (1921) at guards, George Bunge, Jr., (1920) at center, John (Keckie) Moll (1911) at quarterback, Eber Simpson (1917) and Alvah (Rowdy) Elliott (1921) at halfback, and Guy Sundt (1921) at fullback.

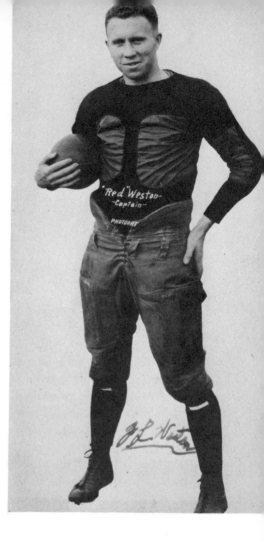

Frank (Red) Weston, an All-American end, and captain of the team in 1920.

On the third team Downer placed Jimmy Dean (1910) and Red Weston (1920) at ends, Al Buser (1911) and Howard Stark (1920) at tackles, John Messmer (1908) and William Mackmiller (1911) at guards, Richard Branstadt (1911) at center, Carl (Coots) Cunningham (1907) at quarterback, Dow Byers (1915) and Steven "T" Gould (1921) at halfbacks, and Al Tandberg (1912) at fullback.

In the *Milwaukee Sentinel* of January 2, 1927, Downer discussed the qualifications of these men, revealing in a small way the demands on players in their day. He wrote:

Carpenter, at center, had everything the position

232

demands, particularly size and speed. He was a keen football mind, a hard charger and an effective man in forward pass defense. When Coach John Richards was stopping the Minnesota shift so effectively, Carpenter was the keystone of Richards' system of defense. No team ever stopped Doc Williams' pet offense so thoroughly as Wisconsin in that period. (Williams' Minnesota shift was one of football's most devastating maneuvers sixty years ago.)

George Bunge on the second team lacked only Carpenter's speed and a spark or two of his fire to be as good.

Flanking Carpenter on the first team we have placed R.M. (Tubby) Keeler and Howard Hancock. Both were exceptional guards. Keeler was a member of the 1912 championship eleven and played three years as a regular. He was a yearly choice for all-conference and all-western honors and we think few will dispute his right to a place. Howard Hancock played guard on the ill-starred 1916 eleven in the "Harvard year" (Coach Withington's year) at Wisconsin. When Richards returned as coach (1917) he placed Hancock at tackle where he played magnificent football. We have heard John Richards speak of him as the equal of any lineman he ever coached at Wisconsin. Because of the wealth of great Badger tackles, we placed Hancock at guard in the sincere belief no Wisconsin guard ever surpassed Hancock's best season.

Wisconsin's other great guards of this period, Bieberstein, Jimmy Brader, John Messmer, William Mackmiller, Carl Neprud and Max Gelein, to mention only the outstanding ones, seem to merit equal consideration. Brader and Bieberstein, our second choices, played football of a grade which no one could deny. Each was an outstanding lineman of his period. John Messmer belongs to the days of 1906, 1907 and 1908. He was conspicuous in his day and was one of the few Badgers given all-conference ratings in those years, but Wisconsin was weak then and Messmer did many things which helped give him this prominence, like passing and running from punt formation, which really do not belong to guard play. However, we shall have no quarrel with any who believe him entitled to second or first team rating.

233

Center Charles Carpenter won All-American honors on John Richards' great teams shortly after the first world war.

When it comes to picking tackles, we were about ready to toss in the towel when forced to choose among Butts Butler, Cub Buck, Ralph Scott, Marty Below, Al Buser, Howard Stark, Eddie Samp, Rip Roberts, Oscar Osthoff, Putty Nelson, Butch Boyle and a few more. There, gentlemen, were a dozen real tackles. Pick any two of them and you would have a pair of rip snorting, roaring linemen to play havoc with any man's football team.

Yet a choice was necessary, and we think we have the right men on the first team, not withstanding the fact that in selecting Cub Buck and Butts Butler we have relegated to the second eleven Ralph Scott, whom Walter Camp picked for his first All-American eleven, and Marty Below, the outstanding western tackle of his time.

Butler was also an All-American chosen by Camp in 1912, and by others — 200 pounds of fighting Irishman and a varsity man for three years. Cub Buck had great weight, astonishing speed for a man of his build, and he was a veritable marvel at diagnosing opponents' plays. He later distinguished himself for 10 years in professional football (Canton and Green Bay).

With Buck and Butler, Below and Scott on the first and second teams, what an array of tackle stars we still have left. With Stark and Buser on the third team we still have Osthoff, Samp and Roberts, whom many may consider almost if not quite as good.

Ends present another difficult problem and here we (speaking of coaches and others who helped in all this) were unable to reach agreement. For all-around excellence of end play, we have placed Paulie Meyers and Gus Tebell on the first team with Merrill Hoeffel and Harlan (Biddy) Rogers on the second and little Jimmy Dean and Red Weston on the third team, not forgetting Jeff Burrus, who in his best game was little inferior to any of them. But in making a choice one has to consider such things as length of service, ruggedness and consistency and we think the men named had these qualities in about the order in which we have chosen them.

Tebell and Meyers were magnificent on defense, fine blockers and expert pass receivers on offense. They were

Ralph Scott won All-American recognition as a tackle in 1920.

100 percent representative Wisconsin men, fighters from head to heel, and withall two of the smartest ends who ever wore the cardinal colors. Hoeffel was captain of Wisconsin's last championship eleven in 1912, and was a great end. He had everything the others had except their speed. Dean, a midget in size, was an all-western choice during most of his college career. Rogers, a brilliant, brainy end, was always more highly thought of at Wisconsin than most of the other ends of his period but did not catch the outside critics' eyes so often. He captained the Badgers in his senior year and was a truly gread end.

And so we come to quarterback, where occurs what is perhaps the greatest difference of opinion to be found regarding any position. The argument as to which was the greater quarterback — Eddie Gillette or the late Keckie Moll — will never be satisfactorily settled. (Moll got his name "Keckie" because as a little tot, he would ask for a cookie but pronounced this "keckie" and the name stuck all through his relatively short life. He died while coaching at Purdue in 1912.) The final decision here in favor of Gillette has the endorsement of the men who coached both, Richard in 1911 and Bill Juneau in 1912.

Gillette was a wonderful leader, a smart general, Rollie Williams' only rival among Wisconsin players as an open field runner, a fine forward passer and a punter who averaged around 40 yards. He played at times when only wrought steel nerve kept him in the game, and he always came through.

Moll at his best played remarkable football and is an easy second choice in our opinion since we chose to regard Eber Simpson, who is classed right up to these two, as a halfback. On the third team, we have given the position to little Coots Cunningham, a similar type of player but not quite the equal of the others. Coots weighed but 130 pounds, was a jack rabbit in the open and a smart leader.

We feel confident that the selection of Rollie Williams and Johnny Van Riper as first team halfbacks will meet with general approval. To praise Rollie's qualities as a runner would be to paint the lily. He was a dependable defensive back and is sure of his place. Van Riper, over the full period of his college football, was Wisconsin's greatest plunging back and he was one of the best men in forward pass defense that Wisconsin ever had. His basketball height and skill also made him a fine pass receiver.

Rowdy Elliott was another great halfback, a hard plunger, a slashing off-tackle runner and 100 percent efficient on defense, including defense against the pass. Eber Simpson, whom we placed as Rowdy's running mate on the second team, was a remarkably fine forward passer, and good on defense — in short an all-around star. (He was also one of Wisconsin's greatest kickers.)

In naming Dow Byers on the third team we have departed from the rule of recognizing length of service in order to do justice to a back of unusual brilliance who played but one year as a regular.

One man never fully appreciated unless it be by his coach was "T" Gould. He was not an elusive runner in the open but was a hard line hitter, good off-tackle and a wonderful defensive player. Wisconsin probably never had a harder tackling halfback than "T" Gould.

Fullback necessitated a choice among four sterling backs — Merrill Taft, Guy Sundt, the late Al Tandberg and Jack Wilce. Wilce belongs to the beginning of the period under consideration and was a notable player. Possibly he deserves a higher rating than we have given him. Coaching counsel was divided among Taft, Sundt and Tandberg. Each played three years. Each was a good kicker, strong on defense and each in his way, a fine ground gainer. Tandberg was one of those fullbacks who is such a joy to a coach and such a help to a quarterback who can always get three or four yards through the line when it is needed. Bill

Guy Sundt was one of Wisconsin's greatest fullbacks shortly after the first world war and served as athletic director from 1950 up to the time of his death in 1955.

Juneau who coached him regards Tandberg as about the best blocking fullback he ever tutored. Guy Sundt excelled on defense, was an excellent blocker and a good plunger besides being one of Wisconsin's all-time great punters.

In the end, however, we have awarded the fullback place to Merrill Taft on his all-around excellence and in particular his great punting ability. In his last year (1924), he gained more ground than any other fullback in the Big Ten, outpunted all opponents and played a fine defensive game. He was better than a fair line plunger and a great off-tackle and open field runner. His kicking was superb, combining great height and distance with excellent placing of his punt. It is an extremely close thing among Taft, Sundt and Tandberg....

In 1969 the University of Wisconsin, seeking an all-time, all-star team in football's centennial year, invited sports editors of all state newspapers and fans to submit their selections.

"When eras die, their legacies are left to strange defenders," a poet once said, and so Wisconsin's all-time, all-star team included only one man picked by Downer: Cub Buck at tackle. The other positions were filled by men of more recent years except at one guard spot, where Arlie Mucks (1914) was named.

Wisconsin's team was composed of Dave Schreiner (1942) and Pat Richter (1962) at ends; Cub Buck, Arlie Mucks, and Bob (Red) Wilson (1949), Dan Lanphear (1959) and Ken Bowman (1963) in the interior line; Ron VanderKelen (1962) at quarterback; and Alan Ameche (1954), Elroy Hirsch (1942), and Pat Harder (1942) in the backfield.

Ameche, 1953 and 1954 All-American and 1954 Heisman trophy winner, was voted by a substantial margin as Wisconsin's all-time greatest football player. Named just behind him and also by substantial margins were Richter, Hirsch, and Schreiner in that order.

Vanderkelen was voted the Big Ten's most valuable player in 1962 and was co-recipient of the outstanding player award in the 1963 Rose Bowl game.

Ends Schreiner and Richter were both two-time All-Americans, Richter in 1961 and 1962 and Schreiner (who was

Arlie Mucks was a 250-pound All-American guard in 1914 whose influence with the alumni association and athletic board brought Dr. Clarence Spears from Oregon as football coach in 1932.

killed in action on Okinawa) in 1941 and 1942.

Wilson, who started out as a center and linebacker under Stuhldreher and was converted into an offensive end by Williamson while remaining a linebacker on defense, is the only Badger ever to be named the team's most valuable player in three consecutive years. He played center in 1946, 1947, and 1948 and end in 1949 and captained the team his senior year. He was named to this all-star team because of his versatility.

Bowman, who was actively recruited by Buck, was center on the 1962 Rose Bowl team. Lanphear was an aggressive and a strong tackle on the 1959 championship team which was so badly battered in the 1960 Rose Bowl game.

In football's centennial year in 1969, every other Big Ten school also named its own all-time team. The combined team lists were then given to the Big Ten skywriters who came up with a 22-man, all-time squad. Every man on it had earned at least one All-American designation, 10 had won Heisman trophy distinctions, and 10 had been named the Big Ten's most valuable player in his playing days.

Alan Ameche was the only Wisconsin man selected. Iowa placed four players in the top 22 and Illinois, Purdue, Michigan, and Minnesota each three. Illinois and Purdue each took credit for Alex Agase, who had made both colleges all-time teams and was an All-American at Purdue in 1943 and at Illinois in 1942 and 1946. (The military had shifted him for training in these years.) Michigan State and Ohio State each placed two men and Chicago and Indiana each one. Northwestern had none.

The all-time Big Ten was as follows: at end, Wes Fesler of Ohio State (1930), Benny Oosterbann (1927) and Ron Kramer (1956) of Michigan, Pete Pihos of Indiana (1945), and Gene Washington of Michigan State (1956); at tackle, Carl Eller of Minnesota (1963), Alex Karras of Iowa (1957), Bronko Nagurski of Minnesota (1929), Leo Nomellini of Minnesota (1949), and Fred (Duke) Slater of Iowa (1921); at guard, Alex Agase of Purdue (1943) and Illinois (1946), Calvin Jones of Iowa (1955), and Jim Parker of Ohio State (1956); at center, Dick Butkus of Illinois (1964); at quarterback, Jay Berwanger of Chicago (1935) and Bob Griese of Purdue (1956); at half-back, Harold (Red) Grange of Illinois (1924), Tom Harmon of Michigan (1940), Leroy Keyes of Purdue (1968), and Nile Kinnick of Iowa (1939); and at fullback, George Webster of Michigan State (1966) and Alan Ameche of Wisconsin (1954).

In addition to the top 22, the skywriters drew up an honorable mention list on which Wisconsin placed three men: ends Dave Schreiner and Pat Richter and halfback Elroy Hirsch, now the university's athletic director.

The question is often asked: What do you think were the greatest games ever played by Wisconsin? Not the greatest victories, the greatest games?

With all the differences in selecting all-time players, there is much unanimity of opinion on the greatest game, which, oddly, was not a victory: the Rose Bowl game of 1963 against Southern California. This was the "VanderKelen" game which Wisconsin lost, 42-37, after one of the most spectacular fourth quarters ever played anywhere. Trailing, 42-14, in the early minutes of the final period, the Badgers rallied for 23 points and even threatened to win in the closing minute.

In order after this, in most opinions, were the Wisconsin victories over Iowa in 1969, 23-17; Nebraska in 1974, 21-20; Ohio State in 1942, 17-7; and Minnesota in 1932, 20-13. The Nebraska game of 1974 was won on a spectacular 77-yard pass play, Bohlig to Mack, with only four minutes left. The victory over Iowa in 1969 was scored with a spectacular rally after trailing, 17-0, early in the fourth quarter. The victory ended a 17-game losing streak and was so joyously hailed that play had to be stopped for four minutes to clear the field of hundreds of exuberant fans.

The win over Ohio State in 1942, probably the high point in Harry Stuhldreher's coaching career, was not only a triumph over an old tormentor but over a team that came to Madison as No. 1 in the press polls and that eventually did finish No. 1. It was a game in which Dave Schreiner particularly distinguished himself. The victory is usually linked with another in the same year over old rival Minnesota, 20-6. It was the first time in the long relationship with the two schools that Wisconsin beat them

From the modest beginning of wooden seats has grown this concrete horseshoe with the field house at the open end and the new Memorial Sports Building at the left. The Wisconsin stadium seats 78,000.

both in one year. Only one other time to the present has this happened—in 1959. The Badgers of 1942, who were named national champions by the Helms Foundation, finished third in the press polls. The surprise defeat at Iowa's hands, 6-0, kept the Badgers from an undefeated season that year, although they tied Notre Dame, 7-7.

Mickey McGuire, the "Hawaiian honey," beat Minnesota almost singlehandedly in Wisconsin's 20-13 victory in 1932. He ran the opening kickoff back 90 yards for a touchdown and then scored two more touchdowns, the third and decisive one on a pass from Joe Linfor in the last minute.

This question is also frequently kicked around by long-time followers of Wisconsin football: Who was Wisconsin's greatest coach? As in the area of all-time players, there is divergence of opinion.

Through the years, going back to 1889, Wisconsin has had 23 coaches, including John Jardine, now in his seventh season (1977). Perhaps the question would be better phrased: Who did the most with his material? Or better still, who did the best recruiting job and then made the most of his material?

Percentages based on games won and lost, with ties counting for a half-game won and a half-game lost, do not always tell the whole story. On this basis, the best coach was Phil King. In eight seasons (1896-1902 and 1905), the "winningest era" in Wisconsin's history, his teams won 65 games, lost 11, and tied one for a percentage of .851. Only one percentage point behind him stands C.P. Hutchins (1906-07), with eight victories, one defeat, and one tie for a percentage of .850. Just behind him was George Little, who in two years (1925-26) won 11 games, lost three, and tied two for a percentage of .750.

In Big Ten games only, King had a 17-8-1 record and Hutchins, 6-1-1. Ivy Williamson had the best Big Ten record with 29-13-4.

This writer has known and observed all the coaches except the very early ones and has always felt that the finest jobs at Wisconsin were done by Ivy Williamson (1949-55) and John Richards (1911, 1917, and 1919-22). Williamson in his seven years won 41 games, lost 19, and tied four for a percentage of .672. Richards in his six seasons won 29, lost nine, and tied four

244

for a percentage of .738.

Only Ohio State, with Wes Fesler or Woody Hayes as head coach, had a better contemporary record among Big Ten schools than Wisconsin under Williamson. Against Williamson's 41-19-4, Ohio State under the two coaches had 46-15-4, including two Rose Bowl victories. The Wisconsin record in this period included one Rose Bowl defeat.

Both Williamson and Richards were good recruiters, tacticians, strategists, and teachers. Both relied heavily on the pass. Richards built much of his attack around the controversial screen pass, on which ineligible receivers would go downfield to occupy defenders while eligible receivers maneuvered into the clear. It was largely because of Richards' effective use of the screen that the rulemakers in the early twenties outlawed it.

Influenced by Michigan's Fielding Yost in all of his coaching, Williamson always built much of his attack around the flight of the ball—the kickoff, the punt, the pass—with just enough running to make the passing work. In practices his passers worked at least half an hour daily on throwing the ball, and Wisconsin had two men who could throw it particularly well—Johnny Coatta and Jim Miller. In four of Williamson's seven years as coach (1950-53), Wisconsin led the Big Ten in team pass completion percentages. Coatta and Miller as individuals each led the league. Coatta led in 1950 and 1951, the former year with a percentage of .642, which is still the conference record. Miller led in 1953 with .529.

Both coaches encountered opposition from within the university, Richards from the faculty and Williamson from overzealous alumni. The alumni, heeding Professor Slichter's suggestion at the turn of the century that alumni always maintain a lively interest in their school's athletic program, intervened, and not always happily. Williamson's last years at Wisconsin were not always serene ones, although he concealed his feelings well.

Richards had his difficulty with Dean Sellery, who at an early convocation stated that he would like to see more Phi Beta Kappas on the football field. The implication was clear. Two years later Richards resigned.

It is only natural that one of the greatest coaches should have turned out what most Wisconsin followers today regard as the greatest team—Ivy Williamson's "Hard Rocks" of 1951.

They did not win any championships; in fact, they finished no better than third in the Big Ten race. But they were still a superb team in every area except luck. They lost the Illinois game, 14-10, in a major heartbreak and tied Ohio State, 6-6, in another. In both games the "Hard Rocks" built up enormous statistical margins that belied the results. Most Wisconsin followers still feel the team should have gone to the Rose Bowl instead of the 1952 team, which lost to Southern California, 7-0.

The criterion of every Wisconsin team until the "Hard Rocks" had been Harry Stuhldreher's 1942 team. The criterion before that was Bill Juneau's undefeated Big Ten champions of 1912. But the "Hard Rocks" have become the all-time standard of great Wisconsin teams.

Appendix

ALL-TIME SERIES SCORES

INDIANA SERIES SCORES

Date and Year	Wis.	Ind.
*Nov. 9, 1907	11	8
Oct. 17, 1908	16	0
*Oct. 23, 1909	6	3
†Oct. 22, 1910	3	12
*Oct. 21, 1922	20	0
Oct. 20, 1923	52	0
*Oct. 23, 1926	27	2
*Oct. 29, 1938 (HC)	6	0
Oct. 14, 1939	0	14
*Nov. 16, 1940 (DD)	27	10
*Oct. 25, 1941 (HC)	27	25
Oct. 23, 1943	0	34
Oct. 4, 1947	7	7
*Sept. 25, 1948	7	35
Oct. 29, 1949	30	14
*Nov. 3, 1951 (HC)	6	0
Nov. 15, 1952	37	14
Oct. 7, 1961	6	3
*Oct. 6, 1962 (W)	30	6
Nov. 4, 1967	9	14
*Nov. 2, 1968 (TV, HC)	20	21
*Oct. 25, 1969 (HC)	36	34
Oct. 24, 1970	30	12
*Oct. 9, 1971	35	29
Oct. 14, 1972	7	33
*Oct. 27, 1973 (HC)	31	7
Oct. 26, 1974	35	25

Wisconsin Won 19, Lost 8, Tied 2
*Games at Madison
†Game at Indianapolis
Games at Madison - 15; Wis. 12-2-1
Games at Bloomington - 13; Wis. 7-5-1
Game at Indianapolis - 1; Wis. 0-1-0

INDIANA SERIES (Cont.)

	Wis.	Ind.
*Nov. 15, 1975 (W)	9	9
Nov. 13, 1976	14	15
	544	386

NO. ILLINOIS SERIES SCORES

Date and Year	Wis.	NI
Sept. 11, 1971	31	0
Sept. 16, 1972 (B)	31	7
	62	7

Wisconsin Won 2, Lost 0

NORTHWESTERN SERIES SCORES

Date and Year	Wis.	NU
†Nov. 26, 1890	10	22
†Oct. 31, 1891	0	0
†Nov. 29, 1891	40	0
Nov. 19, 1892	26	6
†Nov. 24, 1892	20	6
†Sept. 21, 1895	12	6
Nov. 26, 1896	6	6
Nov. 25, 1897	22	0
Nov. 24, 1898	47	0
*Oct. 14, 1899	38	0
*Nov. 8, 1902	51	0
††Nov. 21, 1903	6	6
Oct. 30, 1909	21	11
*Oct. 29, 1910	0	0
Oct. 28, 1911	28	3
*Oct. 12, 1912	56	0
Oct. 18, 1919	10	6
*Oct. 16, 1920	27	7
Oct. 15, 1921	27	0
*Oct. 12, 1929	0	7
Nov. 15, 1930	7	20
Nov. 3, 1934	0	7
Nov. 16, 1935	13	32
Nov. 7, 1936	18	26
*Oct. 30, 1937	6	14
Nov. 5, 1938	20	13

NORTHWESTERN SERIES (Cont.)

Date and Year	Wis.	N.W.
Oct. 21, 1939	7	13
*Oct. 19, 1940	7	27
Oct. 11, 1941	14	41
Nov. 14, 1942	20	19
*Nov. 6, 1943 (HC)	0	41
Sept. 30, 1944	7	6
*Nov. 10, 1945 (HC)	14	28
Oct. 5, 1946	0	28
Nov. 1, 1947	29	0
*Nov. 6, 1948 (HC)	7	16
Nov. 5, 1949	14	6
*Oct. 28, 1950	14	13
Oct. 27, 1951	41	0
*Nov. 8, 1952 (HC)	24	20
Nov. 7, 1953	34	13
*Nov. 6, 1954 (HC)	34	13
Nov. 5, 1955	41	14
*Nov. 10, 1956 (HC)	7	17
Nov. 9, 1957	41	12
*Nov. 8, 1958 (HC)	17	13
Nov. 7, 1959	24	19
*Nov. 5, 1960 (HC)	0	21
Nov. 11, 1961	29	10
*Nov. 10, 1962 (TV, HC)	37	6
*Nov. 9, 1963 (TV, HC)	17	14
Nov. 7, 1964	13	17
Oct. 16, 1965	21	7
*Oct. 15, 1966 (TV, P)	3	3
*Oct. 28, 1967 (HC)	13	17
Oct. 26, 1968	10	13
Oct. 18, 1969	7	27
*Oct. 17, 1970 (P)	14	24
Oct. 2, 1971	11	24
*Oct. 7, 1972 (P)	21	14
*Nov. 17, 1973 (W)	36	34
Nov. 16, 1974	52	7
*Oct. 25, 1975 (HC)	17	14
Oct. 23, 1976	28	25
	1236	834

Wisconsin Won 37, Lost 22, Tied 5
*Games at Madison
†Games at Milwaukee
††Game at Chicago, Ill.
Games at Madison - 25: Wis. 13-10-2
Games at Evanston - 33; Wis. 21-11-1
Games at Milwaukee - 5; Wis. 3-1-1
Game at Chicago - 1; Wis. 0-0-1

ILLINOIS SERIES (Cont.)

Date and Year	Wis.	Ill.
*Oct. 9, 1943	7	25
*Oct. 20, 1945 (DD)	7	7
Oct. 19, 1946	21	27
*Oct. 2, 1948 (W)	20	16
Oct. 1, 1949 (TV)	13	13
Oct. 7, 1950	7	6
Oct. 6, 1951 (TV)	10	14
*Oct. 4, 1952	20	6
*Nov. 14, 1953	34	7
Nov. 13, 1954	27	14
*Nov. 12, 1955 (DD)	14	17
Nov. 17, 1956	13	13
*Nov. 16, 1957 (HC)	24	13
Nov. 15, 1958	31	12
*Nov. 14, 1959 (HC, TV)	6	9
Nov. 12, 1960	14	35
*Nov. 18, 1961 (DD)	55	7
Nov. 17, 1962	35	6
*Nov. 16, 1963	7	17
Nov. 14, 1964	0	29
*Nov. 13, 1965 (W)	0	51
Nov. 12, 1966	14	49
*Nov. 15, 1969 (W)	55	14
Nov. 14, 1970	29	17
*Nov. 13, 1971 (W)	27	35
Nov. 18, 1972	7	27
*Nov. 1, 1975 (P)	18	9
Oct. 30, 1976	25	31
	727	713

Wisconsin Won 22, Lost 22, Tied 5
*Games at Madison
†Game at Milwaukee
Games at Madison - 25; Wis. 12-10-3
Games at Milwaukee - 1; Wis. 1-0-0
Games at Champaign - 23; Wis. 9-12-2

ILLINOIS SERIES SCORES

Date and Year	Wis.	Ill.
*Oct. 26, 1895	10	10
†Nov. 18, 1899	23	0
*Nov. 24, 1900	27	0
Nov. 10, 1906	16	6
*Oct. 26, 1907	4	15
*Nov. 21, 1914	9	24
Nov. 13, 1915	3	17
*Nov. 25, 1916	0	0
Oct. 20, 1917	0	7
*Nov. 9, 1918 (HC)	0	22
Oct. 25, 1919	14	10
*Nov. 13, 1920 (HC)	14	9
Oct. 22, 1921	20	0
*Nov. 11, 1922 (HC)	0	3
Nov. 10, 1923	0	10
Nov. 7, 1931	7	6
*Nov. 5, 1932 (HC)	20	12
Oct. 14, 1933	0	21
*Nov. 17, 1934 (HC)	7	3
Nov. 4, 1939	0	7
*Nov. 2, 1940 (HC)	13	6

MICHIGAN SERIES SCORES

Date and Year	Wis.	Mich.
*Oct. 15, 1892	6	10
Nov. 4, 1893	34	18
†Nov. 30, 1899	17	5
†Nov. 1, 1902	0	6
Nov. 14, 1903	0	16
*Oct. 29, 1904	0	28
Nov. 18, 1905	0	12
*Nov. 12, 1921	7	7
Nov. 18, 1922	6	13
*Nov. 17, 1923	3	6
Oct. 25, 1924	0	21
*Oct. 17, 1925 (HC)	0	21
Nov. 6, 1926	0	37
*Oct. 15, 1927	0	14
Oct. 27, 1928	7	0
Nov. 28, 1931	0	16
Nov. 10, 1934	10	0
*Oct. 19, 1935	12	20
Nov. 13, 1943	0	27
Nov. 18, 1944	0	14
Nov. 16, 1946	6	28

	Wis.	Mich.
*Nov. 15, 1947 (DD)	6	40
Oct. 21, 1950	13	26
Oct. 31, 1959	19	10
*Oct. 29, 1960	16	13
Nov. 3, 1962	34	12
Oct. 30, 1965	14	50
*Oct. 29, 1966	17	28
*Nov. 18, 1967 (W)	14	27
Nov. 16, 1968 (TV)	9	34
Nov. 1, 1969	7	35
*Oct. 31, 1970 (HC)	15	29
Oct. 20, 1973	6	35
*Oct. 19, 1974 (P)	20	24
Sept. 13, 1975	6	23
Sept. 11, 1976	27	40
	331	745

Wisconsin Won 7, Lost 28, Tied 1
*Games at Madison
†Games at Chicago, Ill.
Games at Madison - 14; Wis. 1-12-1
Games at Ann Arbor - 20; Wis. 5-15-0
Games at Chicago - 2; Wis. 1-1-0

MICHIGAN STATE SERIES SCORES

Date and Year	Wis.	MSU
*Oct. 25, 1913	7	12
*Nov. 28, 1918 (T)	7	6
*Oct. 9, 1920	27	0
*Oct. 13, 1923	21	0
*Nov. 14, 1925	21	0
Oct. 2, 1954	6	0
*Oct. 29, 1955 (HC)	0	27
Nov. 3, 1956	0	33
*Nov. 2, 1957	7	21
Nov. 1, 1958 (TV)	9	7
*Sept. 30, 1961 (W)	0	20
Nov. 2, 1963	13	30
*Oct. 31, 1964 (HC)	6	22
Oct. 7, 1967	7	35
*Oct. 5, 1968	0	39
*Oct. 16, 1971 (P)	31	28
Oct. 21, 1972	0	31
Nov. 3, 1973	0	21
Nov. 2, 1974 (HC)	21	28
	176	339

Wisconsin Won 7, Lost 12, Tied 0
*Games at Madison
Games at Madison - 12; Wis. 5-7-0
Games at East Lansing - 7; Wis. 2-5-0

OHIO STATE SERIES SCORES

Date and Year	Wis.	OSU
*Nov. 8, 1913	12	0
Oct. 24, 1914	7	6

	Wis.	Ohio
*Oct. 23, 1915	21	0
Nov. 4, 1916	13	14
*Nov. 10, 1917	3	16
Nov. 23, 1918	14	3
*Nov. 15, 1919	0	3
Oct. 23, 1920	7	13
Nov. 1, 1930	0	0
*Nov. 14, 1931 (HC)	0	6
Oct. 29, 1932	7	7
*Nov. 18, 1933	0	6
Nov. 8, 1941	34	46
*Oct. 31, 1942 (HC)	17	7
*Oct. 14, 1944	7	20
Oct. 13, 1945	0	12
*Oct. 12, 1946 (W)	20	7
Oct. 23, 1948	32	34
*Oct. 22, 1949 (DD)	0	21
Nov. 11, 1950	14	19
*Oct. 13, 1951	6	6
Oct. 11, 1952	14	23
*Oct. 24, 1953 (DD)	19	20
Oct. 23, 1954	14	31
*Oct. 22, 1955	16	26
Oct. 27, 1956	0	21
*Oct. 26, 1957 (DD)	13	16
Oct. 25, 1958	7	7
*Oct. 24, 1959	12	3
Oct. 21, 1960	7	34
*Oct. 28, 1961 (TV, HC)	21	30
Oct. 27, 1962 (TV)	7	14
*Oct. 26, 1963	10	13
Oct. 24, 1964	3	28
*Oct. 23, 1965 (HC)	10	20
Oct. 22, 1966	13	24
Nov. 11, 1967 (TV)	15	17
*Nov. 9, 1968	8	43
Nov. 8, 1969	7	62
*Nov. 7, 1970	7	24
Oct. 23, 1971 (TV)	6	31
*Oct. 28, 1972	20	28
*Oct. 13, 1973	0	24
Oct. 12, 1974	7	52
Oct. 18, 1975	0	56
*Oct. 16, 1976	20	30
	470	923

Wisconsin Won 7, Lost 35, Tied 4
*Games at Madison
Games at Madison - 23; Wis. 5-17-1
Games at Columbus - 23; Wis. 2-18-3

PURDUE SERIES SCORES

Date and Year	Wis.	Pur.
Oct. 19, 1892	4	32
*Nov. 16, 1893	36	30
†Oct. 15, 1894	0	1
*Nov. 17, 1906	29	5
Nov. 16, 1907	12	6
*Oct. 19, 1912	41	0
Oct. 18, 1913	7	7
*Oct. 17, 1914	14	7
Oct. 16, 1915	28	3
*Oct. 24, 1925	7	0

		Wis.	Purdue
Oct.	16, 1926	0	0
*Oct.	22, 1927	12	6
Oct.	20, 1928	19	19
*Nov.	2, 1929 (HC)	0	13
Oct.	25, 1930	6	7
*Oct.	27, 1931 (DD)	21	14
Oct.	15, 1932	6	7
*Oct.	28, 1933 (HC)	0	14
Oct.	20, 1934	0	14
*Nov.	9, 1935 (HC)	8	0
Oct.	10, 1936	14	35
*Nov.	13, 1937 (DD)	7	7
Oct.	22, 1938	7	13
*Nov.	18, 1939 (HC)	7	7
Oct.	26, 1940	14	13
*Nov.	15, 1941 (DD)	13	0
Oct.	24, 1942	13	0
*Oct.	30, 1943 (DD)	0	32
Nov.	4, 1944	0	35
*Oct.	6, 1945 (W)	7	13
Nov.	2, 1946	24	20
*Sept.	27, 1947	32	14
*Nov.	5, 1950 (HC)	33	7
Oct.	20, 1951	31	7
Oct.	17, 1953	28	19
*Oct.	16, 1954 (DD)	20	6
Oct.	8, 1955 (TV)	9	0
*Oct.	20, 1956 (DD)	6	6
Oct.	12, 1957	23	14
*Oct.	11, 1958	31	6
Oct.	10, 1959	0	21
*Oct.	8, 1960 (DD)	24	13
*Oct.	12, 1963 (W)	38	20
Oct.	10, 1964	7	28
Nov.	6, 1965	7	45
*Nov.	5, 1966 (HC)	0	23
*Nov.	6, 1971 (HC)	14	10
Nov.	11, 1972	6	27
*Sept.	15, 1973	13	14
Sept.	14, 1974	28	14
Oct.	11, 1975	17	14
*Oct.	9, 1976 (P)	16	18
		739	**685**

Wisconsin Won 27, Lost 19, Tied 6
*Games at Madison
*Games at Madison
†Game Forfeited to Purdue by Referee
Games at Madison - 26; Wis. 16-7-3
Games at Lafayette - 26; Wis. 11-12-3

IOWA SERIES SCORES

Date and Year		Wis.	Iowa
*Oct.	29, 1894	44	0
*Nov.	3, 1906	18	4
Nov.	2, 1907	6	5
*Nov.	4, 1911	12	0
Nov.	23, 1912	28	10
*Oct.	27, 1917	20	0
*Nov.	15, 1924 (HC)	7	21
Nov.	7, 1925	6	0
*Nov.	13, 1926 (HC)	20	10
*Nov.	12, 1927 (HC)	0	16
Nov.	17, 1928	13	0
*Oct.	26, 1929 (DD)	0	14
*Oct.	8, 1932 (DD)	34	0
Oct.	21, 1933	7	26
*Oct.	16, 1937 (HC)	13	6
Oct.	8, 1938	31	13
*Oct.	28, 1939 (DD)	13	19
Oct.	12, 1940	12	30
*Oct.	18, 1941 (W)	23	0
Nov.	7, 1942	0	6
Oct.	2, 1943	7	5
*Nov.	11, 1944 (DD)	26	7
Nov.	3, 1945	27	7
*Nov.	9, 1946 (HC)	7	21
*Nov.	8, 1947 (HC)	46	14

		Wis.	Iowa
Oct.	30, 1948	13	19
*Nov.	12, 1949 (HC)	35	13
Oct.	14, 1950	14	0
*Nov.	17, 1951 (DD)	34	7
Oct.	18, 1952	42	13
*Oct.	31, 1953 (HC)	10	6
Oct.	30, 1954	7	13
*Oct.	1, 1955	37	14
Oct.	13, 1956	7	13
Oct.	19, 1957	7	21
*Oct.	18, 1958 (TV)	9	20
*Oct.	17, 1959 (DD)	25	16
Oct.	15, 1960 (TV)	21	28
Oct.	21, 1961	15	47
*Oct.	20, 1962 (P)	42	14
Oct.	19, 1963	10	7
*Oct.	17, 1964 (P)	31	21
*Oct.	2, 1965 (P)	16	13
Oct.	1, 1966	7	0
*Oct.	21, 1967	21	21
Oct.	19, 1968	0	41
*Oct.	11, 1969 (P)	23	17
Oct.	10, 1970	14	24
Oct.	30, 1971	16	20
*Nov.	4, 1972 (HC)	16	14
*Nov.	10, 1973	35	7
Nov.	9, 1974	28	15
Nov.	8, 1975	28	45
*Nov.	6, 1976 (HC)	38	21
		1021	**744**

Wisconsin Won 34, Lost 19, Tied 1
*Games at Madison
Games at Iowa City - 25; Wis. 12-13-0
Games at Madison - 29; Wis. 22-6-1

MINNESOTA SERIES SCORES

Date and Year		Wis.	Minn.
Nov.	15, 1890	0	63
Oct.	24, 1891	12	26
*Oct.	29, 1892	4	32
Nov.	11, 1893	0	40
*Nov.	17, 1894	6	0
Nov.	16, 1895	10	14
*Nov.	15, 1896	6	0
Oct.	30, 1897	39	0
*Oct.	29, 1898	29	0
Nov.	18, 1899	19	0
Nov.	3, 1900	5	6
*Nov.	16, 1901	18	0
Nov.	15, 1902	0	11
*Nov.	26, 1903	0	17
Nov.	12, 1904	0	28
*Nov.	4, 1905	16	12
*Nov.	23, 1907	17	17
Nov.	7, 1908	5	0
*Nov.	13, 1909	6	34
Nov.	12, 1910	0	28
*Nov.	18, 1911 (HC)	6	6
Nov.	16, 1912	14	0
*Nov.	1, 1913 (HC)	3	21
Nov.	14, 1914	3	14
*Nov.	20, 1915 (HC)	3	20
Nov.	18, 1916	0	54
*Nov.	3, 1917 (HC)	10	7
Nov.	16, 1918	0	6
*Nov.	1, 1919 (HC)	7	19
Nov.	6, 1920	3	0
*Oct.	29, 1921 (HC)	35	0
Nov.	4, 1922	14	0
*Oct.	27, 1923 (HC)	0	0
*Oct.	18, 1924	7	7
Oct.	31, 1925	12	12
*Oct.	30, 1926	10	16
Oct.	29, 1927	7	13
*Nov.	24, 1928	0	6
Nov.	23, 1929	12	13

MINNESOTA SERIES (Cont.)

*Nov. 22, 1930	14	0	
Oct. 31, 1931	0	14	
*Nov. 12, 1932	20	13	
Nov. 25, 1933	0	14	
*Nov. 24, 1934	3	6	
Nov. 23, 1935	7	33	
*Nov. 21, 1936	0	24	
Nov. 20, 1937	6	13	
*Nov. 19, 1938	0	21	
Nov. 25, 1939	6	23	
*Nov. 23, 1940	13	22	
Nov. 22, 1941	6	41	
*Nov. 21, 1942 (DD)	20	6	
Nov. 20, 1943	13	25	
*Nov. 25, 1945	26	12	
*Nov. 24, 1946 (DD)	0	6	
Nov. 22, 1947	0	21	
*Nov. 20, 1948 (DD)	0	16	
Nov. 19, 1949	6	14	
*Nov. 25, 1950 (DD)	14	0	
Nov. 24, 1951	30	6	
*Nov. 22, 1952	21	21	
Nov. 21, 1953	21	21	
*Nov. 20, 1954	27	0	
Nov. 19, 1955	6	21	
*Nov. 24, 1956	13	13	

Nov. 23, 1957	14	6	
*Nov. 22, 1958 (DD)	27	12	
Nov. 21, 1959 (TV)	11	7	
*Nov. 19, 1960 (TV)	7	26	
Nov. 25, 1961	23	21	
*Nov. 24, 1962	14	9	
Nov. 28, 1963 (T)	0	14	
*Nov. 21, 1964	14	7	
Nov. 20, 1965	7	42	
*Nov. 19, 1966 (W)	7	6	
Nov. 25, 1967	14	21	
*Nov. 23, 1968 (W)	15	23	
Nov. 22, 1969	10	35	
*Nov. 21, 1970 (W)	39	14	
Nov. 20, 1971	21	23	
*Nov. 25, 1972 (W)	6	14	
Nov. 24, 1973	17	19	
*Nov. 23, 1974 (W)	49	14	
Nov. 22, 1975	3	24	
*Nov. 20, 1976 (W)	26	17	
	960	1330	

Wisconsin Won 30, Lost 48, Tied 8
*Games at Madison
Games at Madison - 43; Wis. 19-18-6
Games at Minneapolis - 43; 11-30-2

Date and Score of Every Wisconsin Football Game Played 1889-1976

Date	Played at	Wis.		Opp.

1889 (0-2)

Captain: **Charles Mayer**   Coach: **Alvin Kletsch**

| Nov. 23 | Milwaukee | 0 | Calumet Club | 27 |
| Dec. 14 | Beloit | 0 | Beloit | 4 |

1890 (1-3)

Captain: **James Kerr**   Coach: **Ted Mestre (Yale)**

Nov. 1	Madison	106	Whitewater Normal	0
Nov. 15	Minneapolis	0	Minnesota	63
Nov. 22	Madison	6	Lake Forest	16
Nov. 26	Milwaukee	10	Northwestern	22

1891 (3-1-1)

Captain: **E. H. Ahara**   Coach: **Herb Alward (Harvard)**

Oct. 17	Beloit	40	Beloit	4
Oct. 24	Minneapolis	12	Minnesota	26
Oct. 31	Milwaukee	0	Northwestern	0
Nov. 14	Madison	6	Lake Forest	4
Nov. 29	Milwaukee	40	Northwestern	0

1892 (4-3)

Captain: **J. D. Freeman**   Coach: **Crawford (Yale)**

Oct. 1	Madison	32	Beloit	4
Oct. 15	Madison	6	Michigan	10
Oct. 19	Lafayette	4	Purdue	32
Oct. 22	Milwaukee	10	Lake Forest	6
Oct. 29	Madison	4	Minnesota	32
Nov. 19	Evanston	26	Northwestern	6
Nov. 24	Milwaukee	20	Northwestern	6

1893 (4-2)

Captain: **T. U. Lyman**   Coach: **Parke H. Davis (Princeton)**

Oct. 14	Milwaukee	0	Chicago Athletic Association	4
Oct. 21	Madison	24	Lake Forest	0
Oct. 28	Madison	18	Beloit	0
Nov. 4	Ann Arbor	34	Michigan	18
Nov. 11	Minneapolis	0	Minnesota	40
Nov. 16	Madison	36	Purdue	30

1894 (5-2)

Captain: **T. U. Lyman**   Coach: **H. O. Stickney (Harvard)**

Oct. 6	Madison	22	Chicago Athletic Association	4
Oct. 15	Lafayette	F	Purdue	*W
Oct. 20	Chicago	30	Chicago University	0
Oct. 27	Chicago	4	Chicago Athletic Association	16
Oct. 29	Madison	44	Iowa	0
Nov. 3	Beloit	46	Beloit	0
Nov. 17	Madison	6	Minnesota	**0

*Umpire forfeited game to Purdue.
**Daily Cardinal extra on red paper.

1895 (5-2-1)

Captain: **J. R. Richards**   Coach: **H. O. Stickney**

Sept. 21	Milwaukee	12	Northwestern	6
Sept. 30	Madison	28	Iowa State	6
Oct. 5	Madison	32	Armour	4
Oct. 12	Madison	26	Lake Forest*	5
Oct. 19	Madison	14	Grinnell	4
Oct. 26	Madison	10	Illinois	10
Nov. 2	Chicago	12	Chicago	22
Nov. 16	Minneapolis	10	Minnesota	14

*Also used Rush Medical College players.

1896 (7-1-1)

Captain: J. R. Richards Coach: Phil King (Princeton)

Oct.	10	Madison	34	Lake Forest	0
Oct.	14	Madison	18	Madison High	0
Oct.	17	Madison	50	Rush Medical	0
Oct.	24	Madison	54	Grinnell	6
Oct.	31	Beloit	6	Beloit	0
Nov.	7	Madison	24	Chicago	0
Nov.	21	Madison	6	Minnesota	0
Nov.	26	Evanston	6	Northwestern	6
Dec.	19	Chicago*	8	Carlisle Indians	18

*Played at night in Chicago Coliseum.

1897 (9-1)

Captain: J. P. Riordan Coach: Phil King

Oct.	2	Madison	30	Lake Forest	0
Oct.	6	Madison	8	Madison High*	0
Oct.	9	Madison	28	Rush Medical	0
Oct.	16	Madison	20	Platteville Normal	0
Oct.	23	Madison	29	Madison High	0
Oct.	30	Minneapolis	39	Minnesota	0
Nov.	6	Madison	11	Beloit	0
Nov.	13	Chicago	23	Chicago	8
Nov.	20	Madison	0	Alumni	6
Nov.	25	Evanston	22	Northwestern	0

*Called at end of first half because of rain.

1898 (9-1)

Captain: Pat J. O'Dea Coach: Phil King

Oct.	1	Madison	52	Ripon	0
Oct.	5	Madison	21	Madison High	0
Oct.	8	Madison	76	Dixon (Ill.) College	0
Oct.	15	Madison	42	Rush Medical	0
Oct.	22	Milwaukee	17	Beloit	0
Oct.	29	Madison	29	Minnesota	0
Nov.	5	Madison	12	Alumni	11
Nov.	12	Chicago	0	Chicago	6
Nov.	19	Madison	22	Whitewater Normal	0
Nov.	24	Evanston	47	Northwestern	0

1899 (9-2)

Captain: Pat J. O'Dea Coach: Phil King

Sept.	30	Madison	45	Lake Forest	0
Oct.	6	Milwaukee	36	Beloit	0
Oct.	14	Madison	38	Northwestern	0
Oct.	21	New Haven	0	Yale	6
Oct.	28	Madison	11	Rush Medical	0
Nov.	4	Madison	17	Alumni	5
Nov.	11	Milwaukee	23	Illinois	0
Nov.	18	Minneapolis	19	Minnesota	0
Nov.	25	Madison	58	Lawrence	0
Nov.	30*	Chicago	17	Michigan	5
Dec.	9	Madison	0	Chicago	17

*Thanksgiving Day.

1900 (8-1)

Captain: A. Chamberlain Coach: Phil King

Sept.	29	Madison	50	Ripon	0
Oct.	6	Madison	5	Chicago Physicians & Surgeons	0
Oct.	13	Milwaukee	11	Beloit	0
Oct.	20	Madison	64	Upper Iowa	0
Oct.	27	Madison	45	Grinnell	0
Nov.	3	Minneapolis	5	Minnesota	6
Nov.	10	Madison	54	Notre Dame	0
Nov.	17	Chicago	39	Chicago	5
Nov.	24	Madison	27	Illinois	0

1901 (9-0)

Captain: Art Curtis Coach: Phil King

Sept.	28	Madison	26	Milwaukee Medical	0
Oct.	5	Madison	62	Hyde Park (Ill.) H. S.	0
Oct.	12	Milwaukee	40	Beloit	0
Oct.	19	Madison	23	Knox	5
Oct.	26	Madison	50	Kansas	0
Nov	2	Milwaukee	18	Nebraska	0
Nov.	9	Madison	45	Iowa State	0
Nov.	16	Minneapolis	18	Minnesota	0
Nov.	28*	Chicago	35	Chicago	0

*Thanksgiving Day.

253

1902 (6-3)

Captain: William Juneau   Coach: Phil King

Sept. 27	Madison	11	Lawrence	0
Oct. 4	Madison	24	Hyde Park (Ill.) H. S.	5
Oct. 11	Madison	52	Lawrence	0
Oct. 18	Milwaukee	52	Beloit	6
Oct. 25	Madison	38	Kansas	0
Nov. 1	Chicago	0	Michigan	6
Nov. 8	Madison	51	Northwestern	0
Nov. 15	Minneapolis	0	Minnesota	11
Nov. 27*	Chicago	0	Chicago	11

*Thanksgiving Day.

1903 (6-3-1)

Captain: Allan Abbott   Coach: Art Curtis (Wisconsin)

Oct. 3	Madison	28	North Central	0
Oct. 10	Madison	40	Lawrence	7
Oct. 17	Madison	87	Beloit	0
Oct. 21	Madison	32	Osteopaths	0
Oct. 24	Madison	54	Knox	6
Oct. 31	Madison	6	Chicago	15
Nov. 7	Madison	52	Oshkosh Normal	0
Nov. 14	Ann Arbor	0	Michigan	16
Nov. 21	Chicago	6	Northwestern	6
Nov. 26*	Minneapolis	0	Minnesota	17

*Thanksgiving Day.

1904 (5-3)

Captain: James I. Bush   Coach: Art Curtis (Wisconsin)

Oct. 1	Madison	45	Fort Sheridan	0
Oct. 8	Madison	33	Marquette	0
Oct. 15	Milwaukee	58	Notre Dame	0
Oct. 22	Madison	82	Drake	0
Oct. 29	Madison	0	Michigan	28
Nov. 5	Madison	36	Beloit	0
Nov. 12	Minneapolis	0	Minnesota	28
Nov. 24*	Chicago	11	Chicago	18

*Thanksgiving Day.

1905 (8-2)

Captain: E. Vanderboom   Coach: Phil King (Princeton)

Sept. 23	Marinette	16	Co. I, Marinette	0
Sept. 30	Madison	49	Northwestern College*	0
Oct. 4	Madison	29	Marquette	0
Oct. 7	Madison	34	Lawrence	0
Oct. 14	Milwaukee	21	Notre Dame	0
Oct. 21	Madison	0	Chicago	4
Oct. 28	Madison	17	Alumni	0
Nov. 4	Minneapolis	16	Minnesota	12
Nov. 11	Madison	44	Beloit	0
Nov. 18	Ann Arbor	0	Michigan	12

*At Watertown, Wis.

1906 (5-0)

Captain: W. A. Gelbach   Coach: Dr. C. P. Hutchins (Syracuse)

Oct. 13	Madison	5	Lawrence	0
Oct. 20	Madison	10	North Dakota U.	0
Nov. 3	Madison	18	Iowa	4
Nov. 10	Champaign	16	Illinois	6
Nov. 17	Madison	29	Purdue	5

---

*No longer in the conference.
**Entered conference in 1949.

1907 (3-1-1)

Captain: John Messmer   Coach: Dr. C. P. Hutchins

Oct. 26	Madison	4	Illinois	15
Nov. 2	Iowa City	6	Iowa	5
Nov. 9	Madison	11	Indiana	8
Nov. 16	Lafayette	12	Purdue	6
Nov. 23	Madison	17	Minnesota	17

1908 (5-1)

Captain: Harlan Rogers   Coach: J. A. "Tom" Barry (Brown)

Oct. 10	Madison	35	Lawrence	0
Oct. 17	Bloomington	16	Indiana	0

Oct.	24	Madison	24	Freshmen	15
Oct.	31	Madison	9	Marquette	6
Nov.	7	Minneapolis	5	Minnesota	0
Nov.	21	Madison (HC)	12	Chicago	18

1909 (3-1-1)

Captain: Jack W. Wilce   Coach: J. A. "Tom" Barry

Oct.	9	Madison	22	Lawrence	0
Oct.	23	Madison	6	Indiana	3
Oct.	30	Evanston	21	Northwestern	11
Nov.	13	Madison (HC)	6	Minnesota	34
Nov.	20	Chicago	6	Chicago	6

1910 (1-2-2)

Captain: J. P. Dean   Coach: J. A. "Tom" Barry

Oct.	8	Madison	6	Lawrence	6
Oct.	22	Indianapolis	3	Indiana	12
Oct.	29	Madison	0	Northwestern	0
Nov.	12	Minneapolis	0	Minnesota	28
Nov.	19	Madison (HC)	10	Chicago	0

1911 (5-1-1)

Captain: A. L. Buser   Coach: J. R. Richards (Wisconsin)

Oct.	7	Madison	15	Lawrence	0
Oct.	14	Madison	24	Ripon	0
Oct.	21	Madison	26	Colorado College	0
Oct.	28	Evanston	28	Northwestern	3
Nov.	4	Madison	12	Iowa	0
Nov.	18	Madison (HC)	6	Minnesota	6
Nov.	25	Chicago	0	Chicago	5

1912 (7-0)

Captain: M. E. Hoeffel   Coach: Wm. Juneau (Wisconsin)

Oct.	5	Madison	13	Lawrence	0
Oct.	12	Madison	56	Northwestern	0
Oct.	19	Madison	41	Purdue	0
Nov.	2	Madison (HC)	30	Chicago	12
Nov.	9	Madison	64	Arkansas	7
Nov.	16	Minneapolis	14	Minnesota	0
Nov.	23	Iowa City	28	Iowa	10

1913 (3-3-1)

Captain: Al Tanberg   Coach: Wm. Juneau (Wisconsin)

Oct.	4	Madison	58	Lawrence	7
Oct.	11	Madison	13	Marquette	0
Oct.	18	Lafayette	7	Purdue	7
Oct.	25	Madison	7	Michigan State	12
Nov.	1	Madison (HC)	3	Minnesota	21
Nov.	8	Madison	12	Ohio State	0
Nov.	22	Chicago	0	Chicago	19

1914 (4-2-1)

Captain: R. M. Keeler   Coach: Wm. Juneau (Wisconsin)

Oct.	3	Madison	21	Lawrence	0
Oct.	10	Madison	48	Marquette	0
Oct.	17	Madison	14	Purdue	7
Oct.	24	Columbus	7	Ohio State	6
Oct.	31	Madison (HC)	0	Chicago	0
Nov.	14	Minneapolis	3	Minnesota	14
Nov.	21	Madison	9	Illinois	24

1915 (4-3)

Captain: Howard Buck   Coach: Wm. Juneau (Wisconsin)

Oct.	2	Madison	82	Lawrence	0
Oct.	9	Madison	85	Marquette	0
Oct.	16	Lafayette	28	Purdue	3
Oct.	23	Madison	21	Ohio State	0
Oct.	30	Chicago	13	Chicago	14
Nov.'	13	Champaign	3	Illinois	17
Nov.	20	Madison (HC)	3	Minnesota	20

1916 (4-2-1)

Captain: Paul Meyers   Coach: Paul Withington (Harvard)

Oct.	7	Madison	20	Lawrence	0
Oct.	14	Madison	28	South Dakota State	3
Oct.	21	Madison	13	Haskell	0
Oct.	28	Madison (HC)	30	Chicago	7
Nov.	4	Columbus	13	Ohio State	14

| Nov. | 18 | Minneapolis | 0 | Minnesota | 54 |
| Nov. | 25 | Madison | 0 | Illinois | 0 |

1917 (4-2-1)

Captain: Howard Hancock **Coach: John R. Richards (Wisconsin)**

Oct.	6	Madison	34	Beloit	0
Oct.	13	Madison	0	Notre Dame	0
Oct.	20	Champaign	0	Illinois	7
Oct.	27	Madison	20	Iowa	0
Nov.	3	*Madison (HC)	10	Minnesota	7
Nov.	10	Madison	3	Ohio State	16
Nov.	24	Chicago	18	Chicago	0

*First game played in new Camp Randall Stadium.

1918 (3-3)

Captain: F. Mann **Coach: Guy Lowman (Wisconsin)**

Oct.	26	Madison	0	Camp Grant	7
Nov.	2	Madison	21	Beloit	0
Nov.	9	Madison (HC)	0	Illinois	22
Nov.	16	Minneapolis	0	Minnesota	6
Nov.	23	Columbus	14	Ohio State	3
Nov.	28	*Madison	7	Michigan State	6

*Thanksgiving Day.

1919 (5-2)

Captain: C. H. Carpenter **Coach: J. Richards (Wisconsin)**

Oct.	4	Madison	37	Ripon	0
Oct.	11	Madison	13	Marquette	0
Oct.	18	Evanston	10	Northwestern	6
Oct.	25	Champaign	14	Illinois	10
Nov.	1	Madison (HC)	7	Minnesota	19
Nov.	15	Madison	0	Ohio State	3
Nov.	22	Chicago	10	Chicago	3

1920 (6-1)

Captain: Frank L. Weston **Coach: J. Richards (Wisconsin)**

Oct.	2	Madison	60	Lawrence	0
Oct.	9	Madison	27	Michigan State	0
Oct.	16	Madison	27	Northwestern	7
Oct.	23	Columbus	7	Ohio State	13
Nov.	6	Minneapolis	3	Minnesota	0
Nov.	13	Madison (HC)	14	Illinois	9
Nov.	20	Chicago	3	Chicago	0

1921 (5-1-1)

Captain: Guy M. Sundt **Coach: J. Richards (Wisconsin)**

Oct.	1	Madison	28	Lawrence	0
Oct.	8	Madison	24	South Dakota State	3
Oct.	15	Evanston	27	Northwestern	0
Oct.	22	Champaign	20	Illinois	0
Oct.	29	Madison (HC)	35	Minnesota	0
Nov.	12	Madison	7	Michigan	7
Nov.	19	Chicago	0	Chicago	3

1922 (4-2-1)

Captain: Rollie Williams **Coach: J. Richards (Wisconsin)**

Oct.	7	Madison	41	Carleton	0
Oct.	14	Madison	20	South Dakota State	6
Oct.	21	Madison	20	Indiana	0
Nov.	4	Minneapolis	14	Minnesota	0
Nov.	11	Madison (HC)	0	Illinois	3
Nov.	18	Ann Arbor	6	Michigan	13
Nov.	25	Chicago	0	Chicago	0

1923 (3-3-1)

Captain: Marty P. Below **Coach: Jack J. Ryan (Dartmouth)**

Oct.	6	Madison	7	Coe College	3
Oct.	13	Madison	21	Michigan State	0
Oct.	20	Bloomington	52	Indiana	0
Oct.	27	Madison (HC)	0	Minnesota	0
Nov.	10	Champaign	0	Illinois	10

| Nov. 17 | Madison | 3 | Michigan | 6 |
| Nov. 24 | Chicago | 6 | Chicago | 13 |

1924 (2-3-3)

Captain: **Jack Harris** Coach: **Jack Ryan (Dartmouth)**

Sept. 27	Madison	25	North Dakota	0
Oct. 4	Madison	17	Iowa State	0
Oct. 11	Madison	7	Coe College	7
Oct. 18	Madison	7	Minnesota	7
Oct. 25	Ann Arbor	0	Michigan	21
Nov. 8	Madison	3	Notre Dame	38
Nov. 15	Madison (HC)	7	Iowa	21
Nov. 22	Chicago	0	Chicago	0

1925 (6-1-1)

Captain: **Steve Polaski** Coach: **George Little (Ohio Wesl.)**

Oct. 3	Madison	30	Iowa State	0
Oct. 10	Madison	35	Franklin College	0
Oct. 17	Madison (HC)	0	Michigan	21
Oct. 24	Madison	7	Purdue	0
Oct. 31	Minneapolis	12	Minnesota	12
Nov. 7	*Iowa City	6	Iowa	0
Nov. 14	Madison	21	Michigan State	10
Nov. 21	Chicago	20	Chicago	7

*Played in raging blizzard.

1926 (5-2-1)

Captain: **Doyle Harmon** Coach: **George Little**

Oct. 2	Madison	38	Cornell College	0
Oct. 9	Madison	13	Kansas	0
Oct. 16	Lafayette	0	Purdue	0
Oct. 23	Madison	27	Indiana	2
Oct. 30	Madison	10	Minnesota	16
Nov. 6	Ann Arbor	0	Michigan	37
Nov. 13	Madison (HC)	20	Iowa	10
Nov. 20	Chicago	14	Chicago	7

1927 (4-4)

Captain: **Ed J. Crofoot** Coach: **G. Thistlethwaite (Earlham)**

Oct. 1	Madison	31	Cornell College	6
Oct. 8	Lawrence	26	Kansas	6
Oct. 15	Madison	0	Michigan	14
Oct. 22	Madison	12	Purdue	6
Oct. 29	Minneapolis	7	Minnesota	13
Nov. 5	Madison	20	Grinnell	2
Nov. 12	Madison (HC)	0	Iowa	16
Nov. 19	Chicago	0	Chicago	12

1928 (7-1-1)

Captain: **Rube Wagner** Coach: **Glenn Thistlethwaite**

Oct. 6	Madison	22	Notre Dame	6
Oct. 13*	Madison	49	Cornell College	0
Oct. 13*	Madison	13	North Dakota State	7
Oct. 20	Lafayette	19	Purdue	19
Oct. 27	Ann Arbor	7	Michigan	0
Nov. 3	Madison	15	Alabama	0
Nov. 10	Madison (HC)	25	Chicago	0
Nov. 17	Iowa City	13	Iowa	0
Nov. 24	Madison	0	Minnesota	6

*Doubleheader.

1929 (4-5)

Captain: **John Parks** Coach: **Glenn Thistlethwaite**

Sept. 28*	Madison	22	Ripon	0
Sept. 28*	Madison	21	South Dakota State	0
Oct. 5	Madison	13	Colgate	6
Oct. 12	Madison	0	Northwestern	7
Oct. 19	Chicago**	0	Notre Dame	19
Oct. 26	Madison (DD)	0	Iowa	14
Nov. 2	Madison (HC)	0	Purdue	13
Nov. 9	Chicago	20	Chicago	6
Nov. 23	Minneapolis	12	Minnesota	13

*Doubleheader.   **Played in Soldiers Field.

1930 (6-2-1)

Captain: Milt Gantenbein		Coach: Glenn Thistlethwaite	
Oct. 4	*Madison 53	Lawrence	6
Oct. 4	*Madison 28	Carleton College	0
Oct. 11	Madison 34	Chicago	0
Oct. 18	Madison (HC) 27	Pennsylvania	0
Oct. 25	Lafayette 6	Purdue	7
Nov. 1	Columbus 0	Ohio State	0
Nov. 8	Madison 58	South Dakota State...........	7
Nov. 15	Evanston 7	Northwestern 20	
Nov. 22	Madison 14	Minnesota	0

*Doubleheader.

1931 (5-4-1)

Captain: Harold F. Smith		Coach: Glenn Thistlethwaite	
Oct. 3	*Madison 33	Bradley	6
Oct. 3	*Madison 12	North Dakota State...........	7
Oct. 10	Madison 7	Auburn	7
Oct. 17	Madison (DD) 21	Purdue 14	
Oct. 24	Philadelphia 13	Pennsylvania 27	
Oct. 31	Minneapolis 0	Minnesota 14	
Nov. 7	Champaign 7	Illinois	6
Nov. 14	Madison (HC) 0	Ohio State	6
Nov. 21	Chicago 12	Chicago	7
Nov. 28	Ann Arbor 0	Michigan 16	

*Doubleheader.

1932 (6-1-1)

Captain: Gregory Kabat		Coach: Clarence Spears (Dartmouth)	
Oct. 1	Madison 7	Marquette	2
Oct. 8	Madison (DD) 34	Iowa	0
Oct. 15	Lafayette 6	Purdue	7
Oct. 22	Madison 39	Coe College	0
Oct. 29	Columbus 7	Ohio State	7
Nov. 5	Madison (HC) 20	Illinois 12	
Nov. 12	Madison 20	Minnesota 13	
Nov. 19	Chicago 18	Chicago	7

1933 (2-5-1)

Captain: Harold C. Smith		Coach: Clarence Spears	
Oct. 7	Madison 19	Marquette	0
Oct. 14	Champaign 0	Illinois 21	
Oct. 21	Iowa City 7	Iowa 26	
Oct. 28	Madison (HC) 0	Purdue 14	
Nov. 4	Chicago 0	Chicago	0
Nov. 11	Madison 25	West Virginia	6
Nov. 18	Madison 0	Ohio State	6
Nov. 25	Minneapolis 3	Minnesota	6

1934 (4-4)

Captain: John Bender		Coach: Clarence Spears	
Oct. 6	Madison 3	Marquette	0
Oct. 13	Madison 28	South Dakota State...........	7
Oct. 20	Lafayette 0	Purdue 14	
Oct. 27	South Bend 0	Notre Dame 19	
Nov. 3	Evanston 0	Northwestern	7
Nov. 10	Ann Arbor 10	Michigan	0
Nov. 17	Madison (HC) 7	Illinois	3
Nov. 24	Madison 0	Minnesota 34	

1935 (1-7)

Captain: Ray Davis		Coach: Clarence Spears	
Sept. 28	Madison 6	South Dakota State.................13	
Oct. 5	Madison 0	Marquette 33	
Oct. 12	Madison 0	Notre Dame 27	
Oct. 19	Madison 12	Michigan 20	
Oct. 26	Chicago 7	Chicago 13	
Nov. 9	Madison (HC) 8	Purdue	0
Nov. 16	Evanston 13	Northwestern 3	
Nov. 23	Minneapolis 7	Minnesota 33	

1936 (2-6)

Captain: John Golemgeske		Coach: Harry Stuhldreher (N. Dame)	
Sept. 26	Madison 24	South Dakota State...........	7
Oct. 3	Madison 6	Marquette 12	
Oct. 10	Lafayette 14	Purdue 35	
Oct. 17	South Bend 0	Notre Dame 27	
Oct. 31	Madison (HC) 6	Chicago	7
Nov. 7	Evanston 18	Northwestern 26	
Nov. 14	Madison 27	Cincinnati	6
Nov. 21	Madison 0	Minnesota 24	

1937 (4-3-1)

Captain: Fred Benz		Coach: Harry Stuhldreher	
Sept. 15	Madison	32	South Dakota State	0
Oct. 2	Madison	12	Marquette	0
Oct. 9	Chicago	27	Chicago	0
Oct. 16	Madison (HC)	13	Iowa	6
Oct. 23	Pittsburgh	0	Pittsburgh	21
Oct. 30	Madison	6	Northwestern	14
Nov. 13	Madison (DD)	7	Purdue	7
Nov. 20	Minneapolis	6	Minnesota	13

1938 (5-3)

Captains: Howard Weiss, Vince Gavre		Coach: Harry Stuhldreher	
Oct. 1	Madison	27	Marquette	0
Oct. 8	Iowa City	31	Iowa	13
Oct. 15	Madison (DD)	6	Pittsburgh	26
Oct. 22	Lafayette	7	Purdue	13
Oct. 29	Madison (HC)	6	Indiana	0
Nov. 5	Evanston	20	Northwestern	13
Nov. 12	Los Angeles	14	UCLA	7
Nov. 19	Madison	0	Minnesota	21

1939 (1-6-1)

Captain: Ralph Moeller		Coach: Harry Stuhldreher	
Sept. 30	Madison	14	Marquette	13
Oct. 7	Madison	7	Texas	17
Oct. 14	Madison	0	Indiana	14
Oct. 21	Evanston	7	Northwestern	13
Oct. 28	Madison (DD)	13	Iowa	19
Nov. 4	Champaign	0	Illinois	7
Nov. 18	Madison (HC)	7	Purdue	7
Nov. 25	Minneapolis	6	Minnesota	23

1940 (4-4)

Captain: John Tennant		Coach: Harry Stuhldreher	
Oct. 5	Madison	33	Marquette	19
Oct. 12	Iowa City	12	Iowa	30
Oct. 19	Madison	7	Northwestern	27
Oct. 26	Lafayette	14	Purdue	13
Nov. 2	Madison (HC)	13	Illinois	6
Nov. 9	New York	6	Columbia	7
Nov. 16	Madison (DD)	27	Indiana	10
Nov. 23	Madison*	13	Minnesota	22

*50th anniversary of all-time series.

1941 (3-5)

Captain: Tom Farris		Coach: Harry Stuhldreher	
Oct. 4	Madison	7	Marquette	28
Oct. 11	Evanston	14	Northwestern	41
Oct. 18	Madison (W)	23	Iowa	0
Oct. 25	Madison (HC)	27	Indiana	25
Nov. 1	Madison	20	Syracuse	27
Nov. 8	Columbus	34	Ohio State	46
Nov. 15	Madison (DD)	13	Purdue	0
Nov. 22	Minneapolis	6	Minnesota	41

1942 (8-1-1)

Captains: Dave Schreiner and Mark Hoskins		Coach: Harry Stuhldreher (Notre Dame)	
Sept. 19	Madison	7	Camp Grant	0
Sept. 26	Madison	7	Notre Dame	7
Oct. 3	Madison	35	Marquette	7
Oct. 10	Madison (W)	17	Missouri	9
Oct. 17	Chicago*	13	Great Lakes	7
Oct. 24	Lafayette	13	Purdue	0
Oct. 31	Madison (HC)	17	Ohio State	7
Nov. 7	Iowa City	0	Iowa	6
Nov. 14	Evanston	20	Northwestern	19
Nov. 21	Madison (DD)	20	Minnesota	6

*Played in Soldiers Field.

1943 (1-9)

Captain: Joe Keenan		Coach: Harry Stuhldreher	
Sept. 18	Madison	7	Marquette	33
Sept. 25	Rockford	7	Camp Grant	10
Oct. 2	Iowa City	7	Iowa	5
Oct. 9	Madison	7	Illinois	25
Oct. 16	Madison (W)	0	Notre Dame	50
Oct. 23	Bloomington	0	Indiana	34
Oct. 30	Madison (DD)	0	Purdue	32

Nov.	6	Madison (HC)	0	Northwestern	41
Nov.	13	Ann Arbor	0	Michigan	27
Nov.	20	Minneapolis	13	Minnesota	25

1944 (3-6)

Captain: Allen J. Shafer, Jr.   **Coach: Harry Stuhldreher**

Sept.	30	Evanston	7	Northwestern	6
Oct.	7	Madison	21	Marquette	2
Oct.	14	Madison (HC)	7	Ohio State	20
Oct.	21	South Bend	13	Notre Dame	28
Oct.	28	Madison	12	Great Lakes	40
Nov.	4	Lafayette	0	Purdue	35
Nov.	11	Madison (DD)	26	Iowa	7
Nov.	18	Ann Arbor	0	Michigan	14
Nov.	25	Madison (W)	26	Minnesota	28

1945 (3-4-2)

Captain: Jack Mead   **Coach: Harry Stuhldreher**

Sept.	22	Great Lakes	0	Great Lakes	0
Sept.	29	Madison	40	Marquette	13
Oct.	6	Madison (W)	7	Purdue	13
Oct.	13	Columbus	0	Ohio State	12
Oct.	20	Madison (DD)	7	Illinois	7
Nov.	3	Iowa City	27	Iowa	7
Nov.	10	Madison (HC)	14	Northwestern	28
Nov.	17	Baltimore	7	Navy	36
Nov.	24	Minneapolis	26	Minnesota	12

1946 (4-5)

Captain: Clarence Esser   **Coach: Harry Stuhldreher**

Sept.	21	Madison	34	Marquette	0
Sept.	28	Berkeley	28	California	7
Oct.	5	Evanston	0	Northwestern	28
Oct.	12	Madison (W)	20	Ohio State	7
Oct.	19	Champaign	21	Illinois	27
Nov.	2	Lafayette	24	Purdue	20
Nov.	9	Madison (HC)	7	Iowa	21
Nov.	16	Ann Arbor	6	Michigan	28
Nov.	23	Madison (DD)	0	Minnesota	6

1947 (5-3-1)

Captain: Jack Wink   **Coach: Harry Stuhldreher**

Sept.	27	Madison	32	Purdue	14
Oct.	4	Bloomington	7	Indiana	7
Oct.	11	Madison (W)	7	California	48
Oct.	18	New Haven	9	Yale	0
Oct.	25	Madison	35	Marquette	12
Nov.	1	Evanston	29	Northwestern	0
Nov.	8	Madison (HC)	46	Iowa	14
Nov.	15	Madison (DD)	6	Michigan	40
Nov.	22	Minneapolis	0	Minnesota	21

1948 (2-7)

Captain: Wally Dreyer   **Coach: Harry Stuhldreher**

Sept.	25	Madison	7	Indiana	35
Oct.	2	Madison (W)	20	Illinois	16
Oct.	9	Berkeley	14	California	40
Oct.	16	Madison	7	Yale	17
Oct.	23	Columbus	32	Ohio State	34
Oct.	30	Iowa City	13	Iowa	19
Nov.	6	Madison (HC)	7	Northwestern	16
Nov.	13	Madison	26	Marquette	0
Nov.	20	Madison (DD)	0	Minnesota	16

1949 (5-3-1)

Captain: Robert Wilson   **Coach: Ivy Williamson (Michigan)**

Sept.	24	Madison	41	Marquette	0
Oct.	1	Champaign	13	Illinois (TV)	13
Oct.	8	Madison (W)	20	California	35
Oct.	15	Madison	48	Navy	13
Oct.	22	Madison (DD)	0	Ohio State	21
Oct.	29	Bloomington	30	Indiana	14
Nov.	5	Evanston	14	Northwestern	6
Nov.	12	Madison (HC)	35	Iowa	13
Nov.	19	Minneapolis	6	Minnesota	14

1950 (6-3)

Captain: Ken Huxhold		Coach: Ivy Williamson	
Sept. 30	Madison (W) 28	Marquette 6	
Oct. 7	Champaign 7	Illinois 6	
Oct. 14	Iowa City 14	Iowa 0	
Oct. 21	Ann Arbor 13	Michigan 26	
Oct. 28	Madison 14	Northwestern 13	
Nov. 4	Madison (HC) 33	Purdue 7	
Nov. 11	Columbus 14	Ohio State 19	
Nov. 18	Philadelphia 0	Pennsylvania 20	
Nov. 25	Madison (DD) 14	Minnesota 0	

1951 (7-1-1)

Captain: Jim Hammond		Coach: Ivy Williamson	
Sept. 29	Madison (W) 22	Marquette 6	
Oct. 6	Champaign 10	Illinois (TV) 14	
Oct. 13	Madison 6	Ohio State 6	
Oct. 20	Lafayette 31	Purdue 7	
Oct. 27	Evanston 41	Northwestern (TV) 0	
Nov. 3	Madison (HC) 6	Indiana 0	
Nov. 10	Madison 16	Pennsylvania 7	
Nov. 17	Madison (DD) 34	Iowa 7	
Nov. 24	Minneapolis 30	Minnesota 6	

1952 (6-3-1)

Captain: George O'Brien		Coach: Ivy Williamson	
Sept. 27	Madison (W) 42	Marquette 19	
Oct. 4	Madison 20	Illinois 6	
Oct. 11	Columbus 14	Ohio State 23	
Oct. 18	Iowa City 42	Iowa 13	
Oct. 25	Madison (DD) 7	UCLA 20	
Nov. 1	Houston 21	Rice 7	
Nov. 8	Madison (HC) 24	Northwestern 20	
Nov. 15	Bloomington 37	Indiana 14	
Nov. 22	Madison 21	Minnesota 21	
Jan. 1	Pasadena 0	So. Calif. (TV) 7*	

*Rose Bowl.

1953 (6-2-1)

Co-Captains: Roger Dornburg and Jerry Wuhrman		Coach: Ivy Williamson	
Sept. 26	Madison (W) 20	Penn State 0	
Oct. 3	Madison 13	Marquette 11	
Oct. 9	Los Angeles* 0	UCLA 13	
Oct. 17	Lafayette 28	Purdue 19	
Oct. 24	Madison (DD) 19	Ohio State 0	
Oct. 31	Madison (HC) 10	Iowa 6	
Nov. 7	Evanston 34	Northwestern 13	
Nov. 14	Madison 34	Illinois 7	
Nov. 21	Minneapolis 21	Minnesota 21	

*Night game.

1954 (7-2)

Captain: Gary Messner		Coach: Ivy Williamson	
Sept. 25	Madison (W) 52	Marquette 14	
Oct. 2	East Lansing 6	Michigan State 0	
Oct. 9	Madison 13	Rice (TV) 7	
Oct. 16	Madison (DD) 20	Purdue 6	
Oct. 23	Columbus 14	Ohio State 31	
Oct. 30	Iowa City 7	Iowa 13	
Nov. 6	Madison (HC) 34	Northwestern 13	
Nov. 13	Champaign 27	Illinois 14	
Nov. 20	Madison 27	Minnesota 0	

1955 (4-5)

Captain: Wells Gray		Coach: Ivy Williamson	
Sept. 24	Madison (W) 28	Marquette 14	
Oct. 1	Madison 37	Iowa 14	
Oct. 8	Lafayette 9	Purdue (TV) 0	
Oct. 14	Los Angeles* 21	Southern California 33	
Oct. 22	Madison 16	Ohio State 26	
Oct. 29	Madison (HC) 0	Michigan State 27	
Nov. 5	Evanston 41	Northwestern 6	
Nov. 12	Madison (DD) 14	Illinois 17	
Nov. 19	Minneapolis 6	Minnesota 21	

*Night game.

1956 (1-5-3)

Captain:	Pat Levenhagen	Coach: Milton Bruhn (Minnesota)	
Sept. 29	Madison (W) 41	Marquette	0
Oct. 6	Madison 6	Southern California	13
Oct. 13	Iowa City 7	Iowa	13
Oct. 20	Madison (DD) 6	Purdue	6
Oct. 27	Columbus 0	Ohio State	21
Nov. 3	East Lansing 0	Michigan State	33
Nov. 10	Madison (HC) 7	Northwestern	17
Nov. 17	Champaign 13	Illinois	13
Nov. 24	Madison 13	Minnesota	13

1957 (6-3)

Captain:	William Gehler	Coach: Milt Bruhn	
Sept. 28	Madison (W) 60	Marquette	6
Oct. 5	Madison 45	West Virginia	13
Oct. 12	Lafayette 23	Purdue	14
Oct. 19	Iowa City 7	Iowa	21
Oct. 26	Madison (DD) 13	Ohio State	16
Nov. 2	Madison 7	Michigan State	21
Nov. 9	Evanston 41	Northwestern	12
Nov. 16	Madison (HC) 24	Illinois	13
Nov. 23	Minneapolis 14	Minnesota	6

1958 (7-1-1)

Co-Captains:	Dave Kocourek and Jon Hobbs	Coach: Milt Bruhn	
Sept. 26	Miami, Fla.* 20	Miami (Fla.)	0
Oct. 4	Madison (W) 50	Marquette	0
Oct. 11	Madison 31	Purdue	6
Oct. 18	Madison 9	Iowa (TV)	20
Oct. 25	Columbus 7	Ohio State	7
Nov. 1	East Lansing 9	Michigan State (TV)........	7
Nov. 8	Madison (HC) 17	Northwestern	13
Nov. 15	Champaign 31	Illinois	12
Nov. 22	Madison (DD) 27	Minnesota	12

*Night game.

1959 (7-3)

Co-Captains:	Jerry Stalcup and Bob Zeman	Coach: Milt Bruhn	
Sept. 26	Madison (W) 16	Stanford	14
Oct. 3	Madison (B) 44	Marquette	6
Oct. 10	Lafayette 0	Purdue	21
Oct. 17	Madison (DD) 25	Iowa	16
Oct. 24	Madison 12	Ohio State	3
Oct. 31	Ann Arbor 19	Michigan	10
Nov. 7	Evanston 24	Northwestern	19
Nov. 14	Madison (HC) 6	Illinois (TV)	9
Nov. 21	Minneapolis 11	Minnesota (TV)	7
Jan. 1	Pasadena 8	Washington (TV)	44

1960 (4-5)

Co-Captains:	Henry Derleth and Tom Wiesner	Coach: Milt Bruhn	
Sept. 24	Palo Alto, Calif. 24	Stanford	7
Oct. 1	Madison (W and B)..........35	Marquette	6
Oct. 8	Madison (DD) 24	Purdue	13
Oct. 15	Iowa City 21	Iowa (TV)	28
Oct. 22	Columbus 7	Ohio State	34
Oct. 29	Madison 16	Michigan	13
Nov. 5	Madison (HC) 0	Northwestern	21
Nov. 12	Champaign 14	Illinois	35
Nov. 19	Madison 7	Minnesota (TV)	26

1961 (6-3)

Co-Captains:	Jim Bakken and Don Schade	Coach: Milt Bruhn	
Sept. 23	Madison 7	Utah	0
Sept. 30	Madison (W) 0	Michigan State	20
Oct. 7	Bloomington 6	Indiana	3
Oct. 13	Madison (B) 23	Oregon State	20
Oct. 21	Iowa City 15	Iowa	47
Oct. 28	Madison (HC) 21	Ohio State (TV)	30
Nov. 11	Evanston 29	Northwestern	10
Nov. 18	Madison (DD) 55	Illinois (TV)	7
Nov. 25	Minneapolis 23	Minnesota	21

262

1962 (8-2)

Co-Captains: Pat Richter and
Steve Underwood   Coach: Milt Bruhn

Sept.	29	Madison (B)	69	New Mexico State ... 13
Oct.	6	Madison (W)	30	Indiana ... 6
Oct.	13	Madison	17	Notre Dame ... 8
Oct.	20	Madison (P)	42	Iowa ... 14
Oct.	27	Columbus	7	Ohio State (TV) ... 14
Nov.	3	Ann Arbor	34	Michigan ... 12
Nov.	10	Madison (HC)	37	Northwestern (TV) ... 6
Nov.	17	Champaign	35	Illinois ... 6
Nov.	24	Madison	14	Minnesota ... 9
Jan.	1	Pasadena	37	Southern California (TV) ... 42

1963 (5-4)

Co-Captains: Ken Bowman and
Andy Wojdula   Coach: Milt Bruhn

Sept.	21	Madison (B)	41	Western Michigan ... 0
Sept.	28	South Bend	14	Notre Dame ... 9
Oct.	12	Madison (W)	38	Purdue ... 20
Oct.	19	Iowa City	10	Iowa ... 7
Oct.	26	Madison (P)	10	Ohio State ... 13
Nov.	2	East Lansing	13	Michigan State ... 30
Nov.	9	Madison (HC)	17	Northwestern (TV) ... 14
Nov.	16	Madison	7	Illinois ... 17
Nov.	28*	Minneapolis	0	Minnesota ... 14

*Thanksgiving Day.

1964 (3-6)

Co-Captains: Ron Leafblad and
Ron Frain   Coach: Milt Bruhn

Sept.	19	Madison (B)	17	Kansas State (TV) ... 7
Sept.	26	Madison (W)	7	Notre Dame ... 31
Oct.	10	Lafayette	7	Purdue ... 28
Oct.	17	Madison (P)	31	Iowa ... 21
Oct.	24	Columbus	3	Ohio State ... 28
Oct.	31	Madison (HC)	6	Michigan State ... 22
Nov.	7	Evanston	13	Northwestern ... 17
Nov.	14	Champaign	0	Illinois ... 29
Nov.	21	Madison	14	Minnesota ... 7

1965 (2-7-1)

Captain: Dave Fronek   Coach: Milt Bruhn

Sept.	18	Madison (B)	0	Colorado ... 0
Sept.	25	Madison	6	Southern California ... 26
Oct.	2	Madison (P)	16	Iowa ... 13
Oct.	9	Lincoln	0	Nebraska ... 37
Oct.	16	Evanston	21	Northwestern ... 7
Oct.	23	Madison (HC)	10	Ohio State ... 20
Oct.	30	Ann Arbor	14	Michigan ... 50
Nov.	6	Lafayette	7	Purdue ... 45
Nov.	13	Madison (W)	0	Illinois ... 51
Nov.	20	Minneapolis	7	Minnesota ... 42

1966 (3-6-1)

Co-Captains: Bob Richter and
Tony Loukas   Coach: Milt Bruhn

Sept.	14	Madison (B)	20	Iowa State ... 10
Sept.	24	Los Angeles*	3	Southern California ... 38
Oct.	1	Iowa City	7	Iowa ... 0
Oct.	8	Madison	3	Nebraska ... 31
Oct.	15	Madison (P)	3	Northwestern (TV) ... 3
Oct.	22	Columbus	13	Ohio State ... 24
Oct.	29	Madison	17	Michigan ... 28
Nov.	5	Madison (HC)	0	Purdue ... 23
Nov.	12	Champaign	14	Illinois ... 49
Nov.	19	Madison (W)	7	Minnesota ... 6

*Night game.

1967 (0-9-1)

Captain: Tom Domres   Coach: John Coatta (Wisconsin)

Sept.	23	Seattle	0	Washington ... 17
Sept.	30	Madison (B)	16	Arizona State ... 42
Oct.	7	East Lansing	7	Michigan State ... 35
Oct.	14	Madison (P)	11	Pittsburgh ... 13
Oct.	21	Madison	21	Iowa ... 21
Oct.	28	Madison (HC)	13	Northwestern ... 17
Nov.	4	Bloomington	9	Indiana ... 14
Nov.	11	Columbus	15	Ohio State (TV) ... 17
Nov.	18	Madison (W)	14	Michigan ... 27
Nov.	25	Minneapolis	14	Minnesota ... 21

1968 (0-10)

Captain:	Wally Schoessow		Coach:	John Coatta	
Sept. 21	Tempe*	7	Arizona State		55
Sept. 28	Madison (B)	17	Washington		? 1
Oct. 5	Madison	0	Michigan State		39
Oct. 12	Madison (P)	0	Utah State		20
Oct. 19	Iowa City	0	Iowa		41
Oct. 29	Evanston	10	Northwestern		13
Nov. 2	Madison (HC)	20	Indiana (TV)		21
Nov. 9	Madison	8	Ohio State		43
Nov. 16	Ann Arbor	9	Michigan (TV)		34
Nov. 23	Madison (W)	15	Minnesota		23

*Night Game

1969 (3-7)

Tri-Captains:	Don Murphy, Mel Reddick and Bill Gregory		Coach:	John Coatta	
Sept. 20	Madison	21	Oklahoma		48
Sept. 27	Madison (B)	23	UCLA		34
Oct. 4	Madison	7	Syracuse		43
Oct. 11	Madison (P)	23	Iowa		17
Oct. 18	Evanston	7	Northwestern		27
Oct. 25	Madison (HC)	36	Indiana		34
Nov. 1	Ann Arbor	7	Michigan		35
Nov. 8	Columbus	7	Ohio State		62
Nov. 15	Madison (W)	55	Illinois		14
Nov. 22	Minneapolis	10	Minnesota		35

1970 (4-5-1)

Captain: Bill Gregory			Coach:	John Jardine (Purdue)	
Sept. 19	Norman	7	Oklahoma		21
Sept. 26	Madison (B)	14	Texas Christian		14
Oct. 3	Madison	29	Penn State		16
Oct. 10	Iowa City	14	Iowa		24
Oct. 17	Madison (P)	14	Northwestern		24
Oct. 24	Bloomington	30	Indiana		12
Oct. 31	Madison (HC)	15	Michigan		29
Nov. 7	Madison	7	Ohio State		24
Nov. 14	Champaign	29	Illinois		17
Nov. 21	Madison (W)	39	Minnesota		14

1971 (4-6-1)

Co-Captains:	Bill Poindexter and Roger Jaeger		Coach:	John Jardine	
Sept. 11	Madison	31	Northern Illinois		0
Sept. 18	Syracuse	20	Syracuse		20
Sept. 25	Madison (B)	28	LSU		38
Oct. 2	Evanston	11	Northwestern		24
Oct. 9	Madison	35	Indiana		29
Oct. 16	Madison (P)	31	Michigan State		28
Oct. 23	Columbus	6	Ohio State (TV)		31
Oct. 30	Iowa City	16	Iowa		20
Nov. 6	Madison (HC)	14	Purdue		10
Nov. 13	Madison (W)	27	Illinois		35
Nov. 20	Minneapolis	21	Minnesota		23

1972 (4-7)

Co-Captains:	Keith Nosbusch and Dave Lokanc		Coach:	John Jardine	
Sept. 16	Madison (B)	31	Northern Illinois		7
Sept. 23	Madison	31	Syracuse		7
Sept. 30	Baton Rouge	7	LSU		27
Oct. 7	Madison (P)	21	Northwestern		14
Oct. 14	Bloomington	7	Indiana		33
Oct. 21	East Lansing	0	Michigan State		31
Oct. 28	Madison	20	Ohio State		28
Nov. 4	Madison (HC)	16	Iowa		14
Nov. 11	Lafayette	6	Purdue		27
Nov. 18	Champaign	7	Illinois		27
Nov. 25	Madison (W)	6	Minnesota		14

1973 (4-7)

Tri-Captains:	Mike Webster, Jim Schymanski and Chris Davis		Coach:	John Jardine	
Sept. 15	Madison	13	Purdue		14
Sept. 22	Madison	25	Colorado		28

264

Sept. 29	Lincoln	16	Nebraska	20
Oct. 6	Madison (P, B)	37	Wyoming	28
Oct. 13	Madison	0	Ohio State	24
Oct. 20	Ann Arbor	6	Michigan	35
Oct. 27	Madison (HC)	31	Indiana	7
Nov. 3	East Lansing	0	Michigan State	21
Nov. 10	Madison	35	Iowa	7
Nov. 17	Madison (W)	36	Northwestern	34
Nov. 24	Minneapolis	17	Minnesota	19

1974 (7-4)

Co-Captains: Gregg Bohlig and Mark Zakula   **Coach: John Jardine**

Sept. 14	Lafayette	28	Purdue	14
Sept. 21	Madison (TV)	21	Nebraska	20
Sept. 28	Boulder	21	Colorado	24
Oct. 5	Madison (TV)	59	Missouri	20
Oct. 12	Columbus	7	Ohio State	52
Oct. 19	Madison (P)	20	Michigan	24
Oct. 26	Bloomington	35	Indiana	25
Nov. 2	Madison (HC)	21	Michigan State	28
Nov. 9	Iowa City	28	Iowa	15
Nov. 16	Evanston, Ill.	52	Northwestern	7
Nov. 23	Madison ("W")	49	Minnesota	14

1975 (4-6-1)

Co-Captains: Terry Stieve and Steve Wagner   **Coach: John Jardine**

Sept. 13	Madison	6	Michigan	23
Sept. 20	Madison (B)	48	South Dakota	7
Sept. 27	Columbia	21	Missouri	27
Oct. 4	Madison	7	Kansas	41
Oct. 11	Lafayette	17	Purdue	14
Oct. 18	Columbus	0	Ohio State	56
Oct. 25	Madison (HC)	17	Northwestern	14
Nov. 1	Madison (P)	18	Illinois	9
Nov. 8	Iowa City	28	Iowa	45
Nov. 15	Madison (W)	9	Indiana	9
Nov. 22	Minneapolis	3	Minnesota	24

1976 (5-6)

Co-Captains: Mike Carroll, Ron Pollard, John Rasmussen, Andy Michuda   **Coach: John Jardine**

Sept. 11	Ann Arbor	27	Michigan	40
Sept. 18	Madison (B)	45	North Dakota	9
Sept. 25	Madison	35	Washington State	26
Oct. 2	Lawrence	24	Kansas	34
Oct. 9	Madison (P)	16	Purdue	18
Oct. 16	Madison	20	Ohio State	30
Oct. 23	Evanston, IL	28	Northwestern	25
Oct. 30	Champaign, IL	25	Illinois	31
Nov. 6	Madison (HC)	38	Iowa	21
Nov. 13	Bloomington	14	Indiana	15
Nov. 20	Madison ("W")	26	Minnesota	17

WISCONSIN SINGLE GAME SUPERLATIVES

(Compiled by Sports News Service Staff—Does Not Include Rose Bowl Games in Season or Career Totals)

Rushing Attempts
43 Bill Marek vs. Minnesota, 1974
39 Bill Marek vs. Illinois 1975
37 Jerry Thompson vs. Iowa, 1944
36 Rufus Ferguson vs. Minnesota, 1972

Net Yards Gained Rushing
304 Bill Marek vs. Minnesota, 1974
230 Bill Marek vs. Northwestern, 1974
226 Bill Marek vs. Wyoming, 1973
220 Alan Thompson vs. Oklahoma, 1969

Touchdowns Rushing
5 Bill Marek vs. Minnesota, 1974
4 Rowdy Elliott vs. Lawrence, 1920
4 Bill Marek vs. Iowa, 1973
4 Bill Marek vs. Iowa, 1974

Passing Attempts
48 Ron VanderKelen vs. USC, 1963
44 Mike Carroll vs. Michigan, 1976
39 Chuck Burt vs. Colorado, 1965
38 Jim Haluska vs. UCLA, 1952

Pass Completions
33 Ron VanderKelen vs. USC, 1963
25 Mike Carroll vs. Michigan, 1976
23 John Boyajian vs. Minnesota, 1967
20 Chuck Burt vs. USC, 1965
20 Neil Graff vs. Michigan, 1969

Yards Gained Passing
401 Ron VanderKelen vs. USC, 1963
297 Ron Miller vs. Minnesota, 1961
290 John Boyajian vs. Minnesota, 1967

Passes Had Intercepted
5 Jim Haluska vs. UCLA, 1952
5 Mike Carroll vs. Purdue, 1976

Touchdown Passes
4 Neil Graff vs. Indiana, 1969
3 Gene Rose vs. Iowa, 1926
3 Jim Haluska vs. Marquette, 1952
3 Ron Miller vs. Stanford, 1960
3 Ron Miller vs. Illinois, 1961
3 Ron VanderKelen vs. Iowa, 1962
3 Neil Graff vs. Penn State, 1970
3 Mike Carroll vs. Washington State, 1976

Consecutive Pass Completions
10 John Coatta vs. Ohio State, 1950
10 John Boyajian vs. Minnesota, 1967
9 Ron Miller vs. Stanford, 1960

(Note: Gregg Bohlig completed 12 straight passes over three games in 1974; final one vs. Colorado; all 8 vs. Missouri; first three vs. Ohio State.)

Passes Caught
11 Pat Richter vs. USC, 1963 (Rose Bowl)
11 Jimmy Jones vs. Northwestern, 1964
11 Louis Jung vs. Colorado, 1965

Yards Gained Receiving
170 Pat Richter vs. Illinois, 1961
167 Jimmy Jones vs. Northwestern, 1964
163 Pat Richter vs. USC, 1963 (Rose Bowl)

Touchdown Passes Caught
3 Dave Schreiner vs. Marquette, 1942
3 Dave Howard vs. Iowa, 1955
3 Pat Richter vs. Illinois, 1961

Points Scored
30 Bill Marek vs. Minnesota, 1974
27 Rowdy Elliott vs. Lawrence, 1920
24 Lynwood Smith vs. Marquette, 1915
24 Harold Holmes vs. Indiana, 1923
24 Jerry Witt vs. Northwestern, 1951
24 Louis Holland vs. Illinois, 1962
24 Bill Marek vs. Northwestern, 1974
24 Bill Marek vs. Iowa, 1974
24 Bill Marek vs. Iowa, 1973

Extra Point Attempts
11 Eber Simpson vs. Lawrence, 1915
8 Eber Simpson vs. Marquette, 1915
8 Vince Lamia vs. Missouri, 1974

Extra Point Attempts Made
10 Eber Simpson vs. Lawrence, 1915
8 Eber Simpson vs. Marquette, 1915
8 Vince Lamia vs. Missouri, 1974

Field Goals Attempted
6 Jim Bakken vs. Minnesota, 1961
5 Jim Bakken vs. Utah, 1961
5 James Johnson vs. Indiana, 1968

Field Goals Scored
4   Pat O'Dea vs. Beloit, 1899
4   Vince Lamia vs. Minnesota, 1976

Punt Returns
10   Bill Lane vs. Indiana, 1951
7   Greg Johnson vs. Northern Illinois, 1971
6   Louis Holland vs. Indiana, 1962
6   Roy Burks vs. Iowa, 1951

Yards Punts Returned
158   Earl Girard vs. Iowa, 1947
153   Greg Johnson vs. Northern Illinois, 1971
128   Lou Holland vs. Indiana, 1962
115   Gene Evans vs. Minnesota, 1949

Kickoff Returns
7   Clarence Self vs. Michigan, 1947
6   Tom McCauley vs. USC, 1966
5   Nate Butler vs. Michigan, 1968
5   Nate Butler vs. Minnesota, 1968
5   Danny Crooks vs. Ohio State, 1969

Yards Kickoffs Returned
178   Clarence Self vs. Michigan, 1947
163   Nate Butler vs. Minnesota, 1968
135   Tom McCauley vs. USC, 1966

Punting Average
51.0   George O'Brien vs. Iowa, 1952 (6)
50.0   Frank Bellows vs. Chicago, 1914
49.3   Frank Luksik vs. Ohio State, 1957 (3)
48.7   Dick Milaeger vs. Ohio State, 1975 (6)
48.6   Wendell Gulseth vs. Rice, 1952 (5)

Punt Attempts
12   Dave Fronek vs. Nebraska, 1965
12   Bob Schaffner vs. Iowa, 1968
11   David Billy vs. Arizona State, 1968

Interceptions
4   Clarence Bratt vs. Minnesota, 1954
3   Gene Evans vs. Marquette, 1946
3   Bob Radcliffe vs. Navy, 1949
3   Ed Withers vs. Iowa, 1950
3   Burt Hable vs. Minnesota, 1952
3   Dale Hackbart vs. Minnesota, 1958
3   Tom Schinke vs. Iowa, 1966
3   Neovia Greyer vs. Illinois, 1970
3   Ken Dixon vs. Illinois, 1975

Interceptions Yards
110   Jack Wink vs. Great Lakes, 1942
105   Coots Cunningham vs. Purdue, 1907
103   Bob Radcliffe vs. Navy, 1949
103   Ed Withers vs. Iowa, 1950

Total Offense Plays
57   Ron VanderKelen vs. USC, 1963
       (Rose Bowl)
50   Mike Carroll vs. Michigan, 1976
48   Chuck Burt vs. Colorado, 1965
45   Neil Graff vs. Michigan, 1970

Total Offense Yards
406   Ron VanderKelen vs. USC, 1963
       (Rose Bowl)
314   John Boyajian vs. Minnesota, 1967
309   Ron Miller vs. Minnesota, 1961
304   Bill Marek vs. Minnesota, 1974

SINGLE SEASON SUPERLATIVES

Rushing Attempts
272   Bill Marek, 1975
249   Rufus Ferguson, 1971

Big Ten Only
210   Bill Marek, 1975
184   Rufus Ferguson, 1971

Rushing Yardage
1,281   Bill Marek, 1975
1,222   Rufus Ferguson, 1971

Big Ten Only
994   Bill Marek, 1975
966   Bill Marek, 1974
883   Rufus Ferguson, 1971

Touchdowns Rushing
18   Bill Marek, 1974
13   Bill Marek, 1975
13   Bill Marek, 1973
13   Rufus Ferguson, 1971

Big Ten Only
14   Bill Marek, 1974
10   Bill Marek, 1973

Completion Percentage
.602   John Coatta, 1950
.563   Jim Haluska, 1952
.553   Gregg Bohlig, 1974

Big Ten Only
.642   John Coatta, 1950
.587   Jim Haluska, 1952
.527   Ron VanderKelen, 1962

Passing Yards
1,627   Mike Carroll, 1976
1,487   Ron Miller, 1961
1,410   Jim Haluska, 1952

Big Ten Only
1,171   Mike Carroll, 1976
1,168   Ron Miller, 1961
1,030   John Coatta, 1951

Passing Attempts
262 Mike Carroll, 1976
235 Chuck Burt, 1965
202 John Ryan, 1968

Big Ten Only
201 Mike Carroll, 1976
153 Ron Miller, 1961
146 John Coatta, 1951
146 Ron VanderKelen, 1962

Pass Completions
132 Mike Carroll, 1976
121 Chuck Burt, 1965
112 Jim Haluska, 1952

Big Ten Only
103 Mike Carroll, 1976
80   Ron Miller, 1961

Passes Had Intercepted
22   Chuck Burt, 1965
18   Jim Haluska, 1952
17   Mike Carroll, 1976

Big Ten Only
14   Ron Miller, 1960
13   Chuck Burt, 1965
12   Mike Carroll, 1976

Touchdown Passes
13   Mike Carroll, 1976
12   Jim Haluska, 1952
12   Ron VanderKelen, 1962
11   Ron Miller, 1961
11   Neil Graff, 1970

Big Ten Only
10   Ron VanderKelen, 1962
9   Ron Miller, 1961
8   John Coatta, 1951

Total Offense Plays
335 Neil Graff, 1970
325 Mike Carroll, 1976
286 John Ryan, 1968

Big Ten Only
244 Neil Graff, 1970
243 Mike Carroll, 1976
210 Bill Marek, 1975
198 Ron VanderKelen, 1962

Total Offense
1,627 Mike Carroll, 1976
1,561 Neil Graff, 1970
1,486 Neil Graff, 1971
1,449 Ron Miller, 1961

Big Ten Only
1,260 Mike Carroll, 1976
1,237 Ron VanderKelen, 1962
1,180 Neil Graff, 1970

Passes Caught
47   Pat Richter, 1961
46   Tom McCauley, 1966
42   Mel Reddick, 1967

Big Ten Only
38   Tom McCauley, 1966
36   Pat Richter, 1961
33   Dennis Lager, 1965

Yards Gained Receiving
817 Pat Richter, 1961
702 Larry Mialik, 1970
689 Tom McCauley, 1966

Big Ten Only
656 Pat Richter, 1961
569 Tom McCauley, 1966
487 Larry Mialik, 1970

Touchdown Passes Caught
8   Pat Richter, 1961
7   Larry Mialik, 1970

Big Ten Only
7   Pat Richter, 1961
4   Larry Mialik, 1970

Points Scored
114 Bill Marek, 1974
84   Bill Marek, 1973
80   Bill Marek, 1975
80   Rufus Ferguson, 1972

Big Ten Only
90   Bill Marek, 1974
66   Bill Marek, 1973
58   Pat Harder, 1941

Touchdowns Scored
19   Bill Marek, 1974
14   Bill Marek, 1973
13   Bill Marek, 1975
13   Rufus Ferguson, 1971

Big Ten Only
15   Bill Marek, 1974
11   Bill Marek, 1973
9   Louis Holland, 1962

Extra Points Attempted
41   Vince Lamia, 1974
34   Vince Lamia, 1976
30   Lisle Blackbourn, Jr., 1949

Big Ten Only
27   Vince Lamia, 1974
20   Vince Lamia, 1976
19   Gary Kroner, 1962

Extra Points Scored
40   Vince Lamia, 1974
33   Vince Lamia, 1976
27   Gary Kroner, 1962
27   Roger Jaeger, 1971

26   Vince Lamia, 1974
19   Gary Kroner, 1962
19   Vince Lamia, 1976

Field Goals Attempted
21   Vince Lamia, 1976
16   Jim Bakken, 1961
12   Roger Jaeger, 1969
·12   Roger Jaeger, 1971

Big Ten Only
18   Vince Lamia, 1976
11   Jim Bakken, 1961
 8   Roger Jaeger, 1969
 7   Karl Holzwarth, 1959

Field Goals Scored
14   Pat O'Dea, 1899
13   Vince Lamia, 1976
10   Pat O'Dea, 1898
 9   Roger Jaeger, 1969

Big Ten Only
11   Vince Lamia, 1976
 6   Roger Jaeger, 1969
 5   Karl Holzwarth, 1959

Kick Scoring
72   Vince Lamia, 1976
49   Vince Lamia, 1974
46   Roger Jaeger, 1969

Big Ten Only
52   Vince Lamia, 1976
35   Vince Lamia, 1974
33   Roger Jaeger, 1969

Punt Returns
20   Bill Lane, 1951
20   Roy Burks, 1951
19   Tom Schinke, 1967

Big Ten Only
18   Bill Lane, 1951
17   Nate Butler, 1969

Punt Return Yardage
265   Gene Evans, 1949
206   Roy Burks, 1951

Big Ten Only
175   Gene Evans, 1949
169   Bill Hutchinson, 1952
167   Earl Girard, 1947

Kickoff Returns
25   Greg Johnson, 1969
23   Mike Morgan, 1975
21   Nate Butler, 1968

Big Ten Only
17   Mike Morgan, 1975
17   Nate Butler, 1968

Kickoff Return Yardage
541   Greg Johnson, 1969
540   Greg Johnson, 1971
501   Nate Butler, 1968

Big Ten Only
414   Ira Matthews, 1976
399   Greg Johnson, 1971
391   Nate Butler, 1968
389   Tom Schinke, 1966

Punt Attempts
72   Dave Fronek, ·1965
63   John Krugman, 1970
63   Bob Baumann, 1942

Big Ten Only
45   Bob Schaffner, 1968
43   Dave Fronek, 1965
41   Bob Petruska, 1949

Punting Average
43.8   Frank Luksik, 1957 (13)
43.6   Stan Williams, 1974 (17)
43.0   Mickey McGuire, 1932 (13)
42.2   Dick Milaeger, 1975 (39)

Big Ten Only
42.4   Dick Milaeger, 1975 (30)
42.0   Jim Hammond, 1950 (22)
41.9   Ken Simmons, 1973 (24)
41.5   Jim Bakken, 1960 (28)

Interception Returns
 9   Neovia Greyer, 1970
 7   Scott Erdmann, 1976
 7   Dale Hackbart, 1958
 6   Elroy Hirsch, 1942
 6   Jim Miller, 1954
 6   Tom Schinke, 1966
 6   Jim Embach, 1949

Big Ten Only
 6   Neovia Greyer, 1970
 5   Bill Lane, 1951
 5   Burt Hable, 1952
 5   Dale Hackbart, 1958
 5   Scott Erdmann, 1976

Interception Yardage
175   Jack Wink, 1942
135   Bob Radcliffe, 1949

Big Ten Only
122   Pat Levenhagen, 1955
102   Ed Withers, 1950
102   Dave Fronek, 1965

CAREER SUPERLATIVES

Rushing Attempts
719   Bill Marek, 1972-75
673   Alan Ameche, 1951-54
594   Rufus Ferguson, 1970-72

Big Ten Only
534   Bill Marek, 1972-75
503   Alan Ameche, 1951-54
426   Rufus Ferguson, 1970-72

Net Yards Gained Rushing
3,709   Bill Marek, 1972-75
3,212   Alan Ameche, 1951-54
2,814   Rufus Ferguson, 1970-72

Big Ten Only
2,721   Bill Marek, 1972-75
2,463   Alan Ameche, 1951-54
1,942   Rufus Ferguson, 1970-72

Touchdowns Rushing
44   Bill Marek, 1972-75
26   Rufus Ferguson, 1970-72
25   Alan Ameche, 1951-54

Big Ten Only
31   Bill Marek, 1973-75
19   Alan Ameche, 1951-54

Passing Attempts
551   Neil Graff, 1969-71
432   Jim Haluska, 1952; 54-55
432   John Ryan, 1966-68

Big Ten Only
390   Neil Graff, 1969-71
297   Ron Miller, 1960-61
288   James Haluska, 1952-55

Pass Completions
273   Neil Graff, 1969-71
230   Jim Haluska, 1952; 54-55
201   Ron Miller, 1960-61

Big Ten Only
193   Neil Graff, 1969-71
153   Jim Haluska, 1952-55
152   Ron Miller, 1960-61

Completion Percentage
.542   Ron VanderKelen, 1962
.539   Jim Haluska, 1952; 54-55
.521   Ron Miller, 1960-61

Big Ten Only
.531   Jim Haluska, 1952-55
.531   John Coatta, 1949-51
.527   Ron VanderKelen, 1962

Yards Gained Passing
3,699   Neil Graff, 1969-71
3,093   Jim Haluska, 1952; 54-55
2,838   Ron Miller, 1960-61

Big Ten Only
2,573   Neil Graff, 1969-71
2,134   Ron Miller, 1960-61
2,001   Jim Haluska, 1952-55

Passes Had Intercepted
33   Jim Haluska, 1952; 54-55
29   John Ryan, 1966-68

Big Ten Only
22   Jim Haluska, 1952-55
22   Ron Miller, 1960-61

Touchdown Passes
23   Neil Graff, 1969-71
20   Jim Haluska, 1952; 54-55
19   Ron Miller, 1960-61

Big Ten Only
16   Neil Graff, 1969-71
14   John Coatta, 1949-51
13   Ron Miller, 1960-61

Passes Caught
113   Mel Reddick, 1967-69
110   Pat Richter, 1960-62

Big Ten Only
84   Pat Richter, 1960-62
83   Mel Reddick, 1967-69

Yards Gained Receiving
1,710   Pat Richter, 1960-62
1,320   Mel Reddick, 1967-69

Big Ten Only
1,321   Pat Richter, 1960-62
970   Mel Reddick, 1967-69

Touchdown Passes Caught
14   Pat Richter, 1960-62
10   Jeff Mack, 1972-74

Big Ten Only
10   Pat Richter, 1960-62
7   Jerry Witt, 1951-53

Points Scored
278   Bill Marek, 1972-75
180   Vince Lamia, 1973-76
158   Rufus Ferguson, 1970-72
150   Alan Ameche, 1951-54

Big Ten Only
200   Bill Marek, 1972-75
133   Vince Lamia, 1973-76
114   Alan Ameche, 1951-54
108   Louis Holland, 1961-63

Extra Point Attempts
110   Vince Lamia, 1973-76
96   Lisle Blackbourn, Jr., 1946-49
72   Paul Shwaiko, 1952; 54-55; 58

270

Extra Points Made
105 Vince Lamia, 1973-76
66 Lisle Blackbourn, Jr., 1946-49
61 Roger Jaeger, 1969-71
61 Paul Shwaiko, 1952; 54-55; 58

Field Goals Attempted
39 Vince Lamia, 1973-76
32 Roger Jaeger, 1969-71
26 Jim Bakken, 1959-61

Field Goals Scored
32 Pat O'Dea, 1897-99
25 Vince Lamia, 1973-76
15 Roger Jaeger, 1969-71
14 Tom Schinke, 1965-67

Kicking Points
180 Vince Lamia, 1973-76
106 Roger Jaeger, 1969-71
82 Paul Shwaiko, 1952; 54-55; 58

Punt Returns
43 Roy Burks, 1950-52
37 Jim Miller, 1953-55
32 Tom Schinke, 1965-67

Punt Return Yardage
448 Gene Evans, 1946-49
373 Roy Burks, 1950-52
367 Jim Miller, 1953-55

Kickoff Returns
44 Mike Morgan, 1974-76
44 Greg Johnson, 1969; 1971
40 Tom Schinke, 1965-67

Big Ten Only
31 Mike Morgan, 1974-75
31 Greg Johnson, 1969-71
30 Dan Crooks, 1968-70

Kickoff Return Yardage
1,081 Greg Johnson, 1969; 1971
940 Tom Schinke, 1965-67

Big Ten Only
748 Greg Johnson, 1969-71
724 Dan Crooks, 1968-70

Punts
133 T. A. Cox, 1944; 46-48
116 Bob Schaffner, 1966-68
111 Jim Bakken, 1959-61

Big Ten Only
90 Jim Bakken, 1959-61

Punting Average
41.3 Dick Milaeger, 1975-76
40.9 Jim Bakken, 1959-61

Big Ten Only
40.4 Jim Bakken, 1959-61
40.3 Dick Milaeger, 1975-76

Interception Returns
18 Neovia Greyer, 1969-71
12 Ed Withers, 1949-51

Big Ten Only
14 Neovia Greyer, 1969-71
8 Ed Withers, 1949-51

Interception Yards
285 Neovia Greyer, 1969-71
220 Ed Withers, 1949-51
196 Jack Wink, 1942; 46-47

Big Ten Only
257 Neovia Greyer, 1969-71
150 Ed Withers, 1949-51

Total Offense Plays
876 Neil Graff, 1969-71
719 Bill Marek, 1972-75
673 Alan Ameche, 1951-54

Big Ten Only
620 Neil Graff, 1969-71
534 Bill Marek, 1972-75
503 Alan Ameche, 1951-54

Total Offense Yards
4,134 Neil Graff, 1969-71
3,709 Bill Marek, 1972-75
3,212 Alan Ameche, 1951-54

Big Ten Only
2,972 Neil Graff, 1969-71
2,721 Bill Marek, 1972-75
2,463 Alan Ameche, 1951-54

DEFENSE
SINGLE-SEASON RECORDS

Total Tackles		Year
181 (101-80)	Dave Lokanc	1972
169 (85-84)	Ken Criter	1967
Big Ten Only		
138 (72-66)	Dave Lokanc	1971
130 (74-56)	Dave Lokanc	1972
129 (63-66)	Ken Criter	1967

Solo Tackles		
101	Dave Lokanc	1972
85	Ken Criter	1967
Big Ten Only		
74	Dave Lokanc	1972
72	Dave Lokanc	1971

Assisted Tackles		
84	Ken Criter	1967
83	Dave Lokanc	1971
Big Ten Only		
66	Ken Criter	1967
66	Dave Lokanc	1971

Tackles Forcing Fumbles

6	Jim DeLisle	1968
4	Ed Albright	1968
4	Bill Poindexter	1971

Big Ten Only

5	Jim DeLisle	1968
4	Ed Albright	1968

Most Tackles for Loss (and Yards)

14	(86) John Tietz	1967
13	(77) Ed Albright	1971
12	(64) Jim DeLisle	1968

Big Ten Only

14	(86) John Tietz	1967
8	(52) Jim DeLisle	1968
8	(49) Gary Buss	1968
8	(49) Lynn Buss	1968

Most Passes Broken Up

12	Ken Dixon	1976
11	Steve Wagner	1974
10	Tom McCauley	1968
10	Nate Butler	1970

Big Ten Only

10	Steve Wagner	1974
9	Tom McCauley	1968
8	Nate Butler	1970
8	Neovia Greyer	1970

Touchdown Saves

7	Scott Erdmann	1976
7	Greg Johnson	1971
5	Greg Lewis	1975

Opponent Fumbles Recovered

5	Ed Bosold	1972
4	Jim DeLisle	1968
4	Nate Butler	1970

Big Ten Only

4	Jim DeLisle	1968
3	Ed Bosold	1972

CAREER

Total Tackles

427	(218-209)	Dave Lokanc, 1970-72
358	(198-160)	Ken Criter, 1966-68

Big Ten Only

327	(172-155)	Dave Lokanc, 1970-72
277	(154-123)	Ken Criter, 1966-68

Most Solo Tackles

218	Dave Lokanc, 1970-72
198	Ken Criter, 1966-68

Big Ten Only

172	Dave Lokanc, 1970-72
154	Ken Criter, 1966-68

Most Assisted Tackles

209	Dave Lokanc, 1970-72
160	Ken Criter, 1966-68

Big Ten Only

155	Dave Lokanc, 1970-72
123	Ken Criter, 1966-68

Most Tackles For Loss (and Yards)

30	(164)	Gary Buss, 1968-70
25	(154)	Jim DeLisle, 1968-70

Big Ten Only

21	(113)	Gary Buss, 1968-70
17	(125)	Jim DeLisle, 1968-70

HIGHLIGHTS AND RECORDS
IN WISCONSIN FOOTBALL

PASSING

Most attempts single season—286 in 1967. **Conference** —202 in 1976.

Most attempts single game —49 (vs. USC in 1963 Rose Bowl game). **Conference** —44 (vs. Michigan in 1976).

Most completions single season —143 in 1967 (286 attempts). **Conference** —104 in 1976 (202 attempts).

Best percentage single season —555 in 1952 (117 completions in 211 attempts). **Conference** —582 (74 in 134 attempts) 1952.

Most completions single game —34 (vs. USC in 1963 Rose Bowl game). **Conference** —25 (vs. Michigan in 1976—44 attempts).

Best percentage single game —1.000 (9 out of 9 for 138 yards—vs. Missouri in 1974). **Conference** —1.000 (5 out of 5 for 126 yards vs. Indiana in 1941).

Most touchdown passes single season —13 in 1952, 1961 and 1976. **Conference** —11 in 1961.

Most touchdown passes single game —5 (vs. Cornell College in 1926). **Conference** —4 (vs. Northwestern, 1955), and 4 (vs. Illinois, 1961 and vs. Indiana, 1969).

Most yardage on passes single season —1,772 in 1971. **Conference** —1,377 in 1961. (196.7 yards per game.)

Most yardage on passes single game —419 (vs. USC in 1963 Rose Bowl game). **Conference** — 312 vs. Minnesota in 1961—20 completions in 41 attempts).

TOTAL OFFENSE

Most net yardage gained rushing and passing single season—4398 in 1974 (3162 rushing, 1236 passing). **Conference** —3187 in 1974 (2440 rushing, 747 passing).

Most net yardage gained rushing and passing single game —697 (vs. Lawrence in 1921, 563 by rushing, 134 by passing). Modern record is 630 yards vs. Wyoming in 1973, 548 rushing, 82 passing. **Conference** —608 (vs. Northwestern in 1974—551 rushing, 57 passing).

FUMBLES

Most fumbles single season—44 in 1951. **Conference** —37 in 1951.

Most fumbles single game —12 in 1944 (vs. Michigan, lost 5). **Conference** —same as above.

Most opponent fumbles recovered single game —8 in 1948 (Illinois fumbled 11 times).

PENALTIES

Most penalties single season—74 in 1951. **Conference** —57 in 1951. (8.1 penalties per game.)

Most penalties single game —13 in 1949 (vs. Illinois which declined 3 others). **Conference** — same as above.

Most yardage penalized single season —710 in 1968. **Conference** —575 in 1968.

Least yardage penalized single game —0 in 1950 (vs. Ohio State).

DEFENSIVE

Least net yardage rushing allowed opponents—single season—601 in 1951. **Conference** — 482 in 1951. (68.9 yards per game.)

Least net yardage rushing allowed opponents—single game —Minus 18 yards in 1951 (vs. Iowa). **Conference** —same as above.

Least net yardage passing allowed opponents—single season —661 in 1953. **Conference** —515 in 1953.

Least net yardage passing allowed opponents—single game —None (vs. Indiana in 1951 and vs. Michigan State in 1961).

Least net total combined yardage allowed opponents—single season —1,393 in 1951. **Conference** —1,000 in 1951.

Least net total combined yardage allowed opponents—single game —82 vs. Iowa in 1951 (100 by passing, minus 18 by rushing).

MISCELLANEOUS

Fewest first downs in single game—None (vs. Minnesota in 1926, Wisconsin lost 31 yards by rushing). **Conference** —same as above.

NOTE—Wisconsin made only one first down vs. Iowa (by rushing), 1946.

Most passes had intercepted in single game —6 (by Purdue in 1944, and by Northwestern in 1956).

Most punts returned, single game —11 (vs. Indiana for 96 yards in 1951).

Most yards punts returned, single game —277 yards on 7 returns (vs. Iowa, 1947).

Most punts returned for touchdowns single game —3 (vs. Iowa in 1947).

TEAM RECORDS HELD IN BIG TEN

Best passing completion record for season—.575 in 1952 (77 in 134). **For single game** —1.000 (5 of 5 vs. Indiana in 1941).

Fewest yards penalized single season —91 or average of 15.2 in 1948.

Most opponent passes intercepted single game —7 (vs. Minnesota, 1954).

Most opponent passes intercepted on one individual —6 (vs. Don Swanson, Minnesota, 1954).

PAST WISCONSIN COACHES

(Not pictured — **Alvin Kletsch**, 1889; **Ted Mestre**, 1890; **Herb Alward**, 1891; **Frank Crawford**, 1892; **Parke Davis**, 1893; **H.O. Stickney**, 1894-95).

Phil King
1896-1902, 1905

Art Curtis
1903-04

C.P. Hutchins
1906-07

J.A. 'Tom' Barry
1908-1910

John Richards
1911; 1917; 1919-1922

Bill Juneau
1912-1915

Paul Withington
1916

Guy Lowman
1918

Jack Ryan
1923-24

George Little
1925-26

Glenn Thistlethwaite
1927-1931

Clarence Spears
1932-1935

Harry Stuhldreher
1936-1948

Ivan Williamson
1949-1955

Milt Bruhn
1956-1966

John Coatta
1967-69

University of Wisconsin Football Lettermen
(1889-1976)

This list of football "W" winners was compiled from athletic board minutes, the Badger Yearbook, the National "W" Club office, and other available records. The award winners for the years 1889-1905 include both major and minor "W" award winners, and in some cases the award in football was not made until the year following actual competition.

1889

Blackburn, W., Brooks, W., Bruce, A., Brumder, W., Clark, B., Kerr, J., Logemann, R., Loope, T., Meyers, C., Prael, F., Sheldon, W., Sumner, L.

1890

Ahara, E., Bruce, A., Freeman, J., Kerr, J., McNaught, J., Wiener, M.

1891

Ahara, E., Bruce, A., Coleman, H., Flower, L., Freeman, J., Knapp, G., Kull, F., Onstad, E., Pyre, J., Sumner, L., Thiele, R., Walker, D.

1892

Barth, G., Case, C., Crenshaw, T., Freeman, J., Jacobs, H., Karel, J., Knapp, G., Kull, F., Lyman, T., McGovern, T., Richards, J., Sheldon, W., Sumner, L., Tratt, W., Walker, D.

1893

Bunge, G., Davis, A., Dickinson, H., Freeman, J., Hile, C., Jacobs, H., Kull, F., Lyman, T., Nelson, O., Rendtorff, E., Richards, J., Ryan, J., Williams, D.

1894

Alexander, W., Bunge, G., Cochems, H., Comstock, N., Dickinson, H., Jacobs, H., Kull, F., Lyman, T., Nelson, O., Richards, J., Ryan, J., Trautman, G., Karel, J.

1895

Alexander, W., Anderson, E., Barryman, C., Comstock, N., Dickinson, H., Forrest, H., Gregg, J., Jacobs, H., Karel, J., Kull, F., Pyre, J., Richards, J., Riordan, J., Sheldon, W., Silverwood, T., Thompson, G., Trautman, G.

1896

Atkinson, W., Brewer, C., Comstock, N., Cory, W., Gregg, J., Karel, J., McPherson, C., Nelson, O., O'Dea, P., Peele, H., Pyre, J., Richards, J., Riordan, J., Ryan, J., Sheldon, W., Silverwood, T., Street, L., Trautman, H.

1897

Anderson, E., Cochems, E., Comstock, N., Dean, J., Forrest, H., Fugitt, C., Gould, H., Gregg, J., Hazzard, W., Holmes, H., Jolliffe, W., Lyle, J., O'Dea, P., Peele, H., Riordan, J., Ryan, J., Tratt, P.

1898

Anderson, E., Beddell, M., Bradley, H., Chamberlain, A., Chamberlain, H., Cochems, E., Curtis, A., Holmes, H., Husting, B., Jolliffe, W., Jones, T., Karel, J., Knobel, F., Larson, A., Mather, I., Mauerman, J., O'Dea, P., Senn, G., Shong, A., Stangel, C., Tratt, P., Yeager, C.

1899

Alexander, W., Anderson, E., Blair, E., Chamberlain, A., Chamberlain, H., Cochems, E., Comstock, N., Curtis, A., Driver, E., Jolliffe, W., Juneau, W., Larson, A., Lerum, A., Lyman, F., O'Dea, P., Peele, H., Rogers, C., Senn, G., Tratt, P., Wilmarth, G., Yeager, C.

1900

Abbott, A., Chamberlain, A., Cochems, E., Curtis, A., Dering, C., Door, J., Driver, E., Juneau, W., Larson, A., Lerum, A., Marshall, A., Murphy, M., Richardson, S., Riordan, J., Schreiber, W., Senn, G., Skow, E., Tormey, T., Tratt, P.

1901

Abbott, A., Cochems, E., Curtis, A., Daum, R., Dering, C., Driver, E., Fogg, J., Hammerson, E., Holstein, W., Juneau, W., Larson, A., Lerum, A., Marshall, A., Moffatt, W., Schreiber, W., Senn, G., Skow, E., Westcott, W.

1902

Abbott, A., Bertke, W., Bush, I., Bush, J., Driver, E., Findlay, A., Fogg, J., Juneau, W., Liljequist, L., Long, F., Marsh, C., Moffatt, W., O'Brien, J., Schofield, H., Vanderboom, E.

1903

Abbott, A., Baine, W., Bertke, W., Bush, J., Chamberlain, A., Clark, F., Findlay, A., Fogg, J., Jones, T., Liljequist, L., Perry, C., Peterson, H., Price, J., Remp, R., Robinson, B., Schofield, H., Vanderboom, E., Washer, C., Wrabetz, V.

1904

Bertke, W., Brindley, T., Bush, J., Clark, F., Dering, C., Donovan, L., Findlay, A., Fleischer, O., Grogan, F., Hunt, F., Jones, G., Jones, T., Melzner, A., O'Brien, J., Perry, C., Remp, R., Schneider, W., Stronquist, L., Vanderboom, E., Wrabetz, V.

1905

Brindley, T., Bush, J., Dering, C., Donovan, L., Findlay, A., Gelbach, W., Johnson, A., Jones, T., Levisee, L., Roseth, L., Vanderboom, E., Wrabetz, V.

1906

Bleyer, C., Clark, F., Cunningham, C., Curtin, J., Curtis, H., Dittman, F., Dittman, J., Frank, A., Gelbach, W., Hosler, H., Howard, J., Huntley, L., Johnson, A., Jones, T., Messmer, J., Miller, C., Rogers, H., Soukup, R., Springer, E., Stiehm, E., Whittaker, E., Zeisler, G.

1907

Boyle, F., Cooper, F., Culver, H., Cunningham, C., Davidson, T., Dittman, F., Fucik, R., Hosler, H., Huntley, L., Iakisch, R., Lowman, M., Messmer, J., Mucklestone, R., Murphy, P., Osthoff, O., Rogers, H., Scribner, C., Soukup, R., Stiehm, E., Whitmore, A., Whitmore, J., Whittaker, E., Wilce, J.

1908

Boyle, F., Culver, H., Cunningham, C., Davidson, T., Dean, J., Dreutzer, C., Fucik, R., Howard, J., Lowman, M., Messmer, J., Miller, C., Moll, J., Mucklestone, R., Murphy P., Osthoff, O., Rogers, H., Scribner, C., Springer, E., Stiehm, E., Wilce, J.

1909

Anderson, S., Bunker, E., Buser, A., Culver, H., Dean, J., Frank, A., Fucik, R., Iakisch, R., Mackmiller, W., Osthoff, O., Roseth, L., Wilce, J., Whittaker, E.

1910

Bright, G., Brandstadt, R., Bunker, E., Buser, A., Carter, F., Dean, J., Fucik, R., Gillette, E., Hoeffel, M., Jacobson, C., Mackmiller, W., Moll, J., Pierce, M., Samp, E.

1911

Alexander, A., Arpin, H., Brandstadt, R., Bright, G., Buser, A., Butler, R., Chambers, C., Gillette, E., Hoeffel, M., Lange, R., Mackmiller, W., Moll, J., Murphy, P., Ofstie, H., Pierce, M., Pollock, C., Roberts, G., Samp, E., Tandberg, A., Van Gent, E., Van Riper, J.

1912

Alexander, A., Bellows, F., Berger, L., Breckenridge, W., Bright, G., Butler, R., Castle, L., Gelein, E., Gillette, E., Hoeffel, M., Keeler, R., Lange, R., Moffett, H., Ofstie, H., Powell, T., Powell, W., Samp, E., Tandberg, A., Tormey, A., Wernicke, C., Van Riper, J.

1913

Alexander, A., Bellows, F., Buck, H., Butler, R., Cummings, L., Davy, G., Gelein, E., Keeler, R., Kennedy, M., Lange, R., Martin, J., McMaster, P., Ofstie, H., Powell, W., Stavrum, E., Tandberg, A., Taylor, G., Tormey, A., Van Gent, E., Weimar, A., Zinke, A.

1914

Bellows, F., Breckenridge, W., Buck, H., Cummings, L., Galvin, M., Gardner, M., Keeler, R., Kelly, W., Kennedy, M., Kreuz, L., McMaster, P., Mucks, A., Rau, H., Rieger, H., Schmidt, E., Smith, L., Stavrum, E., Taylor, G., Weimar, A.

1915

Byers, D., Buck, H., Cummings, L., Filtzer, R., Gardner, M., Gunderson, B., Hancock, H., Kreuz, L., Koch, W., McCrory, R., Meyers, P., Pottinger, E., Rau, H., Rieger, H., Simpson, E., Simpson, G., Smith, L., Stavrum, E., Taylor, G., Weimar, A.

1916

Berg, M., Carpenter, C., Cramer, H., Edler, R., Filtzer, R., Gardner, M., Garnsey, E., Graper, L., Hancock, H., Kelly, W., Kieckhefer, H., Koch, W., Kreuz, L., Kralovec, A., McCrory, R., Meyers, P., Olsen, H., Simpson, E., Taylor, G.

1917

Bondi, H., Carpenter, C., Davey, A., Gould, S., Hammen, E., Hancock, H., Jacobi, G., Kelly, W., Keyes, O., Kieckhefer, H., Kralovec, A., Olson, W., Scott, R., Simpson, E., Sivyer, B., Stark, H., Vaughn, H., Weston, F.

1918

Below, M., Brader, J., Brumm, R., Collins, W., Donaghey, J., Leaper, W., Mann, B., Margoles, H., Smith, F., Sundt, G., Usher, E.

1919

Barr, W., Brader, J., Bunge, G., Carpenter, C., Collins, W., Davey, A., Elliott, A., Fladoes, M., Gould, S., Holmes, H., Jacobi, G., Meyers, P., Scott, R., Shorney, G., Smith, F., Stark, H., Sundt, G., Taylor, J., Weston, F.

1920

Barr, W., Barnes, H., Brader, J., Bunge, G., Collins, W., Davey, A., Eggebrecht, O., Elliott, A., Gibson, E., Margoles, H., Nelson, G., Scott, R., Stark, H., Sundt, G., Tebell, G., Weston, F., Williams, R., Woods, J.

1921

Brader, J., Brumm, R., Bunge, G., Christianson, C., Elliott, A., Gibson, E., Gill, R., Gould, S., Hohfeld, R., Kiessling, O., Nelson, G., Sundt, G., Tebell, G., Williams, R., Woods, J.

1922

Barr, W., Below, M., Bieberstein, A., Eagleburger, S., Gibson, E., Harris, W., Hohfeld, R., Irish, R., Miller, C., Nichols, T., Pearse, B., Polaski, S., Schernecker, E., Smith, L., Sykes, R., Taft, M., Tebell, G., Williams, R.

1923

Below, M., Bentson, H., Bieberstein, A., Blackman, T., Eagleburger, E., Gerber, E., Harris, W., Holmes, H., Irish, R., Miller, C., Nelson, P., Nichols, T., Schneider, A., Stipik, R., Taft, M., Teckemeyer, O., Williams, J.E.

1924

Barnum, R., Blackman, T., Bieberstein, A., Burrus, J., Harmon, D., Harmon, L., Harris, W., Kasiska, R., Larson, L., Long, T., McAndrews, H., McGiveran, S., Miller, C., Nelson, P., Polaski, S., Schwarze, H., Slaughter, B., Stipek, R., Straubel, A., Teckemeyer, O.

1925

Barnum, R., Blackman, T., Burrus, J., Cameron, D., Crofoot, E., Harmon, D., Harmon, L., Kasiska, R., Kreuz, R., Larson, L., Leitl, L, Long, T., McAndrews, H., McCormick, H., Nelson, P., Polaski, S., Radke, F., Sauger, F., Stipek, R., Straubel, A., Von Bremer, G., Wilke, E., Wilson, J.

1926

Barnum, R., Burrus, J., Cameron, D., Cole, W., Connor, G., Crofoot, E., Harmon, D., Kasiska, R., Kresky, J., Kreuz, R., Leitl, L., Muegge, W., Rose, E., Schuette, C., Straubel, A., Von Bremer, G., Wagner, R., Welch, M., Wilke, E., Wilson, J.

1927

Binish, S., Cameron, D., Connor, G., Crofoot, E., Cuisinier, F., Davies, J., Gotstein, J., Hayes, N., Hotchkiss, G., Ketelaar, W., Kresky, J., McKaskle, H., Parks, J., Rebholz, H., Rose, E., Shoemaker, L., Smith, L., Sykes, R., Von Bremer, G., Wagner, R., Warren, E., Welch, M., Wilson, J., Zeise, E.

1928

Backus, A., Bartholomew, K., Behr, S., Binish, S., Casey, G., Connor, G., Conry, C., Cuisinier, F., Davies, J., Gantenbein, M., Ketelaar, W., Kresky, J., Linden, J., Lubratovich, M., Lusby, W., Mansfield, A., Miller, C., Oman, T., Parks, J., Price, A., Rebholz, H., Rose, G., Smith, H., Smith, L., Wagner, R., Warren, E.

1929

Backus, A., Behr, S., Casey, G., Dunaway, D., Gantenbein, M., Hardt, H., Jensen, H., Ketelaar, W., Kruger, K., Liethen, A., Linden, J., Lubratovich, M., Lusby, W., Oman, T., Pacetti, N., Parks, J., Rebholz, H., Sheehan, W., Shoemaker, L., Smith, H., Smith, L., Tobias, D., Warren, E.

1930

Behr, S., Bratton, C., Casey, G., Catlin, M., Eggers, V., Gantenbein, M., Gnabah, W., Goldenberg, C., Jensen, H., Kabat, G., Kruger, K., Linfor, J., Lubratovich, M., Lusby,

W., McGuire, F. W., Molinaro, F., Oman, T., Rebholz, R., Schneller, J., Simmons, H., Smith, H., Stout, W., Swiderski, E., Thurner, G., Tobias, D., Wimmer, J.

1931

Begel, M., Bratton, C., Catlin, M., Cuthbert, D., Edwards, C., Engelke, R., Goldenberg, C., Haworth, R., Kabat, G., Kranhold, H., Kruger, K., Linfor, J., Lovshin, R., Molinaro, F., McGuire, F. W., Nelson, P., Pacetti, N., Rebholz, R., Schiller, R., Schneller, J., Simmons, H., Smith, H., Stout, W., Strain, C., Thurner, G.

1932

Edwards, C., Haworth, R., Kabat, G., Koenig, W., Kranhold, H., Kummer, M., Linfor, J., Lovshin, R., McGuire, F. W., Molinaro, F., Pacetti, M., Pacetti, N., Peterson, M., Schiller, R., Schneller, J., Smith, H., Strain, C., Thurner, G., Tobias, D., Willson, M.

1933

Becker, E., Bender, J., Bingham, J., Bucci, F., Deanovich, G., Ferguson, J., Fish, J., Fontaine, J., Golemgeske, J., Haworth, R., Jordan, L., Koenig, W., Kummer, M., Kundert, K., Lovshin, L., Millar, W., Pacetti, M., Peterson, M., Pike, H., Porett, L., Ross, J., Sanger, C., Schiller, R., Schuelke, K., Smith, H., Westedt, P.

1934

Becker, E., Bender, J., Callahan, R., Christianson, E., Davis, R., Deanovich, G., Dehnert, G., Donaldson, J., Fish, J., Fontaine, T., Haukedahl, S., Jankowski, E., Jensen, P., Jordan, L., Kummer, M., Kundert, K., Mahnke, A., Mueller, H., Nellen, J., Null, R., Pacetti, M., Pizer, G., Pohl, N., Schuelke, K., Strain, C., Tommerson, C.

1935

Benz, F., Budde, J., Christianson, E., Clauss, J., Cole, W., Fish, J., Golemgeske, J., Hovland, L., Jankowski, E., Jensen, P., Jordan, L., Lovshin, L., Mahnke, A., Mortell, E., Nellen, J., Null, R., Peak, V., Popp, A., Stanley, H., Tommerson, C., Wilson, J. D., Wilson, J. R., Windward, E., Wright, J.

1936

Bellin, R., Benz, F., Brodhagen, E., Christianson, E., Clauss, J., Cole, W., Davies, W., Gavre, V., Golemgeske, J., Grinde, R., Haukedahl, S., Jankowski, E., Jensen, P., Johnson, E., Lanphear, G., Loehrke, J., Lovshin, L., Malesevich, B., O'Brien, J., Peak, V., Peterson, C., Pohl, N., Tommerson, C., Weiss, H., Windward, E.

1937

Bellin, R., Benz, F., Brodhagen, E., Cole, W., Dorsch, A., Doyle, J., Eckl, R., Gavre, V., Gradisnik, A., Hartman, E., Hovland, L., Loehrke,

J., Malesevich, B., Martin, J.,
Moeller, R., Murray, J., O'Brien, J.,
Paul, H., Peak, V., Pohl, N.,
Riordan, J., Schmitz, W., Weigandt,
R., Weiss, H.

1938

Bellile, K., Bellin, R., Brodhagen,
E., Cibik, V., Davies, W., Dorsch,
A., Doyle, J., Eckl, R., Embick, R.,
Gage, F., Garrott, W., Gavre, V.,
Gile, G., Gradisnik, A., Holloway,
R., Hovland, L., John, R., Lorenz,
A., Moeller, R., Murray, J., O'Brien,
J., Paskvan, G., Schmitz, W.,
Schuelke, K., Tennant, J., Tornow,
E., Wegner, E., Weigandt, R., Weiss,
H., York, C.

1939

Cone, R., Dorsch, A., Doyle, J.,
Eckl, R., Embick, R., Fagerstrom,
E., Farris, T., Fisher, O., Fox, O.,
Gage, F., Gile, G., Gradisnik, A.,
Holloway, R., Kolbusz, D., Kreick,
R., Loehrke, J., Lorenz, A., Miller,
D., Moeller, R., Murray, J.,
Paskvan, G., Peterson, D., Peterson,
R., Sauter, K., Schmitz, W.,
Tennant, J., Tornow, E., Wegner,
E., Willding, R., York, C.

1940

Baumann, R., Bronson, P., Damos,
T., Embick, R., Farris, T., Gage, F.,
Gile, G., Henry, R., Hirsbrunner, P.,
Hoskins, M., Kreick, R., Ladewig,
F., Lorenz, A., Lyons, E.,
McFadzean, J., McKay, R., Miller,
D., Paskvan, G., Peterson, H.,

Phillip, C., Ray, R., Roberts, J.,
Schreiner, D., Tennant, J.,
Thornally, R., Tornow, E., Wasser-
bach, L., Wegner, E., Willding, R.

1941

Anderson, A., Baumann, R., Boyle,
P., Bronson, P., Calligaro, L.,
Damos, T., Dierks, R., Ellis, F.,
Farris, T., Granitz, F., Hanzlik, R.,
Harder, M., Hirsbrunner, P.,
Hoskins, M., Koehler, H., Kreick,
R., Loepfe, R., Lopp, F., Lyons, E.,
Makris, G., McKay, R., McFadzean,
J., Mead, J., Milauc, F., Miller, D.,
Ray, R., Riewer, F., Rooney, H.,
Schreiner, D., Seelinger, L., Thorn-
ally, R., Vogds, F., Vranesh, G.,
Walgenbach, E., Wasserbach, L.

1942

Anderson, A., Baumann, R., Boyle,
P., Calligaro, L., Currier, K.,
Dierks, R., Frei, J., Harder, M.,
Hirsch, E., Hirsbrunner, P.,
Hoskins, M., Johnson, F., Lyons,
E., Makris, G., McFadzean, J.,
McKay, R., Negus, F., Ray, R.,
Regan, J., Roberts, J., Schreiner,
D., Seelinger, L., Stupka, R.,
Thornally, R., Vogds, E., Wasser-
bach, L., Wink, J.

1943

Carolan, P., Clarke, R., Connor, C.,
Dal Sasso, A., Davey, J., Doar, F.,
Dooney, R., Esser, C., Eulberg, J.,
Fischer, S., Heinz, L., Hildreth, H.,
Hodges, D., Keenan, J., Kindt, D.,
Kuenzler, J., Kusa, J., Laird, K.,
Laubenheimer, R., Lee, D., Letz,
R., Lowe, D., Lutz, J., May, W.,
McLaughlin, P., Meyer, R., Piper,

R., Prins, R., Ramlow, R., Reich,
R., Robertson, A., Rowe, C., Self,
C., Vogt, H., Washburn, E., Weber,
B., Weiger, R., Zych, L.

1944

Ackeret, J., Bahlow, E., Botham,
R., Campbell, J., Collias, N., Cox,
T.A., Cusack, D., Davey, J., Elliott,
B., Engle, R., Esser, C., Fee, J.,
Fricke, H., George, W., Girard, E.,
Haese, J., Hanke, D., Hecker, R.,
Holmes, G., Kusa, J., Lauben-
heimer, R., Mead, J., Meyer, M.,
Pittleman, I., Pophal, R., Price, E.,
Schwartz, J., Tarzetti, K., Thomp-
son, J., Weber, B., Weiske, R.

1945

Bendrick, B., Chaney, C., Engle, R.,
Esser, C., Faverty, H., Fricke, H.,
Fuchs, G., George, W., Haberman,
H., Hanke, D., Hanley, R.,
Hubbard, T., John, R., Johnson, E.,
Kindt, D., Kittel, T., Klinzing, V.,
Lehman, C., Mals, R., Mead, J.,
Meyer, M., Nettesheim, D., Nines,
R., Orlich, D., Shea, R., Thompson,
J.C., Thompson, J.H.

1946

Anderson, A., Bennett, T., Bend-
rick, B., Blackbourn, L., Bowers,
D., Cox, T.A., Currier, K., Davis,
R., Dreyer, W., Esser, C., Evans, G.,
Frei, J., Freund, R., Fuchs, G.,
Gallagher, J., George, W., Granitz,
F., Heath, S., Hintz, E., Hoehn, A.,
Kindt, D., Knauff, D., Lee, D.,
Locklin, S., Loepfe, R., Lopp, F.,
Maves, E., Negus, F., Otterback, H.,

Pinnow, J., Rennebohm, R., Self,
C., Thompson, J., Wilson, R., Wink,
J.

1947

Bendrick, B., Bennett, T., Black-
bourn, L., Collias, N., Cox, T.A.,
Currier, K., Donnellan, D., Dreyer,
W., Elliott, B., Embach, J., Evans,
G., Frei, G., Freund, R., George,
W., Girard, E., Hanley, R., Hintz,
E., Hoehn, A., Kelly, J., Kittell, T.,
Knauff, D., Loepfe, R., Maves, E.,
Olshanski, H., O'Neill, E., Otter-
back, H., Pinnow, J., Price, E.,
Rennebohm, R., Rustman, K., Self,
C., Shea, R., Surber, G., Toepfer,
J., Weiske, R., Wilson, R., Wink, J.,
Zoelle, C.

1948

Albright, W., Bendrick, B., Bennett,
S., Bennett, T., Blackbourn, L.,
Christensen, G., Collias, N., Cox,
T.A., Downing, R., Drews, J.,
Dreyer, W., Elliott, B., Embach, J.,
Evans, G., Faverty, H., Gable, W.,
Gilbert, H., Haberman, H., Hanley,
R., Hanzel, L., Huxhold, K., Kelly,
J., Kittell, T., Knauff, D., Mans-
field, R., Meyers, T., Otterback, H.,
Parish, F., Petruska, R., Pinnow, J.,
Price, E., Radcliffe, R., Rustman,
K., Sachtjen, K., Schaefer, J., Self,
C., Shea, R., Smicic, J., Vernon, C.,
Wartinbee, R., Weiske, R., Wilson,
R., Yderstad, C.

1949

Albright, W., Bennett, S., Black-

282

bourn, L., Christensen, G., Coatta, J., Downing, R., Elliott, B., Embach, J., Evans, G., Gable, W., Haberman, H., Halverson, C., Hammond, J., Hanzel, L., Huxhold, K., Kelly, J., Kessenich, P., Knauff, D., Lane, W., Meyers, T., O'Donahue, J., Otterback, H., Petruska, R., Price, W., Radcliffe, R., Sachtjen, K., Schaefer, J., Simcic, J., Staiger, D., Strehlow, R., Teague, R., Teteak, D., Wilson, R., Withers, E., Yderstad, C.

1950

Albright, W., Berndt, C., Burks, A., Coatta, J., Drews, J., Faverty, H., Felker, E., Gilbert, H., Hammond, J., Hansen, D., Hutchinson, W., Huxhold, K., Kennedy, R., Lane, W., Leu, R., Mansfield, R., Meyers, T., O'Brien, G., O'Donahue, P., Petruska, R., Radcliffe, R., Sachtjen, K., Schleisner, W., Simcic, J., Simkowski, G., Smith, J., Staiger, D., Steinmetz, G., Strehlow, R., Suminski, D., Teteak, D., Vanderhoof, W., Withers, E., Yderstad, C.

1951

Ace, N., Ameche, A., Andrykowski, E., Bachman, J., Berndt, C., Burks, A., Carl, H., Coatta, J., Dornburg, R., Faverty, H., Felker, E., Gable, W., Gilbert, H., Hammond, J., Hansen, D., Hutchinson, W., Kennedy, R., Lane, W., Leu, R., O'Brien, G., O'Donahue, P., Peters, K., Prchlik, A., Schleisner, T., Simkowski, G., Smith, J., Steinmetz, G., Stensby, C., Strehlow, R., Suminski, D., Teteak, D., Voss, D.,

Withers, E., Witt, G.

1952

Ameche, A., Andrykowski, E., Berndt, C., Burks, A., Canny, T., Carl, H., Craine, J., Dixon, J., Dornburg, R., Durkin, J., Esser, N., Gulseth, W., Hable, B., Haluska, J., Hoegh, M., Hutchinson, W., Kennedy, R., Locklin, R., Martin, C., O'Brien, G., Peters, K., Prchlik, A., Proctor, T., Rutenberg, W., Shwaiko, P., Simkowski, G., Steinmetz, G., Stensby, C., Suminski, D., Temp, J., Torresani, J., Ursin, D., Voss, D., Wimmer, H., Witt, G., Wuhrman, J.

1953

Ameche, A., Amundsen, N., Booher, M., Bratt, C., Carl, H., Cwayna, M., Dixon, J., Dornburg, R., Esser, N., Gingrass, R., Gulseth, W., Hoegh, M., Lamphere, R., Locklin, R., McNamara, W., Messner, G., Miller, J., Miller, W., Roberts, R., Stensby, C., Temp, J., Ursin, D., Vergetis, G., Wilson, G., Witt, G., Wuhrman, J.

1954

Ameche, A., Amundsen, N., Booher, M., Bratt, C., Dittrich, J., Gingrass, R., Gray, W., Haluska, J., Howard, D., Konovsky, R., Levenhagen, P., Lovklin, R., Lowe, W., McNamara, W., Messner, G., Miller, J., Reinke, J., Shwaiko, P., Stensby, C., Temp, J., Thomas, C., Ursin, D., Wilson, G.

1955

Ambrose, S., Bestor, G.,
Bridgeman, J., Cvengros, J.,
Dittrich, J., Gray, W., Haluska, J.,
Hertel, W., Howard, D., Kolian, R.,
Konovsky, R., Levenhagen, P.,
Lewis, D., Lowe, W., McNamara,
W., Miller, J., Peters, T., Rabas, T.,
Reinke, J., Rosandich, R., Shwaiko,
P., Stellick, J., Thomas, C.

1956

Ambrose, S., Bestor, G., Blackmun,
G., Bloedorn, A., Booher, M.,
Bridgeman, J., Carlson, R., Cinelli,
R., Cooper, M., Gehler, W., Hag-
berg, E., Hill, E., Hobbs, J., Hofer,
K., Howard, D., Kocourek, D.,
Kolian, R., Levenhagen, P., Lewis,
D., Lowe, W., Morris, M., Reinke,
J., Simonson, R., Teteak, R.,
Williams, S.

1957

Allen, J., Altmann, R., Carl, D.,
Carlson, R., Chryst, G., Cooper, M.,
Corcoran, G., Fraser, J., Gehler, W.,
Hackbart, D., Hart, E., Heineke,
J.A., Heineke, J.E., Hill, E., Hobbs,
J., Hobbs, W., Holmes, J., Holz-
warth, K., Jenkins, L., Kocourek,
D., Lanphear, G., Lewis, D.,
Luksik, F., Morris, M., Nicolazzi,
R., Peters, T., Rogers, J., Schoon-
over, A., Stalcup, J., Steiner, R.,
Teteak, R., Walker, A., Williams, S.,
Zeman, E., Zouvas, P.

1958

Altmann, R., Chryst, G., Derleth, H.,

Fraser, J., Hackbart, D., Hart, E.,
Heineke, J. E., Hill, E., Hobbs, J.,
Hobbs, W., Holmes, J., Huxhold,
T., Jenkins, L., Kocourek, D., Kul-
cinski, G., Lanphear, G., Nelson,
R., Perkins, R., Shwaiko, P.,
Sprague, C., Stalcup, J., Steiner, R.,
Teteak, R., Wiesner, T., Williams,
S., Zeman, E.

1959

Altmann, R., Bakken, J., Derleth,
H., Gotta, J., Hackbart, D., Hart,
E., Heineke, J. E., Hobbs, W., Holmes,
J., Holzwarth, K., Huxhold, T., Jen-
kins, L., Kulcinski, G., Lanphear,
G., Moore, B., Nelson, R., Perkins,
R., Rogers, J., Schade, D., Schoon-
over, A., Stalcup, J., Steiner, R.,
Wiesner, T., Zeman, E., Zouvas, P.

1960

Anthony, T., Baer, R., Bakken, J.,
Bangert, D., Bichler, D., Carlson,
R., Derleth, H., Downham, T.,
Ezerins, E., Gotta, J., Grimm, R.,
Hess, W., Huxhold, T., Kellogg, W.,
Kulcinski, G., Kunesh, E., Matthews,
D., Miller, R., Moore, B., Nena, G.,
Norvell, M., Perkins, R., Richter,
H., Rogenski, T., Schade, D.,
Staley, R., Suits, W., Underwood,
S., Vander Velden, D., Vesel, C.,
Wiesner, T.

1961

Baer, R., Bakken, J., Bichler, D.,
Bowman, K., Carlson, R., Fleming,
N., Grimm, R., Hearn, N., Hess, W.,
Holland, L., Jax, J., Kempthorne,